Praise for *Tech-Powered Sales*

"Modern sales technology is baffling, especially for a CEO like me who has no choice but to embrace it but also has no chance of making sense of it on my own—and I run a sales tech company! This book boils it down to this: Some sales tech gives your reps superhuman skills that empower your business to dominate markets at will. You can do it with the team you have. Read it, follow the advice, and dominate."

—Chris Beall, CEO, ConnectAndSell

"You can't be afraid of technology. Building a future-proof sales organization requires a deep understanding of the new power couple—humans and technology. *Tech-Powered Sales* explains exactly how to thrive in the fourth Industrial Revolution by harnessing the power of game-changing technologies today and beyond."

—Tiffani Bova, Growth Evangelist at Salesforce, *Wall Street Journal* Bestselling Author of *Growth IQ*, Thinkers50

"Every sales leader and sales professional needs to read this book in order to thrive in the age of empowered buyers, automation, and disruption. As a leader, I know that the shifts are real, and this book contains the secrets for the operationalization of business-to-business sales at scale."

—Simon Tate, President, Adobe Asia-Pacific

"Justin and Tony's book explores the crucial tech stack elements that are table stakes for an effective sales development strategy. We appreciate their exploration of futurism along with grounding their work in practical research from The Bridge Group and others. In a cacophony of voices, their practical advice and predictions ring true. This book is a fantastic resource for all RevOps leaders!"

—Trish Bertuzzi, Founder and CEO, The Bridge Group

"Reading this book feels like a window into the future of sales. It is ten years beyond anything I've seen, and I've worked with hundreds of sales organizations."

—Steve Richard, Cofounder, ExecVision

"The go-to handbook for all sales professionals who want to multiply their results and maximize their return-on-effort. Justin and Tony have thought of everything for you. The 'Essential Stack' and 'Advanced Stack Additions' alone are invaluable!"

—Marylou Tyler, Speaker. Author of *Predictable Prospecting*

"Justin is the most thought-provoking voice in sales today. His informed, irreverent, and prescient approach makes this THE must-read sales book of this year and beyond."

—Jeremey Donovan,
SVP of Sales Strategy and Operations, SalesLoft

"*Tech-Powered Sales* is filled to the rim with tactics that will stack the odds in your favor for booking meetings with your ideal prospects. Actionable stuff."

—Josh Braun, Host of the *Inside Selling* Podcast

"Justin Michael and Tony Hughes have cracked the code on what will differentiate great sales teams in the coming decades—*Tech-Powered Sales*. The technological capabilities to support sales teams have advanced beyond what anyone would have predicted just a few years ago. Read this book, soak in the recommendations, and stay relevant and effective, now and in the future."

—David Dulany,
Founder and CEO, Tenbound

"*Tech-Powered Sales* blew me away! It delivers practical, evidence-backed strategies salespeople can use to create more opportunities than ever before. If you want to learn how to maximize your ability to develop new business, it's a must-read!"

—David Hoffeld
Bestselling Author of *The Science of Selling*

"*Tech-Powered Sales* highlights the new best practices for RevOps and how to scale blended tech stacks (Tesla) in a point solution world (Model T). The era of tech stack optimization will bring 100x efficiency and truly accelerate sales as I predicted in *The Sales Acceleration Formula*. There is synergistic power infusing humans and machines with data emerging as the 'new oil' fueling strategic targeting and messaging—and Justin and Tony show how to execute in the real world."

—Mark Roberge,
Managing Director at Stage 2 Capital,
Professor at Harvard Business School,
Former CRO at HubSpot, and Bestselling Author of
The Sales Acceleration Formula

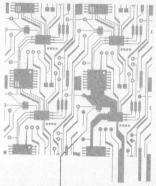

TECH-POWERED **SALES**

Achieve **Superhuman** Sales Skills

JUSTIN MICHAEL
"The Machine of Sales Development"

and

TONY HUGHES
Bestselling Author of *COMBO Prospecting*

HarperCollins
Leadership

An Imprint of HarperCollins

Opt-in, Ethics, and Legal Compliance of Business-to-business (B2B) Outbound

The authors exclusively recommend only the use of automated systems that are built on "privacy by design" principles and architecture, and where possible are also compliant with GDPR, CCPA, CASL, and CAN-SPAM. Data should always be sourced with integrity, and with opt-out and Do Not Contact (DNC) supported. We advocate you place your business address and a link to unsubscribe in every sequenced message. Everything we're suggesting in this book should be implemented ethically and legally in your jurisdiction. Please educate yourself concerning your regulatory obligations.

The leading sequencer companies, data providers, and LinkedIn have gone to great lengths to enable their technologies to operate ethically and securely. As a professional, you must be committed to operating with integrity and intelligence. Send less but more effective and personalized sequences, and split-test more often to smaller batches. Respect the potential customers you are seeking to help by being human in engagement and making it count with brevity and relevance.

ISBN 978-1-4002-2653-5 (eBook)

ISBN 978-1-4002-2652-8 (PBK)

Library of Congress Control Number: 2021935599

Printed in the United States of America

21 22 23 24 25 LSC 10 9 8 7 6 5 4 3 2 1

Contents

Foreword

Sales is a never-ending game of assessing what's working well enough versus what needs to change to outsell the competition and achieve those never-ending new targets.

Standing still means falling behind.

The job of a sales leader is to enable the success of their people for the benefit of customers. Top sellers and teams must operate at previously unimagined levels that require technology—tools designed for their benefit. The right practices are essential, yet the pace of change and array of tools is bewildering.

We all have a love/hate relationship with technology but must master it to remain relevant. Selecting the right technology is tricky, and it is even tougher to deploy it with the right practices that empower salespeople on the front lines.

This book is your guide for blending human creativity and empathy with the technologies that power success rather than creating "just more work."

This is the most important book for selling in the 2020s. Learn from two people who are on the cutting edge of what's possible in selling and sales operations. Tony and Justin combine old-school wisdom with next-generation execution in pushing the technology boundaries of sales.

If this book initially baffles you, read on with an open mind and heart to see the path to an enlightened future. It's possible to orchestrate technology at levels that make you and people on your team superstars in your industry. Study these pages and apply the concepts to transform results.

Aaron Ross
Author of *Predictable Revenue* and *From Impossible to Inevitable* CoCEO of PredictableRevenue.com

Preface

Heart and Purpose

Selling is leadership, plain and simple. It demands the masterful ability to positively influence others and it must be done with integrity. To sell is to be human: it's in our DNA to be heard and to make a difference. To be effective in influencing people, we need integrity and genuine empathy as we step up. For this reason, even as we embrace the digital tools and changing work processes that come from the fourth Industrial Revolution, authenticity and intent is everything. This is our Sales Professional's Creed for opening—the most important and difficult phase of selling . . . are we aligned with your beliefs, attitudes, and mindset?

Professional selling is about making a positive difference in the lives of others—personally and professionally. In doing so, we must provide the necessary level of value that funds our role with our clients and employers. We accept responsibility for the most important and difficult phase of selling—opening. Without the ability to self-generate opportunity pipelines, and open in ways that create value and set the right agenda, all other skills are moot. Real sales professionals are therefore committed to learning and continuous improvement, to being efficient and effective in all aspects of selling, including the systems and tools for sales execution at scale.

This book is not about trickery or gimmicks or fads or the latest sparkly object or tool. It is about saving sales careers and businesses as they seek to help their customers and all those who depend on them, especially in tough times. The success of salespeople drives businesses and the economy. Sales success funds professionals in marketing, product development, production, services, support, accounts . . . and the families who depend on their paychecks and commissions to live. Without sales success, there is no company success.

This is a clarion call and instruction manual to inoculate you against a Skynet future, and written for the pro's pro—that's you if you are reading this. This stuff is inherently complex, really complex, and that's why few can pull it off. It is, however, still the early days and you can get ahead of the curve. We decided to go rogue here, get scrappy, and talk to you with respect by assuming that you've already delved into this topic and are on the technology adoption path.

This work focuses on how to go to the next level in the most difficult and important phase of selling: top of funnel opportunity creation. If you cannot break through and open, you don't get to create solutions or close. The two authors bring an important combination of timeless values, sage wisdom, unrivaled knowledge, insane execution, insider knowledge, and practical advice for the real world. Both have performed at elite levels in their industries. Everything in this book is from the real world and works in the brutal battlefield of competitive business-to-business (B2B) selling.

As a top sales development representative (SDR) mind on the planet, Justin was handpicked by Ben Sardella, cofounder of Datanyze, and Bryan Franklin, CEO of OutboundWorks, to work on an ambitious stealth project seeking to fully automate the SDR function by building an AI model of his brain. This ambitious project at OutboundWorks in 2017 led them to acquire and deploy next-gen Swedish AI tech (Hexa.ai) maxing-out more than thirty-five custom fields to achieve personalization sentences at scale that passed the Turing test. The result was hundreds of concurrent Outreach, SalesLoft, and Reply.io cadences generating over one million emails. It pushed the boundaries of sales automation. The company was successfully acquired, and at the time, Justin was described as "salesborg—man and machine blending human and technology for new levels of sales effectiveness." This book reveals how to harness technology for superhuman levels of tech-powered sales within the bounds of ethical execution.

Tony, already an acclaimed author, met Justin back in 2013 when Justin sought coaching on complex enterprise selling. They became friends and learned from each other with both achieving record-breaking results in their endeavors. Tony became the most read person within LinkedIn on topics of B2B selling. He developed a top of funnel methodology that documented the techniques he teaches for global leaders such as Salesforce, Flight Centre Travel Group, Qualtrics, Adobe, IBM, Red Hat, FCM, SAP, DocuSign, Grant Thornton, and others.

This book assumes a level of sales industry understanding and includes some acronyms and buzzwords. If you become confused, flip to the glossary at the end. If you are brand new to the top funnel role or new to implementing automation, go to the ninety-day SDR checklist, also at the end of the book.

Ironically, some of what you read here will be out of date with the vendors we reference before it is published. Today's amazing technology becomes routine table stakes surprisingly quickly. While we reference (today's) leading technology at the time of writing to provide examples and context to assist you in applying the concepts, we accept that some of the companies and technologies we reference will lose leadership positions or be acquired. It's important to avoid becoming hung up on the specific technologies referenced or the examples provided. Instead, focus on applying the strategies and concepts by leveraging the best technologies available to you in your geography or market.

This book will challenge you in many ways. At times you may feel overwhelmed, like you are drinking from a fire hydrant or playing acronym buzzword bingo. You must have a growth mindset if you are to become the very best seller that you can be. You can become a superhuman salesborg version of yourself with greater reach and effectiveness. Just remember that the things that make us truly human are soul, real empathy, relationships, curiosity, values, intellect—and the effective use of tools, no matter the level of sophistication. Choose to be a builder, not a rock thrower, as you read.

Introduction

Why This Matters ... Your Future Is Here!

"The future of B2B value selling is when buyer sentiment meets seller relevance with human engagement empowered by technology."

—Tony Hughes

The brutal truth is that the majority of salespeople fail. Even in established market-leading companies, we commonly see 60–80 percent of inside and field sellers below their year-to-date targets. All the research supports the fact that business-to-business (B2B) sales failure rates are high and trending worse. The average inside sales rep has a tenure of under 1.4 years down from over 2.2 years in 2014.[1] According to a 2020 survey by Revenue Collective covering more than three thousand inside salespeople and companies generating more than $26 billion in revenue, 83 percent of inside sales reps fail to hit the target and almost 40 percent last less than six months in their role.[2]

Salespeople, on average, invest only a third of their time selling. They fail to consistently hit their numbers because they fail to create an adequate opportunity pipeline, fail to provide insights and value in conversations, fail to close the deals they need, and fail to effectively use the technology and tools designed to help them. It's all punctuated by an epic failure to help clients and customers. It would not be tolerated in other professions such as engineering, building, transport, aviation, medicine, law, or accounting.

Can you see what is happening in the world of sales as sellers ineffectively thrash around, drowning in the very data, technology, and tools available to save them? About 70 percent of what sellers do can be automated by technology. This book will show you the way to elevate yourself out of the morass—and modernize the way you operate for salesborg superhuman revenue performance.

The year 2020 was tumultuous as health and economic pressures disrupted the world. The social impacts were obvious, as distressed and angry hoards protested in the streets and online. Yet it all triggered an acceleration of a silent and invisible trend that is changing humankind forever. It's the fourth Industrial Revolution, where artificial intelligence and technological automation change the very nature of work. This revolution has moved beyond mining, agriculture, manufacturing, logistics, entertainment, retail, defense, and aviation to also transform medicine, health, law, accounting, finance, banking, professional services, and more.

Having made significant inroads into retail sales, the bots are now coming for B2B sellers. If all you do is provide information and help someone transact, you're in trouble: they want a purchasing platform and an algorithm, not a salesperson and pressure. If you think your value is in relationship management, you're deluded. No one worthwhile in business is lonely and bored and looking for another sales friend from supplier land. In 2011, Gartner Research famously predicted that 85 percent of business-to-business (B2B) transactions would occur without human interaction by 2020.[3] It's all happening, quietly.

Make no mistake, beneath all the corporate virtue-signaling about diversity and inclusivity, boardroom executives and power-base players are laser-focused on the economics of survival and prosperity. You may be told that "you are valued," but the brutal reality is that employees, workers, and staff are regarded as *units of production*. Clients, customers, and consumers are regarded as *units of consumption*. Economists use the term *zero marginal product* (ZMP) to describe when someone adds no value at all. There is a cold and calculating heart beating beneath the photoshopped corporate images designed to create warm, emotional connections.

Wake up to what is really going on; the dominos are falling. Cash is finally going away, meetings are moving online, data ubiquity is being accepted, automation is accelerating, high-skill professions are reducing, pay packets are shrinking, and customer engagement is moving away from expensive human-touch to low-cost digital self-serve environments. The term *disruption* has gone from cliche concept to carnage reality. The megatrends of social, mobile, cloud, big data, and artificial intelligence (AI) are combining synergistically to redefine value propositions and go-to-market models.

Have you noticed all the ads offering better prices for buying online or with an app rather than engaging a human? Businesses describe these initiatives as "channel shift" programs to drive customers away from interacting with humans for a much better—and lower-cost-to-serve—experience. Banks have been down this path for years and are now accelerating the closure of premises to reduce real estate and staff costs. One Uber driver we met had a "real job" of being an A380 pilot, another was an SAP programmer, another had just lost a decades-long career as a pathology analyst. Do you think you're safe in sales because you build relationships? Really? In a profession where the majority already fail . . . is that realistic? Self-delusion is not an antidote; hope is not a strategy.

Successful business leaders never let a crisis go to waste. They are driven to maximize their own bonuses and "shareholder value." COVID and the recession of the 2020s provided "social license" to reduce workforce numbers and embrace technology and automation as never before. The business goal is to drive cost out of operations while simultaneously driving up customer and employee experience through technology. Every initiative is designed to reduce costs while increasing revenue and productivity. For the first time in history, capital applied to technology can fully replace expensive and high-overhead humans. Make no mistake, this point in history is like nothing before.

Technology initially augments or complements human work by making individuals more efficient or enabling them to focus on higher-value tasks. But inevitably technology comes to replace many workers, making them redundant. As an example, think about how technology made taxis more efficient and safe with dispatch, tracking, monitoring, navigation, payments, and booking. The drivers became more efficient. Then Uber arrived to drive down cost and improve experience for travelers while wiping out the value of taxi company medallions and reducing driver incomes by disrupting the market and redefining the service. Google self-driving cars will not require a driver at all, just someone willing to provide the capital to fund the vehicle that generates its own income and operates autonomously via the ride platform.

Almost no one is immune from the bots stealing their livelihood. Don't believe the lie that technology simply redistributes jobs from lower-skill and lower-paid work to higher-value and higher-paid careers. In the first two Industrial Revolutions, mills, looms, internal combustion engines, artificial light, and mechanized factories eliminated the vast majority of agricultural and manufacturing jobs or concentrated populations into cities where many lived like battery-hens. Again, technology starts by augmenting human work, and ultimately replaces many human roles completely. Whether it happens is usually not a question of technology being capable of replacing people but is instead a socio-economic question of whether we want it to happen. How do you fund economic models where the vast majority of people are "units of consumption" who depend on a "universal wage," government dole, or charity just to live?

The third Industrial Revolution was enabled by computing with information and communications technology (ICT), driving breathtaking change. The early dumb-bots were driven by human overlords seeking to win during a World War, a Cold War, or to fulfill the dream of human footprints on the moon. In the early days of computing, Alan Turing posited his famous question: Can a machine impersonate real human interaction? The answer to the Turing test is *yes*. Simply go to YouTube and search for "Google Duplex" and see how it happened back in 2018 with a voice call rather than with mere text on a screen. Computers can emulate humans on a keyboard, on the phone, and now also on video.

TQ BOOSTER

Understand what's coming by searching on YouTube for "Google Duplex makes appointments" or "Sophia interview" or "'Obama deep fake." These are old news but should cause your jaw to drop.

All change happens slowly, slowly . . . quickly. The first three Industrial Revolutions reshaped society and how humans interact. Every new development was ridiculed, resisted, and then adopted. The phone is an excellent case in point, with moralists saying it would create an epidemic of lying as people interacted without having to look the other person in the eye. The fourth Industrial Revolution is unique in that it is redefining the very nature of work and the economics on which societies are based. For people to survive and thrive, they need to provide a level of unique value that funds them in their roles. Tradespeople must become artisans; knowledge workers must become insight professionals; leaders must become navigators of ambiguity and disruption. As we will explore at the end of this book, real empathy is the human meta-skill required to thrive beyond table stakes of IQ, EQ, and TQ (Technical Quotient).

The industrialization of modern B2B selling was chronicled by Aaron Ross in 2011 in *Predictable Revenue.* It became the bible of Silicon Valley for scaling, because it showed how to apply Henry Ford's supply chain model to sales via role specialization to unlock exponential productivity. (It included a case study of Salesforce written by Marylou Tyler that was cutting edge at the time.) That industrialization hummed along until 2020 when a Cambrian explosion of tech vendors had emerged to a near choke point of stack overflow.

We are all increasingly working remotely and have some flavor of the tech stack we are underusing. We all have instant access to a supercomputer in our pocket connecting all human knowledge, prospects, and markets in real time. It's up to us to harness this power to unlock unlimited potential and thrive in our roles.

William Gibson (author of *Neuromancer*) is the sage who predicted the internet in 1983 along with just about everything we love about cyberpunk in *The Matrix, Fifth Element, Blade Runner, Minority Report*, and other dystopian movies that sprang from his visionary mind. How close are we to fully automated sales development and then the full-blown AI Singularity event? It's hard to know exactly—probably around 2055. This is the book to bridge you until that point when the bots run the planet, doing all the buying and selling for the remaining humans . . . in their people zoo.

For now, how can human and machine fuse into something synergistic, a whole greater than the sum of its parts? And how can we do it for the greater good, fulfilling the noble purpose of sales—which is making a positive difference in the lives of others, personally and professionally? Like Marty McFly, we will visit the future throughout this book because it is where you and your children will live. Your decisions today will determine the type of existence you experience then.

We are wasting too much time on manual processes that can be automated. We are living in silos among too many disparate systems that can talk to each other if we have a *technology quotient* (TQ) to navigate the array of technological options and pragmatically harness the power of the tools to build a platform for success. The *Harvard Business Review* defines technology quotient as: *Our ability to assimilate or adapt to technology changes by developing and employing strategies to successfully include technology in our work and life.*[4] Someone without TQ today is a dinosaur on the brink of extinction.

Do you have a basic sales TQ? Answer all of these questions honestly:

- Do you have Google Alerts running?

- Can you Google with speed and efficiency to solve your problems?

- Can you construct a Boolean search in LinkedIn Sales Navigator?

- Have you automated the monitoring of sales opportunity trigger events?

- Are you actively using Sales Navigator saved searches?

- Can you create your dashboards and reports in CRM?

- Can you export and import data to your CRM or Sequencer using CSV files?

- Can you build pivot tables in an Excel spreadsheet or run macros?

- Do you have a full understanding of your sales and marketing journeys and all the touchpoints engineered by platforms and technology?

- Could you train someone on all the technologies you use in your job?

- Can you build and execute automated email campaigns with personalization?

- Are you leveraging Tray.io, Zapier, Workato, Automate.io, or Syncari to splice tech stacks together via application programming interfaces (APIs)?

- If you went into business for yourself tomorrow providing "sales as a service" (SaaS), would you have a defined technology stack and automation ready to implement?

- Are you using 80 percent of your time selling versus the average of 36 percent?[5]

If you answered *no* to any of these questions, you need this book. Maybe you can do bits and pieces, but that is not enough. Jill Rowley was right when she said "fools with tools just fail faster."[6] Avoiding competent adoption of the technologies available to you is deciding to fall behind and lose your livelihood. Without technology quotient you're turning up to the gunfight with a peashooter. Instead, choose to become a masterful orchestrator of technology, tools, and platforms of automation and productivity.

You can move from a techno-Frankenstack to revolutionizing your sales process by making one decision—to be less technology avoidant, to embrace your tech stacks whatever they are, and learn them at least 1 to 5 percent more every week. Here you will learn about techno-magical sales enablement, and how to use your tools of the trade as a real professional. Whether you're a Luddite or whiz kid, this is the book for you.

This book explains exactly how to leverage and optimize your JARVIS suit to free up your time to sell again. This is the blueprint to automate yourself to superhuman levels of sales output. Open your eyes, mind, and heart to what is ethically possible.

> "This is your last chance. After this, there is no turning back. . . . I show you how deep the rabbit hole goes. Remember, all I'm offering is the truth. Nothing more. . . . Here we go."
>
> —Morpheus, *The Matrix*

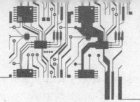

PART I

SALESBORG THEORY

"The best way to predict the future is to create it."

—Alan Kay, former chief scientist at Atari

You've picked up a book that if used correctly will give you real super-powers as a salesperson. No book like this has ever been written in the field of professional selling. You are about to go behind the veil to see how sales pipeline creation can be done at scale by an individual blending the human with the machine. There are some great books on prospecting for today's world, like *COMBO Prospecting* by Tony Hughes, *Fanatical Prospecting* by Jeb Blount, and *Predictable Prospecting* by Marylou Tyler, but none of those books fully explain how to drive strategies at scale—leveraging the full power of technology for the seller.

Read those books and apply what they teach using what you also learn here, and you will be number one in your company, even your industry. Remington Rawlings did, even with all the odds stacked against him, becoming a global top ten power user of Outreach. Working as a young rep trying to learn the tech sales world, while also going to school full-time, he had an unfortunate accident that caused major neck problems. Because he had to work faster and better than all his peers to keep up in school and work, he considered whether there were new ways to find a path to achieving quota. He read and studied, tested, practiced, collaborated, and came up with a system of territory planning that allowed a full connection of his sales tech stack.

After learning every button on every platform, he crafted tons of email content to avoid spam filters, maximize technology use, and connect with his target market in meaningful ways. Doing this hyper-personalization at scale led to 150 percent quota attainment repeatedly, outperforming his peers—and eventually coaching them. Having built $2.5 million in the pipeline in only three quarters with companies including PayPal, Symantec, UPS, Progressive, Gulfstream Aerospace, Smuckers, Bayer, KPMG, and Colgate, he was determined to help others find this same type of success. He contextualized it all for scaling automation and sequencing strategies across other SDR teams. Remi is living proof that the techniques in this book work. You, yes you, young Padawan, can do this too.

Execution is where most things fail. It's not the knowledge that will change your life, it's the doing that makes all the difference. In this book you will see how to operate at a whole new level, leveraging the age of machine automation. In doing so, you'll be reminded of Arthur C. Clarke's Third Law: Any sufficiently advanced technology is indistinguishable from magic.[1]

As a seller, we're often hired to literally create a miracle with revenue, and now, with what you will discover in these pages, you can. It will allow you to fuse with the modern sales stack in an unprecedented fashion— you'll become the orchestrator of your techno-magical performance.

Technology is best at dealing with huge amounts of data, sifting for signals amidst the noise by pattern matching or identifying trigger events, automating repetitive processes or tasks, doing "what-if" analyses, making recommendations, and even rudimentary personalization at scale. In essence, machines can think and do where there are definable parameters with which to work.

Humans, on the other hand, have genuine empathy and can transfer belief and build trust with a real human connection through relevant storytelling. This can create a sense of belonging or community. People are also imaginative, creative, and equipped to deal with ambiguity and hidden agendas in navigating politics and complexity to provide vision and insights. Humans are best equipped to help others feel and decide to drive change, then build a business case for it and secure supporting consensus. Humans can speak to both head and heart with both logic and emotion.

The transference of belief and the creation of emotional resonance in a desire to change is the foundation of sales engagement. Machines think and do. Humans feel and engage. A cyborg-like fusion of both sides is needed for sales success today and into the future for productivity and effectiveness.

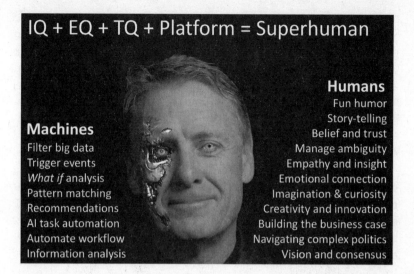

IQ + EQ + TQ + Platform = Superhuman

Machines
Filter big data
Trigger events
What if analysis
Pattern matching
Recommendations
AI task automation
Automate workflow
Information analysis

Humans
Fun humor
Story-telling
Belief and trust
Manage ambiguity
Empathy and insight
Emotional connection
Imagination & curiosity
Creativity and innovation
Building the business case
Navigating complex politics
Vision and consensus

Yet we need to do this in ways that are authentic and ethical. Taking a page out of J. K. Rowling, to access the deep insights contained herein, repeat this aloud: "I solemnly swear that I'm up to real good."

Before you go on, you should know this book *will* challenge you. It is supposed to be hard. It will take you to the very brink of your capacities. You will feel overwhelmed, and you'll wonder where all of this information is taking you. Growth is never comfortable. That's part of the process of evolving—part of the process of becoming a fully cybernetic being.

But if at any time you feel like you're being driven to be a robot, just remember—you're human, and just using the tools available to you to be more productive. That's what has occurred from the Stone Age to the Industrial Revolution and all of the iterations since. We harnessed the power of gravity and water to mill grains, then the steam engine to replace horses, through to mechanical automation and into the information age, and now the fourth Industrial Revolution is being driven by big data, distributed cloud computing and storage, social platforms, mobile everything, sensors within the internet of things (IoT), and artificial intelligence.

There's almost a humanitarian aspect to our mission to free up the human operator from the yoke of the current technology bottleneck, a cage imprisoning the worker to low-value repetitive microtasks, riddled by context switching and ever-increasing KPIs. We see it like Upton Sinclair exposing factory conditions in *The Jungle* in 1905.

Granted, outbound sellers work remotely or in comfy, air-conditioned offices with great coffee and snacks; so there's nothing inhumane about those conditions. But philosophically the system is still inherently so wasteful that over 70 percent of what the human is doing can be automated. About 80 percent of SDRs fall into this job.[2] It's rejection dense, repetitive, and still requires manual configuration. Go buy a top sequencer and load a data list into it and feel your head explode. The process can take hours if you do custom variables and personalization—and this is for the forward-thinking companies that even have the stack.

If you are an operations person, try to make sure everything is syncing perfectly all the time. Have your sales engagement tool matching your marketing automation processes, and make sure that your revenue strategy reflects throughout your whole funnel. It's superhuman for this to be the case, almost unattainable. Yet this is where sales or revenue operations professionals will become orchestrators of the bots, making the tech stack truly sing.

The sales rep of the future? They will be the glue between the CRO (Chief Revenue Officer) and CTO (Chief Technology Officer). Isn't that an API in human form? Internally and externally? Exactly our point! They will be as technical as they are strategic. As much a trusted advisor as a quant analyzing data. The human behind the self-driving Uber, the builder of the business case (ROI). Closest to the code. Sharpest point of the spear. They talk the language of leaders, which is outcomes, numbers, and managing risk—yet they can dive into the relevant detail to silence any critic or justify support. They enable sales and marketing to become one; sales enablement and customer experience to be synergistic; sales evangelism to become sales engineering.

These super-sellers embrace "Smarketing," mapping the entire customer journey across inbound and outbound touchpoints, harnessing the power of intelligent platforms and automation to inject truly human engagement at exactly the right times. (Smarketing is a trademarked term coined by Peter Strohkorb, an amalgam of sales and marketing.) According to SiriusDecisions, B2B businesses that align their revenue engine grow twelve to fifteen times faster than their peers and are 34 percent more profitable.[3] Companies that create a revenue operations team drive unified alignment of their sales, marketing, partner, and customer success teams. Adopting a revenue operations strategy helps unify people, data, and processes across their Go-to-Market (GTM) teams.

What should you be reading or studying to be ready for the rest of your work life? Great at math? Computer science (CS), Mandarin, Node.js, and Python? Great with people, persuasion, and negotiation? How about linguistics, neuroscience, politics, game theory, applied statistics? Right now you should certainly invest more time with your sales engineers to become more technical. Demo your product. Build out your chops in R, Tableau, SQL, JS, and Python. Learn how to properly use your company's CRM and become masterful with spreadsheets. Dust off your entire tech stack. Join GitHub. We're serious; the future will not be televised.

Wesley "Meep" Pennock helps us imagine a prototype of custom software and middleware human sales functions. Part of what we did for early-stage startups was to architect new workflows, sales tooling, and platform features to augment, enhance, and automate disparate systems. It's approachable, even if it feels surreal wiring $100,000 for a small dev team in Kyiv to recode an idea in three months in Python that had taken a year with an army to build in Seattle in PHP . . . and it works!

TQ will be your limitless pill if you have your own house in order with genuine high value in your product/market fit along with a value narrative that creates engagement! By adding TQ, you will become an unbeatable one-human sales engine, a cybernetic salesperson, if you will.

CHAPTER ONE

From Human to Superhuman

Ethical Imperative Amidst New Realities

"With great power comes great responsibility."

—Ben Parker

Some sales leaders perused an early draft of this book and told us to rip it up. Like John Connor at Skynet, "There's just far too much evil these ideas unleash if your goal is to weaponize the top of the funnel." Cries of illegal, unethical, and amoral remind us of the early fears of radio, the internet, television, and the horseless carriage. That's why we have chosen to bring old-school values and new-school techniques together to the final version here.

Read the preface and our creed again. Intent is everything, not just for us as practitioners seeking to help others but for you as a modern, effective seller acting with integrity. We should all embrace positive values and ethical conduct as we seek to break through to help new clients. To quote Jill Rowley, "We live in the age of the empowered buyer." And to echo Dr. Tony Alessandra's Platinum Rule—always "do unto the prospect what you perceive they would want to be done."[1]

It is important here to emphasize the use of automated systems that are GDPR, CCPA, CASL, and CAN-SPAM compliant, built on privacy by design principles and architecture. Data must be sourced with integrity, and with opt-out and Do Not Contact (DNC) easily facilitated. We advocate that you place a link to unsubscribe in every sequenced message.

Everything we're suggesting in this book should be ethical and legal in your country, state, and municipality—so please educate yourself. The leading sequencer companies and data providers have gone to great lengths to enable their technologies to operate ethically and securely. As a professional, you must be committed to operating with integrity and intelligence. Send less personalized sequences that are more effective, and split-test more often to smaller batches. Respect the potential customers you are seeking to help by being human in engagement and making it count with brevity and relevance.

Unbridled technology automation in the hands of amateurs is dangerous. We must use technology intelligently and ethically. This book is not about the "bots running wild" but instead is about running with bots, flying with bots, and even deep diving with them. We are in the age of empathy in light of recent world events so *please* put yourself in the prospect's shoes at every turn. Remember there's a human on the other end fighting their own unique battles in a world that seems to have gone crazy, and you'll be able to keep your white wizard hat firmly in place while performing your techno-magic.

As you read this, you may justifiably feel that this is all about the seller, and you may think, *Isn't professional selling all about the buyer?* Yes it is, but before you can do all the noble initiatives such as setting a vision for a brighter future, exploring and cocreating the business case for change, navigating politics, gathering consensus for support within their teams, and launching a lifelong partnership that provides value . . . you need to find a way to earn their attention. Make no mistake, unless you can find a way to positively break through into the world of the buyer, and do it at scale, you will fail—your skills going to waste.

The trends in the 2020s are conspiring against everyone in sales by reducing attention spans, increasing resistance to change, and hardening the status quo. Decreasing deal sizes, larger quotas or targets, increasing competition, too many choices, slipping close dates, and dreaded non-decision is becoming the order of the day. Garrett MacDonald, SVP at Kochava, one of the greatest Outreach.io power users we've worked with, says: "The status quo is the biggest competitor no one talks about . . . the good sellers can crack the status quo."[2]

Succeeding in sales is tough and the majority fail. The greater tragedy is that they don't do it alone. They fail their top prospects who remain in a "current state" with suboptimal results and jeopardized careers. They fail their bosses who depend on their results. They fail all the workers in their company who need sales revenue to have secure employment.

They fail their families who depend on the income. And they fail themselves. With all this comes lower self-esteem, and their mental health suffers. Yet it doesn't have to be this way!

Many have written about the nobility of selling. Some have even portrayed images of a chivalrous knight jousting the competitor for the sale. But war is not like that. It's all about guerrilla tactics and immersing yourself in the muddy battlefield with blood, sweat, and tears. Jason Hubbard, VP of Partnerships & Alliances at SalesIntel.io, reminds us, "More often than not modern warfare is a game of logistics, and automation is the key to logistics that scale."[3] Real sellers create opportunities rather than just manage the leads handed to them. They embrace the difficult and develop a thick skin. Some prospects will be upset with you and that's okay.

We live in an age of virtue-signaling where everyone wants to appear morally superior. We don't care about that. This book is about helping salespeople emerge from the fog of failure to instead execute at new levels of effectiveness. Most sellers drift along doing enough not to feel guilty instead of doing what it actually takes to succeed. Everyone has access to information at the same time, thanks to an omnipresent Google Search and sales intelligence platform. But if you're strategic, the modern sales cycle isn't linear. It's a Möbius strip, an infinite mathematical meandering that we can intersect. As sellers, we can trigger buying windows. We can create micro-economies and move markets toward us, a quantum leap forward in "time to revenue."

TQ confronts the reality that salespeople drive the economy with the backing of those who innovate and invest to employ them. Sellers do it in brutally competitive environments. To help your clients, you must find a way to break through to them with the right message at the right time, delivered through the right channels. The world is changing rapidly: technology is augmenting or replacing people everywhere. It doesn't have to replace you if you embrace it and wield it wisely. Automation is already becoming table stakes, but you have to know how to deftly employ it.

The fourth Industrial Revolution has brought new challenges for knowledge workers that include adverse impacts on mental health. Even with subspecialization, it's not human to be strapped to the third appendage 250 times per day, the not-so-smart phone with a glaring plastic screen, doing massively repetitive tasks at low skill levels. We have a supercomputer between our ears, the greatest AI ever, that can be used for higher-value activities such as talking to customers. Our mission is to free sellers at all levels from the monotony so they can sell again as free-thinking humans.

Becoming More Than Human

By leveraging all that's possible with machines, we can paradoxically become even more creative and in essence more human. By training the machines to become more human, we gain the superpowers of machines. Maybe we can become Tony Stark.

Remington Rawlings, a fellow tech-powered selling legend and co-founder of Extrovert.io, waxes philosophically:

Read up on "alienation"—and the industrial complex that was created when workers became separated from work. They live to produce results in work they are never able to see to fruition, as they are alienated from a more comfortable lifestyle to make sacrifices for the distant mirage of their next promotion that seems to be dangling right in front of them like a carrot in a rabbit's cage. An SDR could be a career if it's done right. And we certainly think the admins of the future have to understand *Predictable Revenue* by Aaron Ross better if they want to see increases across large user groups creating pipelines.

When someone lives in a world where their life is contingent upon the big bad boss we call "the man" and the world they see is so small. The man cracks the whip—"just dial lots and you will achieve success." Cracks the whip—"just social sell." Cracks the whip—"just be more effective." You start to wonder if we are solving the problem businesses need to solve. It's not about if the outbound sales role is good, it's about how we screw it up sometimes.

In an age where nearly every SDR has felt that the heaviest thing in their day is the dial button and therefore made a "ghost dial" to meet their manager's expectations, we at some point must begin asking the question of how we are preparing the world's future business leaders? By making them smarter? Mmm . . . . By enabling their skillset to expand with tech that universalizes one's ability to achieve meaningful and lasting relationships with customers? Mmm. . . . not that either. By creating bonds of trust between manager and rep, and AE and SDR, so tight that they feel they are a team (thus decreasing turnover)? Not that very often. If it was, we would not have had SDR quota attainment decrease globally five years consecutively. We are asking people to sprint hard for what? So they can try to learn an AE role that may or may not (in general) be something their previous role as an SDR provided them the chance to succeed? No.[4]

Remington continues,

There is a ghost in the machine. And someone is going to need to give it a body and make it come to life. Someone is going to need to handle the change management process from where we are now, to where we can be someday.

I have a vision of a day when product marketing, marketing, sales ops, enablement, SDR leaders, sales leaders, AEs and SDRs themselves, and the executives that lead those functions can all benefit from a brain that removes roadblocks to conversations that must be had the right way with each other internally and with the ideal customer profile everyone is chasing.

And there is power in a goal to democratize and disrupt the tech stack, but that's not the main overarching goal. There is a mission that surpasses anything that has to do with profit. The objective is to disrupt the entire revenue engine and flip it on its head. Knock it out. And when it comes to, teach it a lesson about who and what it really ought to be. If I can do that, I can start to influence businesses to also begin to think in terms of double/triple bottom line business models, their humanitarian impact through their sales org as they get in touch with customers, and create a flourishing of humanity through technology that has never been imagined by these sales leaders.[5]

Remington's insights resonate with us because he has trodden a similar path in wrangling the tools and tech stack for exceptional real-world success. Knowledge and theory may be interesting, but it is an applied effort that reveals the practical truth and creates results. More than that, it must be driven and supported at the top.

According to Alexander Low:

As with any effective change in a business, this has to be led from the top. If the C-suite is not showing any real interest in trying to understand what an SDR has to manage in their day-to-day, why should they bother engaging more than they have to? Without an effective and engaged sales function, a business will cease to exist. Therefore the C-suite needs to invest heavily in understanding what their challenges are, how technology can support them, and what training and enablement are required. By doing this, not only will this help increase top of the funnel, but it will also create more loyalty and longer tenure, which in turn will lead to longer, deeper, and more profitable client relationships.[6]

But not all leaders have the capacity for driving real change when it comes to the sales function because they don't understand it or are fearful of reputation damage from pushing the boundaries. For many leaders, the sales function is an expensive black box that generates inconsistent results. Fixing this problem is a Holy Grail of business that we've been immersed in for decades.

We've been on the bleeding edge of sales automation, taking things to whole new levels. As an example, Justin (coauthor) was approached by a company in stealth mode claiming to hail from the aerospace industry. They swore they could perfectly map his second- and third-degree connections via social media to set appointments programmatically.

Justin explains:

> My CEO went for it and remarkably, we started setting 12+ meetings a day from an office next to a cornfield in St. Louis. We achieved 6 months of output in 6 weeks. We did a 7-figure deal in under 90 days, and a $150K deal in 45 because we hit the entire known universe or TAM (Total Addressable Market) so fast we caught buyers at the white-hot center of their buying window. I was hooked on the mammoth productivity gains! Many lessons learned even then. A few years later, an international search began in Silicon Valley for the top SDR mind to pattern match as a model for artificial intelligence systems by engineers seeking to fully automate sales development itself. I was chosen and it was an opportunity to architect the outbound sales software of the future, the promise of real AI. Then things got interesting.[7]

I suppose this book could have been called *Naked Confessions of a Sales Engagement Platform Power User*, but it needs to be more than that to stay relevant and evergreen through to 2035 and beyond. This is not the book about cold calling versus social selling. This is not the book on the modern sales stack. Those books have been written and are becoming redundant. Some are building out resources to challenge the prevailing worldview of the Ultimate ABSD Tech Stack (account-based sales development), like Lars Nilsson, vice president of global sales at Snowflake, or documenting an almost Sales Lumascape, like David Dulany's V6 of the Tenbound Sales Development Market Map.[8]

What is clear is a Cambrian explosion of vendors that provide "better living through technology" and "bigger, better mousetrap" tools and platforms. The dizzying array of options for the modern seller is paralyzing for most. The recession of the 2020s combined with the acceleration of technology is culling the herd so that the strongest and most relevant survive. It's Darwinian in its brutality, but innovation will continue in this arena because a healthy opportunity pipeline is the lifeblood of every business. Wesley Pennock, technical editor, thinks, "By 2030 most of these companies will be gone and you can quote me on that!"[9]

The modern buyer is equally conflicted. In 2012, the same 200 F1000 CMOs had something like 234 marketing vendors to choose from. In 2020, there are 7,200+ in the Lumascape with fleets of marketers and inside sales reps weaponized with "batch and blast" automation targeting them simultaneously.[10] Epic fail!

The sales engagement platforms (SEPs) have reduced a significant amount of the fragmentation, but the ecosystem of tools is still disparate and they don't talk to each other. SEPs are the next CRM, but they don't always play well with others. That's where you need to become the glue, even superglue, to gain an edge by power-using all of them in a mashup. Consider this book your MacGyver approach to resourcefully using what is around you to achieve the miraculous.

In a world where there are no bidirectional APIs for what is truly needed to thrive in modern selling, you must become the human middleware bringing everything together. Very few know how to do it through masterful orchestration and this is why the overwhelming majority fail . . . talk about pandemics of a metaphorical kind.

Why do more than 80 percent of sales development teams fail?[11] No other profession would tolerate this, yet VCs have pumped $100 million rounds into 40 percent of the startups so drone armies of inexperienced reps must be hired. No time to enable and train so let's hurtle the latest, greatest shiny object at them as pseudo "enablement." Jason Hubbard adds: "It's not much better for bootstrapped startups where limited time and resources mean they don't have the bandwidth to effectively mentor and train and don't have the money to hire expensive, experienced reps. So they inevitably rely on technology to try to fill the gap."[12]

The result? Even less product/market fit because of more competition. CXOs are receiving 250+ emails a day, a sea of sameness from mass blast sequencers. All are making spurious 1,000 percent ROI claims not to be believed. All are clamoring for time that is not available from increasingly busy and stressed senior executive buyers.

The reps responsible are spending up to 65 percent of their time on "non-revenue-generating" administrative overhead. They are tasked to the hilt with inane, automatable things which often include list building, CRM input, programming sequences, researching, emailing, social selling, and calendaring.[13] It is as frightening as it is frustrating from a productivity standpoint: So much of this can be automated or semi-automated with today's tech. And so much more is coming at lightning speed! The awful truth is that most sellers do very little selling at all. They confuse thinking about selling, planning their selling, preparing and researching for selling, talking about their selling . . . with actual selling! It is time for change, don't you agree?

Aaron Janmohamed, Global Product Marketing at XANT, writes: "With the remaining 30 percent of their time supposedly spent on selling, how much of that is actually targeted on the right sales activities? Reps spend 297 percent more time on deals that will never close vs. deals that will. There's an equally strong gap between time spent on non-ideal customers vs. ideal customers. In other words, we need more focus on what really matters."[14]

Depending on the industry and what study you read, less than 50 percent of reps are making their ever-increasing quota number as blowtorch managers put them on performance improvement plans (PIPs). Sales development reps (SDRs), the modern version of inside sales, run hard at becoming field account executives (AEs), where there is the prize of real money on variable commission—usually a 50/50 split. CFOs like the AE role; the big deal can close and the company still preserves margin, even when paying commissions and bonuses to the SDR, AE, even pre-sales, consulting, channel partners, and managers.

When salespeople do get on the phone, contact rates have plummeted to less than 5 percent in the age of robocalls to automated voicemail or "convert-to-a-text" messages. When they actually get live fire, they usually botch the conversation with fake empathy, friending-style rapport building, and then seller-centric messaging. In 2010, it took 4.7 attempts to secure engagement with a prospect. Fast-forward to 2018, and it was 9.1 attempts.[15] (The COMBO Prospecting approach condenses these touches to pattern-interrupt the potential buyer and ensures the seller nails their narrative to execute successfully. Feel free to read the book as a useful companion to this.)

High-growth companies in Silicon Valley spend over $1,000 per month per rep on tech tools in an attempt to better equip their people. And thus we have a cemented SDR/AE industrial complex of inside sales/ field sales, which all really stems from an elaborate snapshot of an effete construct from the early 2000s called predictable revenue. Even the luminous Aaron Ross, and Marylou Tyler (*Predictable Prospecting*), have updated this model for the new guard by blending hybridized models and leveraging new tools and automation with human engagement. The industrial complex approach to B2B selling remains relevant and was inevitable given the tech explosion. We are disciples, rather than detractors, of Aaron Ross.[16]

While simplistic Henry Ford thinking can be applied to the supply chain of demand generation, there are really only two ways to go to shatter the glass ceiling of the SDR/AE industrial complex:

1. More inside sales role specialization (distinct SDR data analyst, content writers, inbound qualifiers, outbound prospectors, etc.) and moving inside sales lower in the funnel doing discovery, qualification, and proposals because automation takes over top funnel outbound to create inbound.

2. Less role specialization with full cycle field sellers enabled with their own top funnel and sales automation stack in order to feed themselves with high-value opportunities to then close. These sellers run their territories like an entrepreneur or franchisee.

The Jungle, written by Upton Sinclair, describes the conditions in factories in 1905. We face a similar existential threat to the sales development role in the 2020s where salespeople's tasks become specialized to a point where all creativity and humanity is at risk of being stripped away.

The inside sales function is an acronym soup swimming in a brew of metaphors and insider jargon. An inside sales rep (ISR) is mainly known as an SDR (sales development rep) for inbound and a BDR (business development rep) for outbound. An inside sales role is sometimes called MDR (market development rep) or MRR (marketing response rep) or LDR (lead development rep) or ADR (account development rep). In large companies, these roles are often supported by SDAs (sales data analysts). The main distinction between ISR roles is whether they are focused on qualifying inbound inquiries or marketing leads, versus driving outbound activity to create qualified leads that are given to more senior salespeople in the field. Inbound reps sometimes report to marketing because they are qualifying the marketing department's leads to move them from MQLs to SQLs. Outbound reps usually report to sales because they feed the field reps (AEs) with qualified leads.

Kenny Madden, Enterprise CSM at ZoomInfo, coined the phrase *the social phone* to describe blending the phone with social platforms for outreach. He prophetically walks us back to the future: "The genesis of the SDR (specialization) came out around the dot.com boom circa 2000 (Oracle, Computer Associates, etc.). Low cost infrastructure software sold on a perpetual basis with upgrade protection."[17] This was a precursor to SaaS, which was nailed by Salesforce, a truly incredible company.

The intention of the inside sales role was to help bridge the black hole between sales and marketing with a massive focus on bringing business insights back to the business. Also a large majority of AEs at that time were frankly bad at new business demand generation . . . sadly, they still are.

Unfortunately, Aaron Ross's fantastic book got confused with a linear "Christmas trees cause Christmas" problem. Put a thousand dials in and get one sale. Therefore two thousand dials equals two sales. A close reading of *Predictable Revenue* never claimed that, yet that is what most sales practitioners sought to implement. It started to slowly break down circa 2008. Now, what has not broken down and never will is the superb "spears, nets, and seeds" approach. More segmentation with metaphors about hunting and farming.

Eric Quanstrom, CMO at CIENCE, is working on novel ways to breathe new life into SDR supply chains with software overlays that can help create a *Moneyball* effect on the team. "Coming from a marketing perspective, it's amusing that sub-specialization is such a big deal. I wouldn't have my lead designer suddenly do SEO."[18] Solving the choke point of context switching is huge, as the brain loathes multitasking. Imagine the power of a system that knows how to dynamically specialize the strongest traits of reps in the workflow. There are a million signals coming from all our tech tools, but which ones effectively suggest what to do next?

Salesforce's Einstein is an AI that analyzes CRM data to identify deal risk and provide forecast accuracy. Einstein can also recommend best next steps with deals based on the data. Sales tool visionary Bryan Franklin is an innovator in articulating where workflow software could go. XANT is approaching this with lead scoring. We need to take a page from RPA (robotic process automation) with machines smarter than us in complex games. Watson won at *Jeopardy* and Go, the most byzantine variable games ever. After the first two moves of a chess game, there are 400 possible next moves. In Go, there are close to 130,000. The search space in Go is as vast as the number of atoms in the universe.

Upstarts like Bloobirds.com are trying to do this. They claim their prospecting platform guides sales development representatives through their workday and helps sales leaders make better decisions. Rahul Rajvanshi from CadenceIQ says: "We want to help sales teams discover the deal winning behavior of their top reps and distribute it as a playbook across their team. We believe a lot of data which is being generated by sales engagement platforms is not being used and with all the activity being done by the reps our recommendation engine aims to process the insights to create customized and intelligent suggestions to the salespeople to drive up conversions."[19]

Futurist Ewing Gillaspy calls this the Seal Team Six strategy, where each contributor has a defined edge to the many blades of the razor. Essentially what will need to be created is some middleware GUI *Minority Report* dashboard that plugs into all the platforms via API. For now we have Tray.io and Zaps to build that glue, or SDR analysts, or VAs behind a Mechanical Turk. Once this is built elegantly, there's room for gamification to drive higher production as well as flight simulator mode.

Stephen Chase highlights how elegantly effective it can be today. "I actually started using Zapier last year when I got hold of Seamless.ai and had a cool setup that automatically populated prospects into a spreadsheet after finding their info in Seamless. Then once they populated into the spreadsheet they went into the Salesforce instance I was using, and then from there they automatically imported to Outreach."[20]

Justin Roff-Marsh, who wrote *The Machine*, posits a brave new era in which the lines of sales are redrawn, with different paradigms for new and existing, reps and CSM (account manager), SDRs and AEs. The model with people looking to drive revenue from the existing install base and the green field must be fundamentally reimagined to reduce waste. He believes the model is broken and we can do better. He calls his process SALES Process Engineering (SPE).[21]

As thought leaders, we hear the near constant refrain of "respect the SDR, take them seriously, elevate them, pay them more, and place them on a career path." But new organizational designs built on the current worldview won't solve the problem. AI and ML (machine learning) are coming at such velocity that we must think like R. Buckminster Fuller to build a new model that shatters the prevailing paradigm.

> "You never change things by fighting against the existing reality. To change something, build a new model that makes the old model obsolete."
>
> —Bucky Fuller

Implement everything that machines can affordably do better than humans in your sales process. Then invest in honing human engagement for winning differentiation. Where's that going, according to futurist Kai-Fu Lee? Empathy, compassion, creativity. Consultative sales, trusted advisor relationships of trust and value, even love—these superpowers are immortal, never to be replaced by machines, as clever as they may be synthesized. One of our favorite stories on Calm App is a modern fairy tale completely written by machine learning algorithms, and it's good, although bizarre and sterile.[22]

Mark Roberge, an engineer by trade, took a page out of Elon Musk's rocketry-first-principles thinking by deconstructing his outbound sales development supply chain and reimagining all the metrics, hiring, and Panama Canal–style locks. He questioned everything as the CRO of Hubspot, taking it from $0 to $100 million in annual recurring revenue (ARR). He adapted an engineer's scientific method and built his own regression analysis to find that grit, coachability, and adaptability matter most to SDR success. He challenged BANT as a qualification method with GPCT (Goals, Plans, Challenges, Timeline).[23] He tested SDR to AE ratios, ABM targeting, and the most effective messaging. We are fascinated with these initiatives because our goal is to help you automate all of them.

Venture capitalist Tomasz Tunguz of Redpoint Ventures provides the best exhortation we've found for reimagining how artificial intelligence can truly transform and enable sales. So engineers, entrepreneurs, and product folks reading here, please go build this:

The startup that disrupts Salesforce will be worth much, much more because instead of simply recording leads and sales, the next CRM will create business for its customers leveraging social proof. It won't be enough for a CRM to inform a salesperson which potential customer to call the way Salesforce's task list operates today. This new CRM will scour the web to find potential customers, discover points of social proof with potential customers increasing close rates and finally record the transactions in the system.[24]

Jason Hubbard comments, "I think at this point [LinkedIn Sales] Navigator is coming closest but it needs to break out of/beyond its own silo."[25] Microsoft has means, but do they have the vision and courage? Yet Salesforce is committed to disrupting themselves. Unlike Kodak, which invented the digital camera but did not act to cannibalize their cash cow of film, Salesforce has real innovation running through its veins.

As you continue reading, you will see a blueprint, a power-user manual on how to self-educate yourself on the most modern tech stacks available on the planet and stay ahead of competition with the power of rapid innovation. What you learn here will bulletproof you for any era. Nail these skill sets and you'll be irreplaceable in any economy . . . bust or boom.

Our *why* should be your *why*. Every sales professional must find a way to succeed in an increasingly complex and difficult environment. An economic downturn is seeking to defeat you, your competitors are gunning for you, client apathy is stalling you, technology is looming to replace you . . . yet you must find a way to up your game and succeed for the sake of everyone who depends on you, including the customers who need your help. Everything else being equal, technology is a mind-blowing game changer and you need TQ to play and win!

CHAPTER TWO

What's Your Technology Quotient?

IQ and EQ are essential, but not enough in the age of automation and AI. We've coached hundreds of reps all over the world, as far as New York, San Francisco, Berlin, London, Seoul, India, and Australia. We've coached on WeChat and even on Gangnam T-Calls. Yep, you can literally show up in person on a screen anywhere. The thing we've noticed in the top reps is agility and nimbleness with the UI/UX itself. They are faster with the tooling and how it all fits together. It's a meta-skill, not unlike the JARVIS Iron Man suit.

The more we tried to automate everything and build AI with OutboundWorks, the more we realized how far away we are from the event horizon of the Singularity and full SDR AI robot replacement of humans. Step one is for us to optimize for humans. Step two is for machines to optimize to humans. Once this feedback loop is closed, we shatter the glass ceiling of the SDR-AE industrial complex like Willy Wonka's elevator.

Anders Fredriksson, CTO of OutboundWorks, puts the vision for 2035 the best. "Imagine a more senior Sales Development 'Operator' that will [eventually] have the efficiency of a hundred person team of SDRs." He goes on to caution: "One of the key challenges is that the market is changing so rapidly so a strategy that worked well last quarter may now not work at all later for various reasons. So the winning reps will be the ones that can operate the technology best while also being good analysts reading the intricacies of the results."[1]

Data czar Greg Meyer adds: "Yes, also one that can pattern match based on a rolling assessment of what's going on today and what is likely to happen in the near future."[2]

In the book *COMBO Prospecting*, Justin was the case study cyborg rep. Back then, it was about using software UIs, and Justin was simply much faster, more agile, and more prescient than most others working with emergent SEP and other platforms such as Outreach, SalesLoft, Outplay, XANT, Groove, LinkedIn Sales Navigator, Apollo, LeadIQ, ZoomInfo, SalesIntel.io, Adapt.io, LeanData, Clari—you name it! The top SDRs are more effective too. We've seen some of the best ever millennials become top AEs, and wow, did we learn a shedload from them reciprocally. Mobile and digital natives operate where this tech is an exoskeleton, a second skin. SDR Trek, The Next Generation, these reps are simply bionic!

How can you have an edge in the modern outbound sales climate? You can't be smart enough, and you can't be empathetic enough to win in the current noisy and weaponized reality. You must master the new sales technology systems themselves—the UI, the UX—to gain a competitive advantage in the Roaring 2020s as we deal with increasingly uncertain economic times and move further toward fully remote selling models at scale.

Greg Meyer knows the importance of the new tech stack when he says: "This is the key to 10X your output!"[3] This is not unlike *The Fast and the Furious*, fine-tuning a five-hundred-horsepower engine with nitro. If you're running low adoption silos set on defaults, and your competitor is running customized, bidirectional APIs, integrated multidisciplinary stacks with 100 percent adoption, next-level personalization, intent data, and triggers—they are going to smoke your results as a competitor off the line every time. Buying this tech isn't enough. Retrofitting it to your use case is where the rubber meets the road, literally and figuratively.

The Essential Stack

Every category here is the price of doing business—table stakes. If you don't have the essential stack nailed, you are underinvesting in your team and already being lapped by competitors. Ensure you're buying all of these. Pricey? The average high-growth startup is spending $1,000 per rep, per month. Ryan Chisholm argues: "We are going to see this number move to $2,000 or even as high as $5,000 per month including VA work."[4]

- **CRM/CX/Marketing Automation.** Salesforce, Microsoft Dynamics, Hubspot, and many others.

- **Social/Networked Intelligence.** LinkedIn Sales Navigator (Navigator or Nav), Twitter, YouTube, even Strava (fifty million users; compare ride stats!).

- **Sales engagement platforms (SEPs).** These are also called sequencers, cadences, flows, or plays. Outreach, SalesLoft, RingDNA, Revenue Grid, Outplay, Groove, XANT, Apollo.ai, FrontSpin, MixMax, AmpleMarket, PersistIQ, lemlist, Autoklose, Airborne, SFDC HVS, HubSpot, Marketo Connect, Pardot, ZoomInfo (Tellwise).

- **Data enrichment.** Cognism, ZoomInfo/Discover.org, Adapt.io, SalesIntel.io, LeadIQ, Seamless.ai, Lusha, Triggr, RocketReach, Infotelligent, ClearBit, Outboundsales.io, CloudLead.co, UpLead, LeadGenius, Modigie, VA's, Custom Built scrapers for event apps such as Slack, and so on.

- **Trigger event monitoring.** ZoomInfo "Scoops," InsideView, Navigator, Triggr.ai, Engagio/DemandBase, and so on.

- **Parallel Assisted Dialers (PADS).** This technology dials thousands of numbers then hot-switches a live caller while screen-popping the data you need for the conversation. ConnectAndSell, ConnectLeader, Orum.

- **Dialers.** RingDNA, Aircall, Dialpad, Truly, RingCentral, ZoomPhone— dial right from the CRM, automate text (SMS), leave prerecorded voicemail drops, and capture call records in CRM.

- **Collaboration.** Remote digital meetings. Zoom.us, Teams, Google Meet, and so on.

Advanced Stack Additions

If the first list is table stakes, the following categories are how you run the game. You will have a limited budget so decide where to place your bets. Remember, we are identifying enhancements or additional layers of the stack. The market changes fast, and the actual vendors most suitable for you will vary at the time of purchase and based on your unique requirements.

- **Intent data.** Bombora, TechTarget, Slintel, and 6sense impute which accounts are searching for a key term. Leadfeeder identifies buyer intent data fueled by revealing the behavior of website visitors after seeing the IP of the incoming web visit and fingerprinting it.

- **Firmographics, psychographics, and technographics.** Orb Intelligence (D&B) for deeper info on businesses including growth and acquisition, HG Insights (formerly HG Data), Triggr.ai for tech stack intel (i.e., technographics).

- **Rep persona and brand management.** Buffer, LinkedIn, Hootsuite, SocialBee, Lately.ai (AI for social media management).

- **Front site chatbot.** Drift, Conversica, and so on to process inbound with interactive AI.

- **Prospect enrichment and ML-driven personalization suggestions.** Nova.ai, Autobound.ai.

- **Research curation.** CheetahIQ, GR8 Insight, and so on.

- **Communication and DM videos.** Drift, Vidyard, Bombbomb, LinkedIn.

- **Calendering.** X.ai, Calendly, Chili Piper, Kronologic, and so on.

- **Better conversations and on-brand messaging.** Grammarly, Lavender, and so on.

- **Email management 2.0.** Superhuman, Hey (Basecamp), Front, and so on.

- **Smart teleprompter and conversation intelligence.** Gong.io, Chorus.ai, ExecVision, RingDNA, Jiminny, Wingman, Fireflies.ai.

- **Real-time call and voice guidance.** Balto, VoiceVibes, Quantified Communications, Verbal Transactions, Beyond Verbal.

- **Presentation and demo Performance.** mmhmm, LivePreso, Open Broadcaster Software (OBS).

- **Content automation.** Descript, Remastermedia, SocialBee.

- **Reply management / sentiment analysis.** LeadGnome, Outreach.io.

- **Affiliate referral automation.** CoSell.io.

- **Account mapping and planning.** Lucidchart (allows reps do strategic prospecting and territory planning visually), Airtable, Trello, and so on.

- **Forecasting.** Clari, Ebsta, Boostup.ai, InsightSquared, AtriumHQ, Einstein within Salesforce.

- **Deal management.** Dealpoint.io, Dooly, Slack/Troops deal rooms, P6 Risk, Slack/Einstein within Salesforce.

- **Proposal contract management.** Docusign, Adobe eSign, CPQ.

- **Win/Loss insights.** Trinity Perspectives.

- **Live crowdsource intelligence.** Guru, Tribyl, and so on.

Sales engagement platforms (SEPs) are a whole new category of tools that are increasingly essential. It's a preprogrammed outbound email software tool that schedules, automates, and orchestrates emails, SMS, VM drops, and LinkedIn actions to prospects. Regardless of which sequencer you use, you need an effective methodology, a way of thinking smartly about A/B testing. John Barrows, CEO of JB Sales, puts it best: "AB test everything!"[5] Something as simple as a subject line can have a dramatic impact on open rates, reply rates, meeting set rates, and ultimately conversion into a bona fide opportunity. But nobody is writing about ways to do effective A/B testing on Outreach.io, SalesLoft, Revenue Grid, Outplay, Groove, XANT (and many more) at scale. And, in many ways, this is still a highly manual process, which will be automated in the future because the technology is so nascent. If you're listening, sales cadence top brass, let's get this on the road map stat!

Per Lars Nilsson, VP Global Sales at Snowflake: "The definition of a sequencer may change, as we know today that sequencers now also include touch pattern functionality (and reminders) for phone calls, LinkedIn InMails, platform sends, Twitter bumps, etc. . . . among other variable touch points. The sales engagement space will continue to add different types of touch points. One outbound campaign can now involve up to twenty-five touch points across five modalities over a three-week time horizon."[6] Wow! A 2020 TOPO report by Craig Rosenberg, "The Age of Multi-Channel Prospecting: Despite the Hype, Nothing is 'Dead,'" argues that all channels are still alive and well; we just need to be blending them more.[7]

There are myriad tools and platforms that enable and integrate outbound activity to make sellers hyper-effective. Aragon Research believes $5 billion will be invested in this category by 2023.[8] There are already more than seventy-five vendors in the G2 grid for sales engagement platforms (SEPs) in 2020.

Many companies are taking Pardot (Salesforce acquisition) and Marketo and flipping those tools outbound (Marketo Connect is the

ToutApp acquisition). Salesforce, with high velocity sales (HVS), is accelerating their leadership by moving deeper into the sales engagement arena. Everybody is getting into the game of proactive outbound sales—as this is where the battle for survival and dominance is fought, especially in tough economic times.

Micah Zayner, demand architect at Teleport, adds: "I took a HubSpot course recently and they revealed their new workflows just released a multivariate if/then option with up to twenty indicators per sequence step to kick people to other workflows and directions. HubSpot workflows are a sleeper. Every single if/then input step can have up to twenty different variants of action based on properties. Their ability to track ad clicks per platform and website page visits makes this a game changer."[9]

Jason Hubbard makes an important point when seeking to drive value from your stack: "It's important to stay on top of the evolving features of your tech stack as often similar products wind up with increasing overlap between platforms and even become direct competitors with virtually identical feature sets. The upshot is that you will often be able to consolidate your tech stack down to fewer vendors if you stay on top of the competitive landscape."[10]

Let's take a look at an actual *tech stack endoskeleton* from Daniel Gray (see Figure 2.1), who is an experienced chief customer officer and uses this framework to drive success.

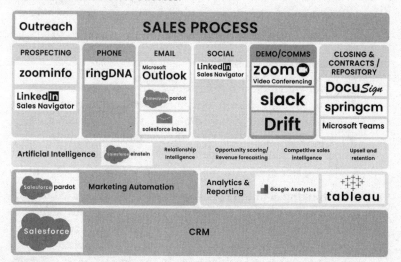

Figure 2.1

Image Source: Daniel Gray

Daniel Gray says: "In the endless sea of sales technology 'blocks' that could be added, I wanted to share a representation of my sales/marketing technology stack developed over the years. Believe it or not, this is a stack I've worked with across multiple companies with more than a billion dollars in annual revenue. It is affordable for smaller businesses and scales for a huge enterprise."[11]

Daniel has a method for building the stack:

First, it takes time. Working backward from our business goals and sales process needs to best serve our customers. I "stack the stack" with the must-have elements such as Salesforce CRM, Pardot, LinkedIn Sales Navigator, and ZoomInfo. Then I augment with insight and productivity enhancers such as Einstein, Tableau, and DocuSign. Then I address the nice-to-have elements including RingDNA and Outreach.

Good ain't cheap, and cheap ain't good. Some blocks like Outlook, MS Teams can come from the IT budget but you must build the business case to fund what you need. Don't under-invest! You also need a mighty Sales/RevOps "Swiss Army Knife" superhero FTE, playing Administrator / BI Engineer / LeadGen / DemandGen / Coder / Integrator / Configurator / Stack manager / Data Integrity / Compliance roles. The tools alone have an average combined cost of $1,000 per month per rep. Maybe as high as $1,500 including fully loaded costing. In a sea of sales technology shiny toys, choice comes back to how best to serve your customers and sellers to remove friction in the sales process.[12]

Here are Daniel's leadership tips:

1. **Arm your warriors.** Inspire customer-obsessed sales "warriors," driven by the company's greater mission and vision, who embrace a "human + technology" sales motion . . . vs. . . . compliant sales "soldiers." To earn and best serve the customer, to maximize value for our stakeholders, to outperform the competition . . . the sales / marketing tech stack is the endoskeleton of today's sales team!

2. **Stop thinking about the vendors or even the available budget.** Instead, ask all the right questions: What process is to be followed by the sales team? How do they qualify and conduct discovery? What is the deal risk management methodology? What paperwork needs to be done to execute a deal? What is the average selling price? And when all of those questions are answered,

start asking about the process required to get a customer through the funnel as quickly as possible.[13]

Remington Rawlings adds to this by saying: "It is really easy to be loyal to a certain vendor in our day and age, and even to get fixated on making things work to bring that vendor on wherever you go. And that works most of the time. But sometimes, your company's processes dictate that loyalty to a vendor is a mistake. Before the technology, you must understand the problems being solved. You create this understanding by truly knowing your customers and competition. You go deeper with your culture during coaching, knowing your metrics, knowing your people."[14]

According to Remington: "As you build this process, you might find that you have budget constraints and that there are cheaper vendors or that you can consolidate existing suppliers. You probably have existing tools in place with different contract end dates but the trick is learning to build the plane while you fly it and nail your process through iteration, testing, and user feedback. Ultimately you can find the right solutions after you spend time evaluating vendors with your must-haves that match your processes."[15]

In every technology category there are many contenders. You might find that you happily use one vendor only to be surprised when the technology falls in its ranking, or when you realize how many other options there were before you signed your current supplier contract.

We've been bombarding you with a bewildering array of tech tools and platforms, yet CRM remains the bedrock of any tech-powered sales strategy. This is because you must have a single source of truth about the prospect journey and customer life cycle. This platform must bring marketing, sales, professional services, and support together for a truly customer-centric view of revenue operations (rev-ops).

TQ TAKEAWAY

CRM such as Salesforce, plus sales engagement such as Outreach or salesLoft, plus sales intelligence tools such as LinkedIn Sales Navigator and ZoomInfo are essential. Make CRM your single source of truth and the center of your universe for sales and marketing automation.

Beyond being competent and committed to CRM, sellers need a meta framework to utilize all the sales tooling: marketing automation, BI, sales intelligence, social, triggers, calls, emails, InMails, and programmatic campaigns. The very best sellers assimilate the latest technology to be intuitively proficient. There are several aspects of leveraging new sales systems that become axiomatic. Think about meta-frameworks. Think about unconscious competence.

Do you have a visual map of the SDR transformational journey that can illustrate maturity and show the steps to programmatically improve TQ? The best example of maturity of the stack comes from Lars Nilsson when at SalesSource (see Figure 2.2).[16]

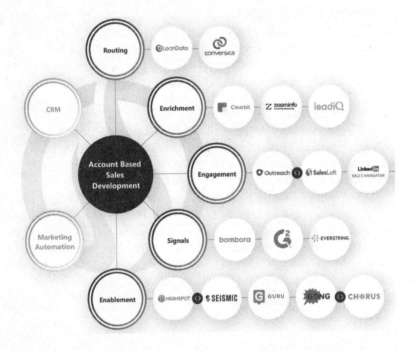

Figure 2.2

Cropped illustration from https://salessource.com/resources/the-ultimate-absd-tech-stack-infographic/. Copyright exclusive to Lars Nilsson and SalesSource.com, experts in modern ABSD tech stacks.

Some Nostradamus predictions from Lars Nilsson when at SaleSource and David Dulany at Tenbound "We will see the role of the CSDO (chief sales development officer) emerge. If I were the CEO of a SaaS company with a product that has an ASP of $20K+ and a sales cycle of more than one month, I myself would hire a CSDO and pair them with a revenue operations specialist (Sales Operations—SOPS & Marketing Operations—MOPS combined) and blow the demand gen door wide open with this lethal combination."[17]

There are so many avenues a company *could* take in regards to sales development, and all routes entail a marketing, personnel, and technology spend that is extensive. They also require substantial time and patience to return an effective ROI. All this amidst insane rates of change. It means that we need to make careful decisions with absolute clarity on the problems we are solving, and then strategize and execute with a high TQ.

Another reason why this type of role might emerge can be illustrated by this quote from Remington Rawlings: "The revenue operations teams of the future won't be so focused on being loyal to their favorite vendor from the past. Especially as new technology emerges, and we see the transition of SDRs from list building and trying to glue together a tech stack that keeps falling apart at times, admins and data gurus, as well as executives, are going to increasingly focus (or should increasingly focus) on matching people and processes to proper technology. For nailing and scaling as early stage startups, high growth unicorns who have nailed their ICP, even large enterprises who have a strong brand, and everything in between, the processes that are part of the company's path to success will be supported by technology, not the other way around."[18]

It is this true-to-process focus that could demand a higher-paying executive to help shoulder the plan and strategy for an increasingly important function. The strategic pipeline creation process plays deeply into CAC (customer acquisition cost), "Rule of 40" for tech companies, and company valuation. These quasi-operational hybrid prospecting geniuses turned executives will help this true-to-process reformation stick in industries that need higher-performing sales development.

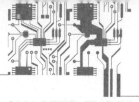

CHAPTER THREE

The Rise of the Machines

The existential threat is that AI in the fourth Industrial Revolution will take our jobs.[1] We've posited that by 2035 there will be cutting-edge startups fully running the top funnel via automation and prepro-grammed sequences. By then, software will have matured in being able to write itself. *Sans SDR* . . . can you imagine? How do we know this? We already did it when working at OutboundWorks. They had outreach sequences with personalization injection, mobile responsive design enabled, that looked so natural and convincing that they were indistin-guishable from something written by a human. Sales Ex Machina (hat tip Victor Antonio and James Glenn-Anderson). It passed the Turing test!

Lars Nilsson predicts: "In the next five to ten years, we will either see a renaissance where creativity, value, and personalization is the new norm with the help of data and automation. Or, we'll choose to ignore what's right in front of us and continue executing blind campaigns that our bosses trained us on because their bosses trained them and so on. If we go down the second path, AI wins and we lose."[2]

Advances in ML, AI, NLP (natural language processing), and deep learning neural nets will synthesize decision trees. The result will be "if this, then that" rules engines that *trip the light fantastic* of machine with human dancing to be indistinguishable from real human interaction. Next-level chatbot automation is coming. Rather than a decision tree, category leaders such as Drift are moving into AI where ML interacts live with prospects, leveraging true artificial intelligence to hold dynamic conversations. Automation of effective Q&A is the future!

Imagine a bot working 24/7 on your website, interacting with your prospects in real time and setting up your humans to call those who could actually buy from you. Almost like a wiki preprogrammed to handle most common objections and FAQs. Rather than form-fill, Drift empowers prospects to immediately schedule a meeting with their assigned sales rep (without human intervention). Drop the Drift-bot on the site, and reps get alerts when target accounts and ideal buyers are on the site and jump into conversations with interested buyers. Space-age stuff and it makes a huge difference to sales results because 78 percent of customers buy from the first responder.[3]

Pushing the envelope even further, Drift Automation (Drift's AI offering) is like cloning your best rep so they can greet every visitor on your website 24/7 and answer any questions your buyers may have.[4] Companies including Okta, Zenefits, Tenable, and Smartling are already leveraging this technology. You can also create interactive landing pages with Drift-bots running on them live; can you imagine? Game-changing interactivity.

At one company we had an outsourced team in Medellin, thanks to Amir Reiter, that sat on Drift all day warming up deals into our funnel front of site. It became a very lucrative, real-time channel. Without the Drift-bot style technology, the average conversion rate on a landing page is 2.3 percent. If you have thousands of unique visitors and you only convert 2 percent of these, you're leaving a ton of opportunities on the line because your website isn't giving real-time experience for potential buyers. But how about filling that site with rich inbounds based on your SalesLoft outbound activity? Machines can replace low-value repetitive work to more effectively augment high-value human value creation.

Look at Google Duplex, an outbound AI that calls people on the phone and has conversations. It can call a restaurant and book a table or call a client and set an appointment, and the human on the other end can't tell that it's an AI-powered voice robot. The natural speech capability is breathtakingly realistic. It's programmed to handle most interactions—and even uses *ums*, *ahs*, and colloquialisms. This is already a reality. Imagine in five years with Moore's law acceleration. IBM's Watson went from the size of a bedroom in 2012 to the size of two pizza boxes in 2020. The rate of change is staggering—98 percent of the information on the internet was created in the last twelve months.

If your startup is in seed, angel, or A-round mode, you could plug in an SDR robot or automated sales development engine and you suddenly just start to automatically get the qualified meetings you need? What happens to the SDR layer then? Well, sellers morph into sales engineers designing messaging and programming those sequences, refining based on the analytics, and helping to architect the software road map. They operate like an analyst or data scientist, even product manager. The meta-skill of future salespeople? Maybe you guessed it? Messaging and coding!

Aaron Janmohamed writes: "Buyer Intelligence powered by Collective Data enables reps to be fed insights on buyer behaviors, suggesting who to engage, how to engage, when to engage, based on the interactions of the collective interactions of buyers and sellers in real time."[5] The future of sales automation is perpetual cycles of outbound that generates inbound that generates engagement that results in customer acquisition. Check out Conversica, an intelligence virtual assistant that leverages AI to process all your inbound leads, and also Zoe Bot cadence and chat for enterprise-grade sales engagement automation.[6]

Imagine delivering exactly the right message, right place/channel, at precisely the right moment. The future of buying and selling may actually go full-blown AI on both sides of the aisle where the top funnel is gone and it's just bots moving at the speed of high frequency trading via blockchain in the cloud . . . buying and selling sentient AI entities. But for now there's a long way to go with *human meets tooling*!

Lars Nilsson is one of the world's leading consultants on ABSD (account-based sales development) frameworks, a code he cracked at Cloudera. He says: "If you're part of those 15 percent of companies that are more likely to spend on more advanced tools, choose wisely. It's much easier to choose a tech tool than it is to implement it in your existing system in order to truly help your reps. AI tools are not designed to solve your problems. Instead, they are designed to help focus on what matters most. There are newer players in the field that are taking AI to the next level to better equip SDRs. Tools such as Nudge.ai (recently bought by Affinity), People.ai, Gong.io/Chorus and Conversica are helping teams identify target personas and even identify active buying signals that come from them at target accounts."[7]

The big four in the arena of sales engagement platforms (SEPs) are currently XANT, SalesLoft, Groove, and Outreach; and the category will continue to proliferate before consolidating.

The Future of Sales Engagement: From Static to Active and Predictive

What the sequencer companies are building is in many ways version 1.0. The beauty is, without disclosing their road maps, they are all driving strategies to move from static to active themes. It's not just about pre-programming a sequence, cadence, flow, or play to determine when sequences and touches will happen. The systems can now optimize the right touch, to the right person, at the right time. There is also propensity modeling. Imagine you look up a CXO and you can see she typically responds to four emails, two cold calls, and her average ACV is $26,300. Don't forget timing either, as she may only respond to emails between 3:40 p.m. and 5:15 p.m.

If you launch a dozen cadences, can the system automatically surface sentiment analysis on the replies? Can I get beyond the analytics so that the ones working better rise to the top? Which insights and recommendations can the system provide in real time? That's the rub because it determines where humans can invest their time for maximum results.

Companies such as Revenue Grid are already starting to make these connections, not by developing all of the functionalities themselves, but by integrating with a wide variety of tools that already exist to let you make complex interconnections. Here is an example: Meetings are going digital more and more, and the medium provides an opportunity. Plug in a tool such as Gong, Chorus, or Fireflies.ai to the online meeting to transcribe everything. Then let Revenue Grid analyze it and alert specific team members or trigger automations immediately, based on the outcome. The stack is already forming a web, providing synergistic outcomes.

Also check out Everstring: "The company's predictive analytics platform helps companies identify and engage with their best customer prospects. EverString captures 20,000 unique signals per company and keeps data current by scouring the web with the capacity of 1,000,000 humans, by creating new data through machine learning, and by ingesting data from every relevant source. When the platform encounters something it's unsure about, it deploys parallelized human workers through a proprietary Human Intensive Task (HIT) system. This enables the platform to teach itself anything it doesn't already know. Once it learns, it never forgets."[8]

Aaron Janmohamed, Senior Director of Product & Content Marketing at XANT, believes the brave new world is prescience. "Our focus has always been accelerating revenue growth for customers, so we continue to build beyond cadence to complete sales execution. One of the key challenges for vendors is that digital and data disruption have not only upended buying and selling but have specifically given buyers a surge in their access to information, pushing them further along their decisionmaking process before sellers enter the picture. But direct engagement remains the most likely method of influencing a purchasing decision. So getting in front of buying groups as early in the buying process as possible is key. Sellers have no shortage of things to be busy on but the key is to be busy on the right things."[9]

If you're reading this, stuck on inbound, it's your time. Time for outbound action, even mastery, where you become the most valuable person in your company. Top of funnel pipeline creation that actually converts to revenue is highly valued by those who make the decisions on who to retain or promote in tough times. Revenue creates cash flow. New-name logos are the holy grail for any business. If you're the one creating the magic, you'll be secure and have a bright future.

Secrets Learned from Sending One Million Emails

Having personally sent over one million emails compliantly using a vast sequencer array, we know the realities. It required Outreach and SalesLoft instances in the hundreds, plus hundreds more Gmail accounts. There are many unexpected black swan considerations at this scale—unknown unknowns. Warm the domains that you side load and don't run off your root domain. Gmail has a 250-per-day sending cap. Maybe you can get away with 500 but don't push it; it sucks to get your account suspended. There is nothing illegal or unethical about this but pick your tools carefully and be willing to do a shedload of work. ReturnPath is a technology that has enabled financial institutions to send billions of bank statements and stay whitelisted.

Data czar Greg Meyer provides valuable advice: "Note that your mileage may vary and you should plan to use less than this while focusing on making your emails less bot-like in tone."[10] So if you want to send a thousand emails a day out of Outreach, you need four Gmail accounts and to warm them up. It's esoteric, but in appointment-setting parlance we call this *feathering*. You need to be very careful of your core domain, Acme. com, so you don't get dinged or blacklisted by the global internet service provider (ISP) community. So grab Acme.io instead.

Sam Feldotto, head of sales and growth at SalesHive, adds:

> Deliverability is becoming harder and harder and changes faster than most people can keep up with. Even the numbers Greg added above for a thousand emails per day across four domains wouldn't cut it today, when

it would have last year. Unless the domain has been steadily increasing in activity for months, taking four domains and trying to push a thousand emails across them per day within a few months is a great way to get flagged as spam. Plus, the domain is just one piece of the puzzle for deliverability. Open tracking pixels, especially when the pixel is using a subdomain shared by other companies using the same email service (SalesLoft/Outreach) are one of the biggest reasons emails go to spam. Using excessive HTML, link tracking, or even using spam trigger words like "Savings" or "Call" can be enough to trigger a spam filter, and that's before you even look at the domain. After the domain, you also need to be aware what IP your emails are being sent from. A good domain on an IP that's flagged as bad because another company sent spam on that IP (similar to the shared subdomain for open tracking) can and will result in your emails never getting through to the inbox. The main takeaway of this is not that high volume cold-email is impossible, but unless you have a very strong understanding of the intricacies of deliverability then you should not rely on it as your main outbound channel, but rather a piece of a multi-channel puzzle.[11]

We recommend sending your sequence out of Gmail versus Outlook, which has more problems with deliverability. Stephen Chase uses memes within his emails and has seen more success with that approach within sequences sending from Gmail versus Outlook, due to the fact that Outlook auto defaults to needing to click to view images.

Comically, we've seen a James Bawden email move around with a cute animal like a baby sloth and using a cuteness factor to get response rates. We're not sure about the relevancy, but it's quite funny and can work. This is like "the Bieber close" heard 'round the world. True story: On the rep's last day, he sent just the lyrics of the Bieb's "What Do You Mean." Meeting gets set, the deal closes, and it's significant revenue. That stunt and rep are still famous with thousands who bore witness and forwarded.

When you send emails at macro scale, you see many patterns. The real goal of all sequences, cadences, flows, and plays is to think about the Turing test. The implications of this are not yet understood. A CEO we know once sagely pointed out that consumers will demand a warning label for fully AI-written communication, and that will reduce efficacy. For now, you should make it look so human the recipient can't tell that it came out of a sequencer. We've done all sorts of experiments with short subject lines. Controversially, funking the grammar (making the syntax look ugly) and also testing deliberate spelling mistakes resulted in more engagement because it looked really human rather than from automated marketing. It's all a wide variety of spectra where you A/B test everything but hold a control to benchmark.

Think of spectra as follows: funny to serious, colloquial to formal, facts and figures to touchy-feely soft stories, qualitative to quantitative, right brain to left brain, super long form to hyper short. When considering all this, Jason Hubbard says:

> This is obviously really complex. It's where AI-powered solutions promising sentiment analysis, personality insights, etc., hopefully hold the key for being able to target these spectrums to the individual automatically. In the meantime, leverage segmentation both at the company and at the buyer persona level to find the types of content and tone that generally connect best. For instance, while hardly uniform, SaaS marketers interact with other SaaS marketers and as a result there will be themes to the type of communication they are used to and will respond to.[12]

The Hemingway App makes your writing bold and clear like Ernest! Don't forget to run Grammarly natively in Gmail to fix spelling and grammar, but A/B test funky grammar structures. We've done a litany of readability experiments using the Flesch-Kincaid scoring method, which is basically a proxy of complexity of the text. Leverage Lavender (trylavender.com) as an AI-powered, computational linguistics virtual copyeditor to craft more thoughtful, sensible emails with real-time scoring on the quality and relevancy. It can tell you your Flesch-Kincaid score and adjust your tone for the sentiment of the prospect. Like Grammarly on steroids, Lavender tells you how succinct and effective your writing is while you write!

Beyond improving your writing, technology can now even do it for you so that you edit its work, not the other way around. Autobound is a company automagically creating contextualized email content managing serious complexity around industry vertical, buyer persona, and injected contextualized personalization. Another example of how advanced things are is OpenAI's GPT-3 "language generator," which is being used as a sophisticated chatbot and also to write press releases, stock analysis reports, short stories, even poetry and songs. It is advancing at stupendous speed. In 2019, GPT-2 had 1.5 billion parameters in its neural network. In 2020, version 3 had 175 billion. How's that for blowing Moore's Law away for disruptive inhumane growth?

GPT-7 is coming soon and will go to a whole new level in AI email writing that integrates with other platforms for killer automated outbound. The next sales copywriting revolution is about AI delivering content on a silver platter for personalization. Examples are Lavender (trylavender.com) for email intelligence and Sharetivity that automatically suggests what the rep should write. Also check out Otherside.ai, compose.ai, copy.ai and Autobound.ai. Oh . . . yes, OpenAI's GPT-3 also creates computer code and actually does a better job speaking its native tongue, coding and numbers, than working with the horrendously difficult English language.

Yet computer writing for adults does not need to be all that sophisticated. The readability of US newspapers has gone from the sixteenth- to the eleventh-grade level, where it remains today. Humorously, or brilliantly, Donald Trump consistently articulates at a fourth-grade level. Jeremey Donovan has done some groundbreaking measurement of millions of emails at SalesLoft and looked at their Flesch-Kincaid scores to confirm that writing at an elementary school level, or *USA Today* level, wins.

Computers are now emulating humans with self-generated content that is staggeringly good. Players such as Lately (www.lately.ai) use AI to read your original blogs and articles, and watch your audiogram podcasts and also your videos.[13] It then technomagically creates a multitude of posts across all your social platforms that are pre-tested to contain messaging it knows your targets will engage with. Working with your base content, their platform creates snippets and publishes them beautifully across different social channels. It's run by an AI bot for "content-driven social selling" to build your brand and following to attract leads. This is *Star Trek*–style ideation in this space: "Lately.ai is *social publishing, Jim . . . but not as we know it.*"

Pushing these extremes with content automation and sequences will help you find sweet spots where you see an increase in performance as judged by open rates, click-through rates, reply rates, and ultimately conversion to qualified opportunities generating revenue. When working with sales engagement platforms (SEPs), add custom fields in Salesforce or other CRMs to pull relevant data into an Outreach.io cadence to A/B test. This is especially powerful with ABM for existing clients. Outbound analytics is the new science of pipeline and revenue velocity as measured by the "campaign touches" themselves coming out of your sales engagement platform.

Jason Vargas, in the book *Sales Engagement*, highlights these top variables to A/B test:

- Subject lines.

- Send schedules/time of day (weekday business hours, weekday morning versus evening, weekends, etc.).

- Value proposition order (which emails and value propositions drive the most engagement).

- Tonality (formal versus informal, etc.).

- Testimonials and case studies (analyze if certain testimonials perform better than others within the same message).[14]

Our suspicions confirmed in our testing that any response is a positive response. Even *remove, take me off the list*, or *not interested* is still better than nothing. We recommend still seeking a referral off this person. At very large scales of sending, over fifty thousand emails a week, you really should be looking at reply specialization or reply management. Hire a dedicated SDR/MDR for inbounds, reply management, and data cleansing. Start pulling all the replies into spreadsheets and attributing KPIs to them. See if you can infer which types of subject lines create which response families. The whole idea here is to look for patterns and streaks both empirically and quantitatively. You can break up the revenue supply chain into even further granularity with role specialization.

There are companies that create and clean lists with real-time data validation. One team in India prides itself on 98 percent list accuracy by putting each email through rigorous manual testing, firing a test signal at the IP range, and so on. Email verification is an art form unto itself if you can believe it. It's why data companies have become unicorns. One has three hundred reps in Portland just calling businesses all day verifying direct dials and emails. SalesIntel leverages their patented AI engine to verify their data and then runs it through a team of researchers to hand-verify every record and guarantee 95 percent accuracy. They can even automatically enrich Salesforce or other CRM with that up-to-date accurate information.

The emerging role in 2020 is the SDR analyst. Their job is simply to ensure perfect targeting and the most accurate calling and email data. Garbage in, garbage out. If you put an SDR who usually does outbound prospecting on inbound functioning as an MDR, and get an SDR analyst doing the list building, validation, verification, and hygiene—game over on efficiency. Massive productivity gains. Fine-tune your engine for greater success through granular role specialization! You're taking the Aaron Ross and Marylou Tyler SDR-AE complex a step further in revenue supply chain optimization.

Certain companies are already adopting an SDR-specific operations role, where instead of the traditional broadly focused sales operations role, it's instead some of that with a main focus on sales development. This is beneficial in a few ways, and it is most beneficial when you have a person with a large amount of understanding regarding sales development because they have personally done it and are proficient.

Workfront pioneered this role with Remington Rawlings, who got his start in operations after being very successful in the SDR function in multiple companies. He was able to know the tech they used, the data they needed, and the problems they faced on a day-to-day basis. Companies like this, especially those selling into the enterprise, really need the expertise of someone who can provide this air cover across the organization while the market adjusts to having more and more data analysts who work in tandem with the SDRs.

The focus on revenue operations changes when someone knows how to create enablement programs, optimize sequencing triggers / automation workflows in CRM, and configure the prospecting strategy with sequences that span multiple personas and title levels. Operations people who are sales-minded and understand what it takes to be a top performer (what it's like to feel the rush of when that executive answers the phone and you have one shot to do your up-front contract and value pitch) know what it's like to watch operations screw up your data because they just don't understand all the systems well enough.

It's these people who are going to be the pioneers of the future of sales engagement. Their operational understanding as well as their discontent with the problems are going to cause them to invent and iterate, and find new ways to apply and benefit from the thought leadership of Aaron Ross, Lars Nilsson, and other amazing minds mentioned in this book.

In one company, we spent $1 million plus in driving LinkedIn white paper downloads, targeted and tailored them by industry vertical (retail saw retail white paper, fintech saw fintech, etc.), and then ran Marketo ABM against them for drip and scoring and had a dedicated MDR firing on every lead. This strategy tended to yield lower-level people in the customer organization so we pioneered triangulating who that analyst-type reported to in the marketing organization, then used DiscoverOrg (now part of ZoomInfo) to map the power-base and call in above to see who deployed the person doing the research. The senior decisionmakers were ingesting the white papers in the LinkedIn feed and delegating their team to actually read and provide nuggets back to them.

Micah Zayner contributes:

> At my last role we were able to get up to sending 1,500 emails per day per seat with six seats running for almost a year. We smashed outbound and inbound, but I didn't have a good relationship with demand-gen or marketing so failed in the ad aspects. This time I am rebuilding it out so that all emails coincide with ad campaigns and all individuals in the system will be programmed to be receiving something at some point within a rule set based on their digital empathy score. MQL is too binary of a definition. Digital Empathy Score reminds us to remember who they are and what they are telling us.[15]

Now, imagine aligning your inbound ABM per vertical so that the content download reflects their industry. For example, fintech brands get the fintech case study. Then aligning that to the ads and retargeting they see. Then aligning all of this to the personalized cadences you build. This is true full-funnel marketing.

Guillaume Moubeche, cofounder, lemlist, knows how to push the boundaries in platforms, and says: "This is one of the biggest mistakes salespeople make with cold emails. When their open rates fall, they identify subject lines as the main issue. However, the real problem is email deliverability. Prospects aren't receiving emails because they're ending up in promotion or spam folders. Those places are like the second page of Google. Nobody goes there and you can't make a sale, no matter how good your email is."[16]

If you want to land in the primary tab, there are three aspects of email deliverability you need to pay attention to.

1. Technical setup (e.g., custom tracking domain, SPF, DKIM)

2. The way you send emails

3. Warming up your email domain

Initially, people used to manually warm up their address, which was way too time-consuming. Today, you can do it automatically with products such as lemwarm to maximize deliverability without breaking a sweat.

> ## TQ TAKEAWAY
> Email automation at scale is fraught with blocking problems. Choose the right specialist partner who has effective strategies, along with the right tools, to evade ISP blockers and customer spam filters.

TQ Is a Separate Meta-skill from IQ and EQ

Aptitude is a funny thing. For years there have been SATs and assessments even for sales. When it comes to MCATs (Medical College Admissions Tests) and passing the Bar, the truth is, no matter how many sales books you study, it's just like heliskiing. If you get dropped out into steep powder, you better have deep, prior, real-world experience or you're going to turn into a human avalanche after you face-plant. Being smart used to matter along with having empathy and reading people. They are both table stakes now.

We're coming back to technology quotient (TQ) here because it is the game changer. It is the meta-skill that unlocks sales excellence and the flywheel effect. If two people are as smart, as charismatic, intuitive, likeable, gritty, and dynamic, and one has a Gatling gun while the other has a knife, who will win in a fight is painfully obvious. And that Gatling gun is the ability to take your ingenuity on setting meetings and project it out into the future. To visualize a series of eight to twelve touches over thirty days to a thousand contacts.

You need to visualize the narrative of these messages, how often they bump up and nudge. Also how close they apply per vertical they address, per persona. It's putting yourself into the mindset of the future and programming, like a sales engineer considering how your prospects will respond. Thinking from the viewpoint of the fish, you'll optimize the bait. Bait is scientifically A/B tested with the classic "scientific method," which has stood the test of time with a hypothesis and controls.

Always sequence at the board and C-level too. Tim Ferriss is right: "The fishing is best where the fewest go and the collective insecurity of the world makes it easy for people to hit home runs while everyone is aiming for base hits."[17]

All aptitude is considered equal—it comes down to sheer technical skill that differentiates competing reps. Work ethic has always mattered, but the best operators know to work hard *and* smart. TQ is the new smart and hard because the technology does most of the work. We've seen reps give up trying after a single campaign in Outreach. We've seen reps take three hours to build the perfect one. Conversely, we know sellers that launch epic campaigns in ten minutes, pulling a custom contact list inside Salesforce, pushing it to Outreach or SalesLoft or Outplay, and boom . . . send.

We've equally seen great agility with LeadIQ, building a very tight Boolean search in Sales Navigator, and then pushing all the optimal direct emails right into Outreach. This stuff sounds really easy to do but actually takes some real TQ skill and dexterity. You are nodding your head in agreement if you've tried it. In every demo of a vendor's sales kit, simplicity gets advertised—but few customers actually fully utilize the bulk uploading, integration, and fast automation components of these systems. The ones that have high TQ and are competent (even unconsciously competent) have an enormous edge. Power users rule.

TQ TAKEAWAY

You're wasting money on tools if you don't have real power users in the team as exemplars, trainers, and coaches for everyone else. If you sell technology, make sure your customer understands this; otherwise they are unlikely to renew.

And what happens when power users rule? What happens when you can master the ins and outs of the tech stack more fully? The answer is simple: You will talk with more people and increase sales. You get on to doing the job that you may have wanted to do the whole time. This task of creating TQ in teams rests with the leader, starting with who they hire. Do they architect their onboarding process to include technology-intensive modules that engage the reps in activities that force them to see how the tech fits into the company's processes? It continues with the ways managers are encouraged to coach utilizing the technology to help reps maximize their efficiency. The new breed of SDR hires must become technology ninjas to be effective at scale.

The experts we talk with agree that the first phase for creating the future of sales engagement is just to start creating sophisticated work-flows to handle newly routed leads once the LeanDatas of the world do their part. Create triggers to get things where they need to go based on deep connections between databases, and then use other triggers or workflows to automate the data entry that reps typically would have to do. Create hyper-visualizations of data all along the sales process, all while creating hyper-personalization at scale because of the messaging strategies involved in the various sequences being used.

These ideas are essential for orchestrators of systems who focus so deeply on using funnel metrics to prove out the model that they build and understand what areas of training are needed. This includes the full tech stack to be harnessed by SDRs, their managers, sales leadership, operations admins, marketing leadership, and executives alike.

The future of sales engagement according to Remington Rawlings is:

> Move beyond the simple binary emails and calls you make to connect with a prospect after adding them on LinkedIn. The future is multi-threaded, omni-channel opportunities created based on key pieces of data served up to a rep, or given to a rep by the lower-level prospects, data that are then disseminated to higher-level executives in prospect accounts in such a way that they influence a buying motion that is more meaningful. You take away some of the manual nature of their jobs, then SDRs can live a life of creating relationships at scale, backed by extreme air cover from increas-ingly capable revenue operations and enablement functions who are using technology to its maximum potential and training reps to do the same.[18]

Tallying up his metrics from his most recent role in 2018 before Remington began running operations for SDR initiatives in a new role, he achieved more than 150 percent of his annual quota, showing a 96 percent conversion rate from appointment to opportunity because of his approach with the decisionmakers he was working with. In this most recent role, 9 percent of the calls he made connected, and he converted 15 percent of calls into appointments. He created $2.6 million in the pipeline in just three quarters. He shared with us a couple of the ways he optimized the tech stack for his own use as an Enterprise SDR (Outreach, Sales Navigator, Salesforce, Ambition, Marketo, etc.).

Remington started with a hypothesis that he would need to do less manual activity and more automated outreach if he was more organized account by account, and therefore get to more people just because he was organized. So he utilized old deprecated fields in Salesforce to batch his entire territory through mass updates and filter criteria in contact views based on a plethora of factors. This was in order to make his reports easier to manage and to build lists with ease to import to sequences for months to come.

He then identified all previous inbound leads, people who had opened emails, people who had been closed/lost, people whom he had seen answer the phone at one point, people in certain title levels and buying centers, industry, revenue, and so on. Even people with whom it looked like he could strike up a conversation based on their interests on Facebook or LinkedIn. He created account-based email templates; then he spent more time researching while his sequences worked on his behalf. Using email opens, intent data, and Marketo interactions, he also focused on accounts with the highest propensity to buy—and the people most likely to answer. Figure 3.1 is a diagram that Remington shares.

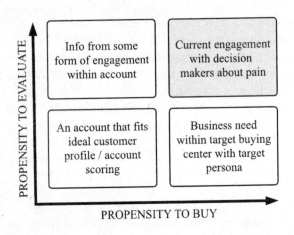

Figure 3.1
Source: Remington Rawlings, Advanced Revenue Consulting

After batching the data in the CRM, he utilized smart views and sequencing throttles to push people through to sequences on a timely basis to ensure deliverability didn't take a hit, and organized exactly which people and accounts needed to be engaged with via LinkedIn activity as the sequences progressed through the various titles and batches of people in each account. He hypothesized that if he could speak with more people in lower titles through their responses, taking a social engineering approach, and then reach up higher into the org earlier in the deal cycle with a relevant message, he could get more decisionmakers into play prior to the opportunity actually being created.

TQ TAKEAWAY

Automate things that are lower value to spend time on the things that are higher value. Listen to calls and get coaching and feedback to improve soft skills, and move higher in the prospect organization faster.

The results of this aren't shocking: as you can expect, executives took his calls. Here is what a typical email could look like:

Hey ____ , You don't know me yet, but it would be great to connect. I know a lot about your org because I talked with so and so, who said X, Y, and Z, and it sounds like there are already some people discussing getting these things changed. These issues probably matter to you and I won't waste your time. I'll call you this afternoon to share some ideas.

Because many lower-order activities were automated, Remington could focus on higher-value activities that truly engaged potential buyers in a strategic manner. He would lead with value pitches as bold as: "Give me thirty seconds to explain why I am calling and I promise if you don't like what you hear, I will never call you again." And they would listen. Why? Because he was automatically transcribing data across his accounts in sophisticated ways, using technology to reach as many people as possible to get all the data he could about pain, technology, budget, current initiatives, and so on. before he ever talked with an executive. When he got to an executive, he knew their business, and they listened.

This approach of social engineering created a sort of information funnel that led to accounts quickly gaining interest because high-level leaders notice how important things are to some of the lower-level people that report to them. "Showing them that you know them" creates a level of instant trust because it isn't a generic sales pitch. Pragmatic research can be made practical with LinkedIn Sales Navigator saved searches and saved accounts; pair it with maximum utilization of InMails, and constant persistence with phone calls to the right people during "power hours," which makes it easier to talk with warmed-up people in the account.

By doing this at scale, using email variables and snippets to insert the data from the account research or previous conversations to make emails hyper-personalized, you can also reach out to fewer people in a certain account with more impact, and protect the Gmail domain of their company. Ultimately, using all these practices, Remington created a legendary pipeline including some of the biggest enterprise accounts in the world, and it led to large deals closing.

The coolest part about his story, though, and what makes this encouraging for anyone who is in an SDR role now, or is trying to create a team of people who can do this, is Remington was newly married to his wife, Christin, going to school full-time during all of this at Utah Valley University as a philosophy major, working full-time as an SDR, helping serve as a leader in his local church congregation, all while dealing with health issues that made it difficult for him to work as much as he wanted to. By necessity, he optimized the tech stack and produced realistic, sustainable results across some of the biggest brands in the world because he learned how to automate low-value tasks, learned every button in every technology, and used every feature of the available tech to his advantage to set himself up to build quality relationships with his prospects.

The point in Remington's story is that the future of selling is not about SDRs trying to piece together all the necessary components of a tedious process, but rather about everyone (sales, marketing, operations, and leadership) growing the pipeline by optimizing scalability of their processes to reach their target personas. This is what will lead to a sustained winning sales pipeline with less effort. This is TQ. This is possible.

When Remington got promoted to run SDR Operations at Workfront, he also developed enablement training plans in conjunction with his colleague Eddy Morris, who now leads much of the sales enablement for PluralSight. They merged their combined talents in technology and enablement to solve the tech stack and end-user adoption issues they were facing.

They put together onboarding and ongoing education training geared toward helping the new SDRs and veterans alike to see the tech as an ecosystem. With a blend of strategic leadership involvement, improving sequence messaging through the diligent efforts of many people involved, and working deeply on understanding where each feature of the tech matched the sales process, they created an eight-hour technology training program that each SDR went through. Was it perfect? No. But they learned a lot about the importance of these two worlds colliding.

Help your people see the technology as an ecosystem. Remington elaborates:

> I managed user licenses and vendor relationships for 200 to 250 end-users consistently, depending on which software was org-wide or not. I knew which features were most important for an SDR to be successful and move fast through the tech, and I knew the gaps or how it fitted together. So I could tell, especially with top performers and low performers, why their technology understanding and capabilities played into their performance. I even tried to put together what I called a "technology awareness score" using the compiled data on an individual's technology usage which helped me to craft the technology training.[19]

Remington then watched the user data and correlated it with the number of opportunities created to then identify the top practitioners. Something interesting also emerged as the SDR managers became more aware and more savvy with the tech: they improved the way they coached. Dashboards were created to run a world-class sales-development team. These activities in onboarding are examples of the future of sales engagement and sales development. Constantly ask yourself: How well are reps doing with the technology? Which users are doing well and which are struggling?

TQ TAKEAWAY

You cannot manage what is not measured, yet not everything measured can be managed. Focus on the core activities or input metrics that make a difference and decide which skills to coach. You cannot succeed if you're running blind or drowning in irrelevant data.

Remington and Eddy drew flowcharts and diagrams to illustrate the way people needed to use the tech to be effective in opportunity pipeline creation. They broke it down visually because they wanted everyone to see the purpose and function of each technology within their core responsibilities and the sales process.

Remington explains:

> Even if a creative team didn't build this perfectly to be all pretty for us, we were able to use Lucidchart to enumerate the full playbook we created in step-by-step, layer-by-layer presentations. We started with Salesforce showing on the page, and then we talked about how to get contacts in Salesforce and showed them. And then we showed the sales engagement platform, and then the call coaching platform and how they fit together. Even if it was drinking from a firehose, we sent them off to their new desks with a clear picture of how their tech stack was set up to enable them to perform well. Others may have mastered this better without even using one of the WalkMe or Pendo technologies, or whatever, though we're sure those help. The point is getting through to your end-user that these technologies are for their benefit, and here's how you can optimize them. Then you take away anything manual from them that you can: automate data entry, triggers to auto sequence people, coaching smart views, call coaching views for managers, etc.[20]

Sales management is typically the weak link in the revenue chain for most businesses. To drive effective adoption of sales technologies, leaders should ask these questions: How many use effective smart views / lead lists with top accounts, or have dynamically updating prospect lists they can sequence from leveraging auto-import features that run at a set schedule? This allows sellers to surface freshly created inbound prospects in a centralized location. How many admins have created a plethora of triggers with automated data entry, including contact status? How many admins or leaders can point to the exact gaps in their account-based selling (ABS) motion and then train the SDRs to use every feature they need to in the right way? Are sellers able to quickly load new people into sequence with hyper-personalized messaging based on relevant triggers, attributes, or trusted relationships? Can their sellers execute rapid pragmatic research? Are new SDRs and sellers being onboarded in the effective use of their tools in the first thirty days? It's not okay for reps to take six to nine months to be fully "ramped" in their roles.

Remington is right concerning the future of sales engagement and sales development demanding new ways of looking at things, including individual, team, organizational, and even leadership-specific TQ to aid in quota attainment. The collision of enablement, sales ops, marketing ops, sales leadership, SDR leadership, SDRs, and AEs presents huge challenges. Only those nimble enough to learn about the processes entailed with being faster and better will reap the rewards.

Stephen Chase says: "There is a need for a new training segment, a subset of sales enablement that primarily focuses on tooling and progressing tech stack usage. I don't think those sessions should be optional either . . . it should be mandatory skill training."[21]

> "Education without application is mere entertainment"
>
> —Luigi Prestinenzi.

Ryan Chisholm adds, "It's unbelievable how many reps don't understand how to use technology to produce reports that intelligently target to save time, increase sales production, or improve the customer experience. It's also incredible how many reps don't attend internally offered education sessions."[22]

As expensive *field sales* resources transition to *inside sales* at lower cost, and reliance on technology for digital outreach becomes the rule not the exception, TQ becomes table stakes to stay in the game. Outreach.io gets it: "Triple your salesforce, without making a single hire," intones their native advertising. One ad claimed to increase by ten times the productivity of sellers. How is this number so high? The answer is TQ and platforms blended with old-school principles of value creation, relationship mapping, political alignment, and strategic selling. We've done this and created campaigns in weeks that generated results a team of ten old-school cold callers would have taken six months to rival.

Your future depends on your TQ . . . not just knowing but doing. The bots are coming and you must choose either to be their master or have them replace you. Let's now dive into the practicalities of salesborg execution that technomagically drives creation of a high-quality sales opportunity pipeline at scale. If you can crack this code, you will become the most valuable person in your company, maybe even your industry.

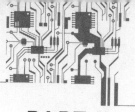

PART II

SALESBORG ACTION

"The successful person makes a habit of doing what the failing person doesn't like to do"

—Thomas Edison

Let's be clear: using any technology platform like a Gatling gun to blast spammy, botched messaging into the market just destroys your brand and annoys potential buyers. The foundation of sales success is strong product / market fit, clarity concerning ideal customer profiles (ICPs), knowing your buyer personas, and then nailing your message and narrative with insightful questions!

CHAPTER FOUR

Your Value Narrative

Before we jump into how to execute outreach at scale, let's first touch on what you will be delivering into the market. If "tech-powered automation" is the gun, then the ammunition is your value narrative, or the message you load into it. All messages and conversations must be about the buyer, not about us. We best earn the right to engage by having relevance and a worthwhile point of view. Here is a summary of the power laws for effective outbound before you start thinking about enabling yourself with technology:

- All communication must be relentlessly about the target persona's opportunity to drive improved results in their role. Do *not* open by talking about yourself, your company, your product, your service, or your solution. Anything that looks like sales or marketing spam is deleted.

- Be brief and communicate like a peer rather than a needy seller. No sales cliches such as "provide value" or "solution." It's okay to be slightly cryptic and assumptive. Get to the point fast because your buyer suffers from executive ADD. They are thinking, "What do you want and why should I care?" They also want you to "be brief and be gone." Anything too long is just ignored. Be easy to do business with by having a clear call to action that is simple.

- Relevant personalization is the force multiplier. As the legendary Marylou Tyler says, "Show them that you know them, right from the very beginning."[1] Make sure you reference a common relationship, a trigger event, or a relevant attribute as the reason for the approach. Quote them back to themselves if they've published something salient. Evidence any claims using other customers that they will regard as relevant. Anything generic damages our attempt to break through.

- Provide genuine insights. Be confident yet humble. Be consultative but with a worthwhile point of view. Rather than behaving like a "professional visitor," aspire to be their trusted advisor. (It's not a mythical unicorn role: it is possible and we know CEOs who publicly acknowledge some of their supplier partners in this way.)

- Have a clear and simple call to action.

Here is an example of an email that would actually work if you wanted to get to me (Tony). It's brief, references a relevant relationship to open with trust, and is about the opportunity for improved results (double-edged benefit of more revenue with less time or effort). It also talks "the language of leaders"—$250,000 revenue and shows that you've done your research by referencing the 99 percent heart blockage that was stented. Doesn't say anything about what is being sold (eLearning). Amazing . . . selling without talking about yourself, your company, or your product. It works.

> Subject: Justin COMBO $
>
> Hey Tony. Justin suggested we speak about some ideas on how you can drive more revenue from COMBO Prospecting. I think $250k is doable in year 1 and with less time and effort—probably important to transition revenue model given you dodged a bullet with your heart. How's Thursday 2:15 for a quick chat? Cheers, Trevor. PS. Book is brilliant, love the honey badger!!!

It's three sentences rather than three paragraphs and can be read in a few seconds. It hooks the person at a glance and is an example of exactly the approach you need for busy people—brief, relevant, researched, hyper-personalized, mentions a trusted relationship, is about them and their opportunity for better results, and with a simple call to action.

TQ TAKEAWAY

You can go crazy driving gazillions of outbound sequences across an array of channels, but if the message is wrong, you'll just be an annoying spammer. Delete, block, disconnect. Clumsy automated personalization that has low relevance has the same negative effect.

Beyond the words you use, written and spoken, it's the way you say it that makes all the difference. Wharton business school and others have done studies, and the consensus average statistic is that only 7 percent of received communication comes from the actual words. The rest is all about the way you say it with your body language and tone of voice. Steve W. Martin, a professor at USC who wrote the book *Heavy Hitter Selling*, highlights that C-level interactions actually work best when you humbly assume equal business stature (EBS). This weaves into the principle of uninterest or non-hunger because you need to be willing to respectfully challenge around a relevant business case for change.

We would advise you to become a student of business writing to get into the mindset and parlance of the ways these folks think, write, and make power moves. Oto.ai can analyze and suggest how to read emotion and improve the human voice during calls. Read the business journals, *Barron's*, 10K and 10Q filings, the CEO's and chairperson's annual reports, *Fortune*, *Forbes*, anything from the C-suite. Despite age or background, anyone can acquire genuine gravitas and business acumen if they set their mind to it. In the digital age of selling, you must be able to write; otherwise you have a distinct disadvantage.

Once you have clarity on who you should be targeting (ICP and buyer personas), and also nailed your narrative or value message, you can start to build lists of target prospects and people in those organizations. Here are some tips:

1. Run advanced Boolean searches leveraging Bombora intent data to find accounts closer to buying windows because they're already searching for your company.

2. Break your ICP into five to ten personas, then break those into title cloud arrays (VP, CEO, COO, CFO, CIO, CMO, CSO, EIEIO, etc.) to cluster for baseline messaging highly relevant to each in their role.

3. Personalize your cadences with injected custom fields based on firmographics or technographics. This can identify the prospect where you can replace inferior competitive or ancillary technologies, or augment and enhance other tech, which influences the targeting and scripts.

4. A/B test two dozen sequences and run sentiment analysis on the replies. Use the Crystal Knows Chrome extension to predict the sentiment and personality traits of each prospect. Leverage Lavender, which is an AI-powered virtual copyeditor, to craft

more thoughtful, sensible emails with real-time scoring on the quality (Flesch-Kincaid method) and relevancy. Match the tone against DISC personality.

According to Jason Hubbard, who saw our list above: "A data solution like SalesIntel can facilitate steps 1 to 3 by combining Bombora intent signals (along with reverse IP visitor lookups from your website traffic) with firmographic details (along with the contact information you need for your decisionmakers) which can then be pushed directly to your sequences all in one integrated solution."[2]

Crystal Knows uses AI to assess an individual's personality to accurately predict their operating style and behaviors. The AI analyzes text samples ingested from publicly available data such as LinkedIn, blogs, articles, or social media published by the person. The result is succinct summaries of the best way to engage the person . . . pure gold for sellers. Here is just the beginning of what a seller would see with Crystal Knows to inform their outreach.

Crystal

Tony Hughes
Co-founder and Sales Innovation Director

Tony is likely to be an ambitious and persuasive achiever with a casual and direct communication style.

(CONFIDENT) (SPONTANEOUS) (PERSUASIVE)

A Crystal Knows report goes on to provide summaries on the alignment or gaps in personality and operating style for the seller and buyer. Then Crystal coaches on the best way to communicate. The incredible thing here is that it is surprisingly accurate and beats sending your prospect a forty-minute personality assessment questionnaire as prep for the very first call to qualify any potential opportunity.

Technology is the key to unlocking personalization, which makes all the difference in opening a sales opportunity. Ewing Gillaspy predicts: "Targeting accounts will be like email verification once ML models mature. It will give sellers the confidence to not give up on the right accounts."[3] We believe Bombora and G2 crowd data is like reply rate pixie dust for automated email templates. Here is an example of personalized outreach from Ewing.

*Ms. Executive, I noticed that four people from your Denver office researched
Workday competitors in April (and that's after Covid started). This signals
to me an active research process that is fundamental and not seasonal to a
downturn.*

*We have a fresh POV about companies that [Insert another distinguishing
characteristic or industry or known pain point].*

Should I connect our teams for a few hours to see what we both hear back?
—Ewing, VP / GM (Not Sales)

*P.S. We have an executive headcount slotted for [Buyer's Title] event in Q4,
if you'd like to chat about that.*[4]

Yet personalization without relevance is folly. In seeking to automate
personalization, Greg Meyer says:

The most advanced approach includes access to a data scientist, or at least
a learning model that can ingest a variety of sources and provide signals.
Be cautious of people who say they can predict the future, and welcome
the people who suggest a model that can be tuned based on inputs to
produce better results than random.

The most advanced framework hasn't been written yet. It will use
some sort of machine learning (ML) model that will take data sources
(job posts, search intent data, press releases, social media posts, and
more) and provide a ranked list of the top accounts that should be prioritized for contact. If this framework is truly advanced it will be able to
produce a list of lookalike companies that will convert at a better than
average rate.[5]

As you automate and dramatically increase the volume of outreach,
you may wonder how much outbound persistence is too much. Again,
over-assertiveness or inappropriate personalization can get you removed.

*Hi John, I noticed we both live in Los Angeles and I'm reaching out because
our market leading plumbing lead generation service could give you more sales
as a proctologist. Can we explore opportunities together?*

Any epic miss will drive them to choose *do not contact* and *not interested* faster, especially if your tone, technique, or message is wrong. If
that happens, you can suppress lists in Outreach / SalesLoft / Revenue
Grid / Outplay / Groove / XANT / FrontSpin, and so on, but prevention is
better than any remedy needed from negative responses.

Yet, honestly, if you fear negative feedback or being removed, you're doing it wrong. According to Billy Sturgis: "Sales is binary and prospects are more likely not to give you a shot. It's important to find people who are ready to discuss, then find ways to make people refuse to say no."[6] You need to be able to go back to your boss and advise them concerning the status of all stakeholders in your named accounts. That's power, no vague optimism, in your account-based marketing / targeting / selling, instead just data driven reality!

The enemy of every seller is false hope. The sooner you know where you really stand with a prospect, the better off you will be. Believe in your message and the value you provide even if they don't become a customer. You must have a worthwhile point of view that drives conversations and is at the heart of all your outreach. Be willing to push for a real *no* and persist through false objections and smoke-screen excuses. Be brave and bold while making it all about them.

Your mindset needs to be *give me a real no or give me a conversation.* Press in and press hard. Don't let them ignore you. It's okay to be un-friended or deleted by people who are not going to buy. If you push hard enough, you will qualify where to invest your precious time and secure fast referrals and even some yeses within the 3 percent who are in the buying window or the 40 percent of the marketplace willing to entertain switching.

AEs and SDRs should collaboratively maintain a Google sheet where dream accounts are listed along with the six or seven stakeholders within each account. Make sure they're all in custom, personalized sequences with details that can be given to the boss.

Acme = Going with a competitor
Beta Corp = follow-up Q2
Delta Corp = willing to entertain augmenting an incumbent with our solution!

As soon as you possibly can, move from Google sheet to CRM. Any contact with "proof of life" or that you want marketing support for invi-tations to events, lead nurturing, and so on, needs to be in CRM!

When you understand *learning how to learn* and improve your TQ deliberately, the sales tech will fall away. The CRM, sales intelligence plug-in, sequencer, the latest auto-dialer, marketing automation . . . you'll flow through them and be human middleware. Imagine that. TOPO Research points to adoption of tech stacks as a major indicator of quota overachievement.[7] Better performance through technology is often about upgrading to a bigger, better mousetrap. In our view, the pinnacle is to see the technology fall away and enhance the analog experience. The best leaders and real visionaries have always understood this.

TQ TAKEAWAY

The ultimate sophistication in technology is the radical simplification of its presentation, to where it is almost invisible and intuitively enables the thing you are seeking to do.

The sales rep of the future needs to move from "Excel to S-Q-L," which highlights the need to move from manual processing to being data science savvy—from the Henry Ford production line to the Iron Man JARVIS suit. We are all seeking that "*Minority Report* meets *Iron Man*" interface that makes us omnipotent at selling, delivering the right prospect with the right pain and in the right buying window with a shiny red bow.

If you can master the most modern systems, you will transcend any competitor. One enabled sequencing master can eclipse a team of six, maybe even fifteen. We're reminded of Bruce Lee taking on fifteen goons in the round. Real deal! It also reminds me of Neo in *The Matrix* bending over backward, moving faster than the bullets he is dodging. "Nothing quite gives a business an edge like having a sales rep process fifty leads per hour instead of five; all without making sacrifices on their quality of work," says Vlad Voskresensky of Revenue Grid.[8]

It is possible to move rapidly, blowing away the mediocrity of statistical averages. Imagine lifting your game to move from selling 30 percent of the time to 80 percent of the time and even higher! You'll be living up to your full selling potential. A limitless pill? No, power laws are very real . . . we must embrace Pareto.

When you master automated sequencers, it's the ethos of "make money while you sleep." You can program a cadence that is as effective as six unenlightened reps because of volume and specificity with personalization, relevance, and timing. Decades ago, phone book advertising proclaimed, "Let your fingers do the walking." Now you can have ten sets of fingers, even a hundred, walking prospects up the ladder of engagement with "outbound that creates inbound"!

We know how to outperform peers, typically because we became so facile with all the sales tech, leveraging the signals from these novel platforms to break into the 3 percent of those inside the buying window based on trigger events. Steve Richard points to these Chet Holmes statistics: "Three percent of people in most markets are actively buying, whereas 40 percent of your prospects are susceptible to looking and potentially poised to switch. Anyone can get the 3 percent. How well you get to the 40 percent and shape their buying vision determines your success with outbound."[9]

Your ability to do all this at the necessary scale depends on how effectively you leverage the best tech stacks. This is where systems such as ConnectAndSell (parallel assisted dialing—bazooka) and Outreach (the cannon!) come in. They enable the true 10X moonshot for modern sales. Yet why are so few going full-bore applying this?

A sales manager is furious with a salesperson who arrives late, leaves early, and is failing in every area. Almost screaming, the manager says: "Your results are unacceptable and you're the lowest performer on the team! Is it apathy or ignorance that's the problem?" The rep just stares back, deadpan: "I don't know, and I don't care." Not a true story but maybe you're feeling bewildered, or maybe a little complacent. Set the goal of topping the performance charts, or maybe decide not to lose your livelihood . . . either way, spur yourself into the uncomfortable zone.

When we set out to write this book, we thought we'd share our experience and opinions on cracking TOFU, the top of funnel, which we've done for dozens of startups and more than a hundred market leaders. What we've discovered is that most sellers are using as little as 5 percent of the capabilities of the systems there to help them—even in LinkedIn Sales Navigator, which is devised like a Bloomberg terminal.

Greg Meyer knows that technology adoption is difficult and says: "But the gains accumulate geometrically or exponentially."[10] This is not unlike Excel macros, SQL pulls, and pivot tables that data scientists hack in their sleep with great sophistication and aplomb. You need to be power-using the platforms to truly gain a competitive edge. For top of funnel, applying high TQ gives you a huge advantage with:

- **Targeting.** You are finding the deals faster.

- **Messaging.** You are curating and sharing insights that are literally more relevant, piquing more interest (create real desire to meet!).

- **Personalization.** Showing relevance (opportunity, not just pain- and fear-driven) and building trust right from the beginning through common relationships, triggers, or playing back to them relevant attributes.

- **Conversion.** The perfect storm of "in the buying window meets relevance."

Let's dive into how you can transform results quickly by understanding and then harnessing the power of trigger events to target the right people at the right time.

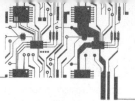

CHAPTER FIVE

Target for Relevance

Trigger Events

A trigger event is something that creates buyer awareness concerning opportunity for change or the need for what we sell. Trigger events can occur in the client's industry, within their company or department, or in their personal career. Trigger events can also occur in the marketplace and can include competitor activity, environmental or economic changes, reputational issues, new regulatory requirements, and more.

> "Everyone is drowning in the very data that can save them. Yet most don't even notice, let alone take advantage of what is available to them."
>
> **—Tom Rielly, CEO of Triggr.ai**

It is important to understand that an attribute is not the same thing as a trigger. Within your ideal customer profile (ICP) you will have the attributes of organizations that represent an ideal fit for what you sell. This then informs you concerning what you should seek to monitor in terms of trigger events.

Here is an example. Imagine you're a Salesforce rep selling CRM and you've identified "scale-up tech business" as being in your ICP. You've also decided that "Hubspot software use" is an attribute that matters because, as good as Hubspot is, you still have a strong track record of successfully displacing that product for companies with changing needs as they become larger and more complex. Again, an attribute that defines if they are in your ICP is "high growth," and you look for triggers that are associated with accelerated growth. Even though these smaller companies are not listed, and therefore do not publish their financial results, you can identify the growth trigger event by monitoring for 1) capital raising announced in the press or 2) hiring additional sales and marketing roles on recruiting websites or within Sales Navigator. Another trigger around the Hubspot attribute could be forced upgrades, price increases, acquisition, and so on. In the simplest terms, the main attribute within the ICP is the competitor product being used, and the primary trigger event is accelerated growth.

Here are other examples that show the difference between an attribute and a trigger. Remember that attributes help define ICP and triggers equip you to have conversations within the right context with people in those organizations. The trigger event contextualizes why you are reaching out to the potential buyer now.

ATTRIBUTE	TRIGGER
Has role of chief customer officer	Hires new chief customer officer
Based in my city or territory	Opens new office in my territory
Uses a weak competitor product	Competitor supply contract expires
Uses a weak competitor product	Competitor is acquired or fails
Uses a weak competitor product	Competitor rep or relationship leaves
High growth business	Announces strong growth results
Invests in staff training	Hires new head of people and culture
High compliance environment	New compliance regulations
High compliance environment	Major failure or breach announced

Trigger events are essential within our outreach narrative because they warm up the conversation with context. Referencing a trigger event shows them that we have done some research and that we have relevance.

Adding a referral from a common trusted relationship amplifies the effect by layering trust to the context and relevance created by a trigger event. Craig Elias writes about triggers in his book *Shift!* (coauthored with Tibor Shanto) and says that the average CXO deploys $1 million in capital on new solutions in the first ninety days in their role.[1] Now, this number looks incredible, but I'd say for sure the assessment and intent to switch it up happens that quickly. This is because new senior people are hired to effect change, and they also have a limited window of time in which they have high levels of support from their boss.

In our opinion, there are four types of trigger events relevant for sales:

1. **Bad experience with incumbent suppliers.** The decisionmaker has a negative experience with a current provider's product, service, or people. Dissatisfaction makes them open to considering other options, but the window of opportunity is usually small. Time is of the essence.

2. **Role-based change.** A senior decisionmaker or influencer leaves our existing customer or someone new joins a target buying organization. We should follow our supporters to their new employer and also defend our existing account against our competitor doing the same to us with the new person coming in.

3. **Change in results or strategy.** The customer organization has a significant change in results or announces a change in their strategic direction impacting priorities and operations. There is an appetite for change and desire to explore options for improving results.

4. **Operating environment changes.** The decisionmaker becomes aware of the need to change for competitive, risk-avoidance, economic, social, legal, or compliance reasons. There is an opportunity to provide insight and aspire to be a trusted advisor shaping their business case for change and influencing their requirements.

In business-to-business sales, the most powerful trigger event is a decisionmaker role change because executives hired into new roles are expected to drive improvement. The next most powerful trigger event is a change in results or strategy, because it necessitates change. Competitor dissatisfaction can be alluring, but we must ensure their pain or unhappiness is strong enough to sustain the perceived effort and risk of change; never underestimate the power of an incumbent. The weakest trigger events are within the operating environment category because there is usually less urgency.

Role-based trigger events can be interrelated as the changes cascade through an organization and in the market. Here is an example.

1. Our support leaves and goes to another employer. We have a

trusted relationship and congratulate the person on their move and ask how we can help them in their new role.

2. Our supporter is replaced by a new external person. We create elevated engagement with the new person, saying that we were working closely with their predecessor and have some ideas on some quick wins by extracting more value for our existing relationship.

3. That person came from somewhere. As we build a trusted relationship and provide value for them in their new role, we ask about their previous employer and how we could potentially help them also (if not their competitor). This provides us with coaching and a referral.

In the above example we have identified two "new logo" sales opportunities, managed an account risk (competitor follows new executive into our existing client), and created an upsell or cross-sell opportunity in an existing account (elevating the level of engagement with the new person). Although tracking job changes is easy to do in Sales Navigator, it's an underutilized feature. The most basic thing you can do to improve your TQ is to dive deep into Sales Navigator and build saved searches to leverage triggers.

Importantly, the key to working with trigger events is the use of technology. Triggr.ai is an excellent example, with their platform using the internet as the sales pipeline database to search and filter based on intelligent combinations of attributes and trigger events to provide salespeople with context and relevance in their sales outreach. Triggr detects technologies, identifies hiring trends, finds contact details, and more. It then serves those details in a consumable format for sellers in a web browser or pushes the data into CRM or marketing automation systems.

Amidst the tsunami of data in the world, we see what we look for. Modern sales professionals identify triggers and automate detection and notification to open opportunities with "warm" conversations. The very, very best go to the next level in automating at scale to harness the power of technology in driving productivity and accelerated success. LeadIQ or Apollo.io are further examples of how you can also efficiently build lists based on trigger events. For example, you can pull the saved search for job changes last week, suck those leads into a cadence, and you're off to the races.

Honorable mention to SifData and User Gems! According to Nelson Gilliat: "UserGems automates the job change trigger so you can sell to newly hired buyers, especially previous relationships (e.g., champions, users) and achieve personalized, timely, and relevant outreach at scale. Previous customers are more likely to buy again and buy faster. New hires are also likely to optimize things, have unspent budget, and aren't speaking to the competition."[2] It's a Yogi Berra paradox, but "buyers buy."

TQ TAKEAWAY

The fastest path to a sale is found when combining trigger events with referrals. Referencing a common credible relationship starts the conversation with trust and a trigger event provides context. Following trusted relationships creates amazing synergies.

Automation of Ideal Customer Profile Identification

Tom Rielly is CEO of Triggr and believes that data, and how we use it, is everything. "Sales leaders can no longer afford to run their teams on hunches, assumptions, and educated guesses. Being data-driven is therefore essential and must go beyond in-house systems to using data strategically to create opportunity pipeline, inform decisionmaking and drive effective action to transform the way we do business and drive success."[3]

A strong ICP is the foundation of building a solid data-driven sales strategy because it allows you to focus on high value clients where there is alignment and greater propensity to buy. Targeting those within your ICP reduces wasted sales and marketing efforts, and instead increases predictability, increases average revenue, and reduces the cost of sale.

Traditionally, when developing an ICP, sales leaders focus on firmo-graphic attributes of a business such as company size, revenue, and industry as data points to describe what a perfect customer looks like. However, the rapidly growing volume of information available on potential prospects such as technology attributes, news mentions, hiring trends, announcements, financial performance, and much more means business profiles are dynamic.

Technology can search and correlate ICP data in seconds compared with what a mere human could do in days. Triggr employs big data, AI, and algorithms to match characteristics of known ICP customers with new organizations that could become potential buyers. It makes sense of all the information out there and then provides you with a list of targets with whom you can drive contextualized outreach.

With technologies like Triggr you're also able to connect your CRM and the platform, and it will take a look at closed/won and closed/lost accounts over a defined period of time. The platform then benchmarks against public data to automatically generate a constant, up-to-date profile of what an ideal customer looks like to then notify you of key trigger events for driving sales opportunities in real time. The result is that your ICPs never become out-of-date and remain relevant while fueling effective sales activity.

TQ TAKEAWAY

Platforms such as Triggr can automatically analyze ICP based on the URL of a target prospect or customer, to then provide you with a list of look-alike companies to target. This starts you fishing in a pond where they are more likely to bite. Revisit your ICP and buyer personas, as they are always changing. Identify the attributes and trigger events most relevant to your sales success. Evaluate the platforms that can automatically identify the best prospects to contact.

The Role of Pain and Fear Drivers on Effective Messaging

Let's revisit messaging in the context of trigger events. Sales is a game of change management, and we must identify where the pain of the current state is greater than the pain of change. The easiest thing for a prospect to do is consume your time by evaluating and then just doing nothing. The only way to pique interest methodically, almost programmatically, is a pain-centric message. This is true even if that pain is the fear of missing out, of not realizing that killer opportunity in front of them if they open their eyes.

Fear works as a facet of pain: Tony Robbins talks about humans being pain- and fear-driven when the optimal state is love and success. Only a small percentage of buyers will buy for incremental improvements; most have pain that drives a faster sale for another seller. At the end of the day, if there is not a serious problem to be solved, why make the effort? In the land of laziness, fear and pain is the most effective motivator . . . sad but true.

Cory Bray and Hilmon Sorey from ClozeLoop always say that tailoring the message, in a way that addresses the pain that typically exists for a certain persona, provides all of the personalization most prospectors need to find success.[4] For sellers who have large market segments with a seemingly endless stream of prospects, individual personalization is not necessary to get someone's attention. If an email specifically describes the pain points solved for someone like the recipient, and they actually have that pain, enough folks will pay attention to fill the pipeline. If they don't have any pain, a further conversation is likely a waste of time anyway, so "attention-getting personalization" that has nothing to do with the recipient's needs can take everyone nowhere.

The trick is not to come across as a doom-mongering purveyor of fear. We must leverage their pain for their own benefit by setting a vision for a brighter future. There are only four reasons to buy software and most other things in the world of business-to-business sales: make money, save money, reduce risk, or maintain compliance. Steve Richard talks about this with what he calls the four demand types: commodity, better mousetrap, evangelical, and, his favorite, government regulation where the buyer has to take the meeting to cover their tail.[5]

So if you are approaching your market by leveraging fear or pain messaging and targeting stakeholders who have changed jobs, this is the most powerful approach to initiate buying windows. Remember, latent pain—the pain they don't even realize they have—is what creates the interest and drives sales. Steve Jobs, the world champion of predicting consumer desire, once said: "They never knew what they always wanted." He was a phenomenal demand generator, producing inexplicable pent-up demand for risky tech with lines around the corner like a *Star Wars* premier for an iPhone Steve Ballmer at Microsoft panned and predicted would flop.

It is vitally important, however, to use fear and pain in an intelligently nuanced manner. Ensure you have "social proof." This is a concept from Dr. Robert Cialdini, one of his timeless *6 Principles of Influence.*[6] Reciprocity, commitment and consistency, social proof, authority, liking, and scarcity all play a role in powerful automated messaging. Specifically which social proof? Ideally, send both qualitative and quantitative ROI results from very similar customers (optimally direct competitors) in similar verticals. This will achieve the fastest response as no one wants to be left in the dust by their competition.

Relative customer size is also crucial. You don't want your prospect saying: "Of course your solution works for Ford, they're Ford, but we are small and don't have their resources!" Good case studies are stories, and stories sell since the dawn of time. Joseph Campbell, who influenced George Lucas on "The Force" in *Star Wars*, pretty much nailed how to write "bomb sales copy."

According to Sam Feldotto:

> Another approach is to consider the person you are trying to establish your credibility with and provide them with an example of how you helped a similar persona, rather than focusing entirely on the industry they are in. Some prospects could care less about how you solved a pain for another company in their industry. If they're a VP of Sales, they probably care just as much about how you helped another VP of Sales with a specific pain they may also be facing. Even if it's in a completely different industry, that pain and social proof will resonate far better than relying on logos. This is especially true for companies that are targeting SMB-Mid Market companies. If you're using a client like Adobe for your social proof to a company with fifty employees, it's not going to be compelling. In fact, it may do the opposite. Since you may not have social proof for a company similar to them that's recognizable, focusing on the pains of the persona you are reaching out to and drawing social proof from a similar persona can be extremely productive.[7]

We created another set of techniques with job changes that everyone should be using who is new into a sales territory or struggling with the pipeline. First, run the deadwood and find everyone who's considered the product in the past year. Sequence to them en masse with "I see you've considered our solution in the last year . . ." You'll be amazed how many prospects boomerang back. It's a simple play you can execute as automated outbound that creates inbound. Run a report in your CRM of all the opportunities closed/lost over the past year. Find the stakeholders again on LinkedIn, pull their direct emails out of your preferred sales intelligence tool, and design a custom email sequence for win-back.

The other logical corollary technique here is to find every customer who has ever purchased your tech in company history and run a "where are they now" search to locate them currently on LinkedIn so they can be champions for your solution in new places. Sales Navigator has a "past company" advanced search to make surfacing this data simple. Often, past buyers move up in the industry because they succeeded using your tech and understand it the most. The users of today are the decisionmakers of tomorrow.

CHAPTER SIX

Design, Test, Refine

A/B Split Test Everything

Philosophically, be committed to quality but abandon perfectionism. We've seen companies, marketing departments, and sellers all get stuck in paralysis by analysis. The whole beauty of technology is that you can easily design A/B tests of subject lines right into a cadence in platforms such as Outreach. You can test six variations of the same message to six different verticals and buyer personas. It's endless. If anything, the core sequencer companies need to make better systems for the automation of full A/B testing.

If you launch twelve sequences, it would be great for the software itself to shift leads from one bucket into the other depending on how well they are doing. The sequence with the best-performing analytics lights up green and sends more, while red pauses or slows down. Imagine the cadence list stack ranking the best sequences right in the UI! That's the future. For now, you as the operator must review to make the crucial calls and adjustments. What's really hard is that "high open rates" are often a false proxy for "high rejects."

Figure 6.1 is from Outreach.io, and according to Max Altschuler, vice president of sales engagement, "Buyer sentiment is a first-of-its-kind, machine-learning technology that classifies buyer attitudes and opinions to accurately measure sales engagement. Buyer sentiment analysis classifies a buyer's email reply as a positive response, referral, objection, or unsubscribe request."

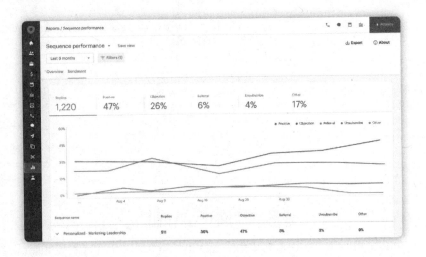

Figure 6.1

Source: Max Altschuler, vice president of sales engagement, Outreach.io

The future of sequencers will be programming the types of personalization for experimentation. You would send a thousand emails and for each email it would see the best connection in common and inject it into the sequence—university in common, common charity affiliation, relevant groups, and so on. Remember, avoid inane personalization . . . it must be relevant! There have been forays into this type of personalization using technology such as Hexa.ai that became part of OutboundWorks. That is the closest thing we've ever seen.

Apparently, Nova.ai is getting into the game using machine learning to auto-generate injectable snippets. Snippets are just a simple template you can load fast into an automated outbound set of email touches to personalize them to an individual prospect or persona or group of similar prospects within the ideal customer profile. We're also aware of some tech at Outreach that's doing sentiment analysis of replies so you can see if you're getting an overall reaction, negative or positive. They're heavily investing in AI specialists and serious data science.

Tactical things to split test include: time of day, day of the week, subject line length, super short copy and long copy, blends of short and long copy, test all lowercase, and so on. Test imagery in the second to eighth touch—it can be made quickly with CloudApp so it's compressed and features a wow moment. Test injection of custom fields. Test GIFs and emojis. Test fear-based or gain-based sentiment. Test every pattern interrupt you can think of at the front of the email. Example: "Hey hey hey . . . {{customer.name}}." Test a single sentence in the subject line of the email. Test song lyrics. Test humor. Test customer quotations. Test grammar formatting—very formal, super compacted, or funked out like poetry. Test purposeful misspelling (yes, controversial!). It often performs higher, looks plausibly human and not spat out of a sequencer . . . even if it was!

Sequencer 2.0 to 3.0 and Beyond— Static to Dynamic and Predictive

The sequencer of the future predicts the next best action. Should you use the phone? If so, which number (dialed from local area code), how many calls? Should you leave a voicemail? What's the optimal cadence of call, vmail, email, InMail, direct mail? What's the appropriate frequency of the cadence? Day 1, 3, 5, 7, 12? SalesLoft's SVP, Jeremy Donovan, experimented with the Fibonacci sequence on a cadence, which is mind boggling: 1, 2, 3, 5, 8, 13, 21.[1]

The future of semi-automation will take into account an omni-channel perspective. Companies like XANT have enough anonymized big data to be able to understand a "baseball card" summary per user. Imagine if you got into work, the system served up the appropriate customer list that day, optimized it per region, gave you the right playbooks and scripts to approach these leads, and knew when to stop the automated cadence so you could inject more personalized real human interactions. Even recommended ideas about what to personalize and a propensity score on the personalization angle. This is the future!

Aaron Janmohamed of XANT writes, "There's such a push toward buying groups and away from leads, although still most firms speak in terms of leads. We're quickly shifting to speaking broadly of customers and committees more so than just leads. . . . But this is a great summation of our point of view. Understanding buyer behaviors is really what it comes down to, and harnessing collective insights is the key to unlocking buyer intelligence. Who to target, how to engage, when to engage, what to do next."[2]

Luís Batalha, founder of Amplemarket, has developed groundbreaking sales engagement software that allows you to start hyper-personalized multi-channel sequences (yes, LinkedIn; touches included). You can leverage dozens of buying intent data points like someone that liked or commented on a specific LinkedIn post or ad and then start a sequence to that person that starts by visiting their LinkedIn profile, followed by a personalized connection request, and finally an email. LinkedIn is always closing doors of automation to outsiders so it's a tricky space to play.

Amplemarket incorporates fallback logic in dynamic scripting so you can set up smart parameters that go beyond curly brackets for custom fields. Imagine one call-to-action (CTA) for directors and another for VPs, or adding a customized case study depending on the industry of the company. They apply ML to help reps with repetitive nurturing tasks and get the most meetings out of the prospects you are targeting. As an example, the platform follows up with leads that are "Not the right person" or "Out of the office," automatically opting out anyone that responds with a hard no but doesn't click on the opt-out link.

The future of all the tech stack players will include "converged systems." As the price of building this tech comes down (G2 already lists seventy-five sequencers), we can see blended models across the long tail. For example: ZoomInfo has a super strong data set for dials and emails. They could acquire and release a sequencer and start their journey in this area by acquiring and integrating a company called Tellwise.

But what if a provider offered a blend of dialer, sales engagement, conversational intelligence, and a chatbot interface plus intent data? Although there will always be the best of breed point solutions, buyers are focused on reducing cost, increasing efficiency, and getting more bang for their buck by consolidating these Frankenstacks. The future is holistic offerings that are purpose-built for vertical industries, various budget types, and customizable all-in-one systems. Interseller. io is a great example of sequencing for recruiting, just as ChurnZero does sequencing for customer success in order to retain and renew key accounts.

The magic is in pulling all these disparate systems into a middleware dashboard for some flavor of robotic process automation (RPA). If there is enough big data and pattern recognition, through your training of the algorithms, you will be given recommendations for the next best or logical action with the customer. This is where AI assistants come in to solve the right problem. Salesforce Einstein is already doing this within CRM. Predictive analytics requires big data but companies like XANT have the Neuralytics InsideSales data sets anonymized to crunch at this level today.

According to John Girard, CEO of CIENCE: "We need to be applying machine learning and AI to the right problem."[3] Perfect personalized email automation may be about as useful as a Google Duplex call synthesizing a human voice; if we get good at fooling the prospect with AI, it will get regulated and require a warning label. "This message from Justin was sent by a robot with artificial intelligence." Just as we say, "You're on a recorded line," she'd have to say, "This call is placed by an AI; press 1 to accept." That's if the regulators even cleared the tech.

What's really missing? As a rep, do you know which touch patterns worked well in the past for other colleagues? What about currently? Couldn't learnings be brought back to you across the team? How about a template builder that suggests optimal steps in the sequence based on collective data? Why are the top 20 percent of reps so vastly outperforming the rest when all have the exact same tools? Software can answer this. Even with the same number of calls, emails, and identical skill sets, it can remain a mystery.

Effectiveness can be assessed and optimized through conversation intelligence analyzing tone, question style, intent, pitch, listen-to-talk ratio, and more. Yet in all these systems, we still don't know as the rep what to do next. We hate to reference Microsoft Clippy, because it was such an epic fail, but the AI assistant crunching in the background and giving you tips like KITT the talking car on *Knight Rider* helping the Hoff solve the mystery is where all this tech needs to go!

The problem is that the current products are built for individual users. They are not built to handle an agency's workflow generating leads for multiple brands or clients. Airborne is the first sales engagement platform designed and built for agencies: they solve multiple problems to make operations significantly more efficient. This includes managing multiple accounts, scheduling calls, setting up automated triggers, managing teams, and keeping client data separate in secure silos. If you're an agency or in house seeking to serve multiple masters in the sales-dev role, have a good look at Airborne.

On Sequence Design Architecture

When we built a hundred concurrent Outreach and SalesLoft campaigns, we had copywriters but there was an initial bet we made: brevity would rule. We dubbed the sequences *spears*, which is really a morphed term from Aaron Ross. Instead of a long-form marketing brochure, the sequences were painfully short, even to an extent that it was often a bit tricky to get clients to agree to sending them.

> *Day 1—Spear:*
> *Subject: Growth*
> *Hey Jim, Curious how it's going with Competitor X [HG Insights techno-graphic insert]? We notice they have [limitation 1], which drives [customer pain 2] to augment or switch to our solution. We differentiate by value prop A and B. Customers like Acme and Beta Corp have seen a 263 percent lift in performance due to [technical proofpoint 3] and reduced their risk. When's a good time to hop on a call? Thanks.*

> *Day 2 Bump:*
> *Subject: Thoughts?*
> [Hit reply all to previous email.]

Jeremey Donovan, SVP of Sales Strategy, believes in spacing cadences and making them unpredictable, which is another form of pattern interrupt. Read his book, *Leading Sales Development*, for a breakdown of some sales geometry.

Our theory of everything in outbound email is to always have mobile responsive design. Can it shine in the subject line and preview text on your friend's iPhone X? In our experience, the best subject lines are one to three words. We prefer single action words like *growth*. There's a whole conference called grow.co after this idea. Who doesn't want to grow, right? Jeremey Donovan tested five million emails and found reducing subject lines to one word increased reply rates on average by 87 percent. The other huge tip is, be willing to end every single email closing with *thank you*. There's a 20 percent increase in response rate for displays of gratitude.[4]

As far as the structure of the emails, three sentences maximum with the third being a call to action. No bullets, dashes, or wingdings. No italics, bold, or funky fonts. Hit the strip font key. Emojis are cool to use in emails two and three. Usually the body copy is just mentioning social proof of compelling business case outcomes and measurable results for similar clients.

We adapted something we called *tap-outs* from Bryan Kreuzberger at breakthroughemail.com, although nobody has ever defined this except maybe Art Sobczak from Smart Calling with *weasel words*.[5] Essentially, there's nothing more *trusted advisor* and nonchalant than, "If it makes sense to talk, how does your calendar look?" It's in the family of, "Well, we might not be a fit." As lacking in confidence as this sounds, it's the signal you are not arrogant and don't have commission breath. No one likes pushy or desperate sales strangers. Tap-outs let the customer walk out of the used car lot octagon.

The buyer is in control in the modern era; sellers simply can't Alec Baldwin, *Glengarry Glen Ross*, manipulate their way anymore ... and they shouldn't! Always write from a place of empathy and respect that caters to the prospect's intelligence and self-interest. Talk up to the prospect and show positive intent in seeking to help achieve a far better state of affairs for their organization and them in their role.

This begs the question of jargon—what's its role? We've heard pundits talk about removing all jargon and gobbledygook. Yet some industry-specific jargon adds massive credibility . . . if it is theirs and not yours! If you are selling to trucking supply chains and you know an acronym that is uniformly used across that industry, dropping that into an automated email will lift results. Guaranteed! This is because you are showing them that you know them and it creates the feeling that you are from their world.

Let's talk about architecting a value narrative arc. We went deep when designing thirty-day sends. Think of it this way. Send an email, bump it the next day. Wait forty-eight hours. New subject line (thread), bump it the next day. Continue assertively like this until you get removed, no, not interested, or referred, even yes. Visualize it and draw it out on a white-board or in an illustration that paints the picture to your team.

Remember that sales sequencing is not marketing or demand-gen. You don't want perfect expository essay paragraphs and formal structure in iambic pentameter. It needs to be compacted, the concept of *spears*. If you have three paragraphs per message, you're doing it wrong because it looks like drip marketing to a mailing list. You'll get deleted. A golden rule is that deliverability depends on brevity.

Remember that the people you seek to break through to are hyper busy. Whenever anyone "springs from the bushes" with an unexpected conversation, whether an employee at their office door or a seller on the phone or an email in the inbox, they're thinking: *What do you want and why should I care?*

Each spear and bump (a fast reply the next day to the original message) is broken into narratives in accordance with your own style. The first sequence cluster could be value narrative one. The second sequence cluster, value narrative two. The third sequence cluster could be diagrams or imagery. The fourth cluster, customer testimonial. The fifth cluster, an upcoming event and a calendar invitation. In accordance with *COMBO Prospecting*, condense touches within a sequence to pattern-interrupt viewers' habit of ignoring strangers and sellers.

This is where you need a vast array of creativity around the structure, the narratives, communication channels, and ways that the emails flow with multimedia. It becomes modern art! We've found that by switching the subject lines every forty-eight hours and keeping the body copy hyper-short, we were less likely to be shunted to a spam folder, opted-out, or deleted.

When we're writing sequences, we always go for that visceral gut response. The best possible outcome is when they just respond to the subject line and text in the preview pane. Then you've passed the Turing test and they don't even realize you sent an email out of a sequencer. They forget what touch they are on and it feels human. Then conversion rates go through the roof. Your goal is to be more human than a human messaging from the tech. Admit it, you don't want to see David Copperfield's mirrors.

Once we were asked to work with an entire CRM opt-in list. We sent one message with a subject line that read: *Throwing a VIP party, who should I invite from your team?* No body copy, just the opt-out link from a sequencer. Three hundred thousand people received it. We received seven hundred responses from CEOs of top tech companies deferring to the right VIPs within two hours. Unreal and unprecedented for those who know the outbound business. Ludicrous speed and overwhelming glass shattering response rate!

It's possible to leverage best-in-class messaging and sequences with REGIE, a sequence creation tool. You can choose your workflow and buyer persona, and then REGIE feeds you recommended messaging variables and sequence designs. The recommendations are built on over two billion rows of sales engagement performance data, plus their workflow allows you to take sequence creation from up to ten hours down to ten minutes.

Sam Nelson at Outreach.io swears by the Agoge Sequence to double results (see Figure 6.2). Agoge was inspired by the Spartan training programs for warriors in ancient Greece. Here is an example applied to sales, and it drives amazing results.

The Agoge Sequence

Step	Task	Day	Automated
1	Manual Email	1	No
2	LinkedIn Follow	1	No
3	Phone Call	1	No
4	Email Reply	3	Yes
5	Phone Call	3	No
6	Phone Call	4	No
7	Email Reply	4	Yes
8	LinkedIn InMail	7	No
9	Phone Call	10	No
10	New Email	14	Yes
11	Reply Email	15	Yes
12	Reply Email	17	Yes
13	Phone Call	19	No
14	Phone Call	21	No
15	Breakup Email	27	Yes

The Opening Emails
Middle Emails
Social Touches
Calls
Breakup Email

Figure 6.2 by Sam Nelson at Outreach.io.[6]

According to Sam Nelson:

The vast majority of the power of an entire sequence is in the first email and associated reply emails. . . . A great first email will increase the power of the rest of the sequence like compound interest: The more attention you get from the prospect at the beginning, the more effective the rest of the steps will be even if you don't get a response initially.

In the past we were afraid to have our reps customize because we were worried that it would cause them to spend too much time on individual emails. This was a huge mistake. The fresh-out-of-college SDRs were surprisingly good at customizing emails for high open and response rates. The key is to make it systematic to prevent misallocation of time.[6]

Part of the sequence architecture that Remington Rawlings shared (ultimately a product of a sophisticated, data-based approach collectively decided upon by enablement, operations, sales leadership, and marketing) was breaking the sequence types into a structure that made sense for segmentation based on personas within buying centers. See the example in Figure 6.3.

SEQUENCE STRATEGY

Sequence	Description	Use Case	Description
OUTBOUND	custom, targeted sequences to top cold prospects	Persona Executive Sequence	Persona/ Authority based Sequences
		Persona Champion Sequence	
INBOUND	warm sequences to inbound leads	Persona Executive Sequence	
		Persona Champion Sequence	
ENGAGEMENT	more generic auto sequences to cold prospects	Persona Based sales messaging drip campaign to lower levels - packed with content and less direct CTA's (to generate email opens and feed Level 1 Outbound)	
QUALIFYING	generic actions on people who've responded, but no meeting yet	Generic tasks every two days that remind a rep to reach out and keep the process moving with those who've responded from any sequence	
NURTURE	auto sequences to rejected/no response prospects to re-engage	Messaging that keeps a relationship alive even after a rejection or someone didn't answer to the initial sequence	

Figure 6.3
Source: Remington Rawlings, Advanced Revenue Consulting

Remington Rawlings says:

Within these sequences, there were specific templates that were tailored to various roles within that persona (i.e., within Marketing: Creative Director, Controller, Creative Project Manager, Campaign Manager, etc., and doing that for each buying center based on the targeted value pitch from the product marketing team). When you start to build sophisticated lists and route things appropriately based on those lists, you can take a top-down TQ approach just in the fact that your content strategy matches the needed focus for your SDR outfit.[7]

Each template was customized based on the specific pains and value pitches they knew the prospect was open to hear. Additionally, each rep was given the chance to personalize the first message in that template with a focused approach of giving account-based triggers and outlining a key knowledge of account-based attributes that showed the prospect they not only knew the business, but they also knew them in their role.

As good as the Agoge Sequence is, you can drive even better results by applying *COMBO Prospecting* techniques. We added COMBO to Agoge with a sales team of five people that were setting six qualified opportunity meetings (total) per month (epic failure rate) . . . to sixty! That's 10X improvement by adding COMBO with the right value narrative and with stronger touch clusters to pattern-interrupt and break through. We simply added COMBO philosophy to Agoge days one, three, and seven with a minimum of three pattern-interrupts within ninety seconds and always with the phone included . . . kaboom!

TQ TAKEAWAY

Sequences only work if you have the right message. Back up and make sure you've nailed your ICP, buyer personas, and relevant messaging to load into the Gatling gun of automation. Adding COMBO triples creates exponential results and can take 2X Agoge into 10X to 20X results.

When you are doing all of this in a sophisticated way, the key to success becomes your systems and your messaging. There are ways to make this really impactful, but it's not as easy as people sometimes think. And when you hit walls with lower open or reply rates, or your emails don't convert to meetings, you have to get creative. Jason Bay at Blissful Prospecting shares a checklist to fix cold emails that aren't working:

LOW OPEN RATE

- Open rates should be 30 to 50 percent at a minimum (ideally, you're at 60 to 70 percent or more).

- A/B test the subject line. Try using their first name or company name. We also have success using one-word subject lines.

- Make sure the first line of the email is personalized and relevant. This shows up in the preview on their email client.

LOW REPLY RATE

- Reply rates should be 5 to 10 percent of total prospects contacted at a minimum.

- Share relevant results you've created for others. Leverage social proof and case studies.

- Use an empathy-based approach by leading with the prospect's challenges. Prospects are much more likely to respond when you lead with *their* challenges, not *your* product or service.

- Keep your outreach laser-focused. Use only one CTA and keep the email to around three to five sentences, or fewer than 120 words.

LOW CONVERSION RATE INTO MEETINGS

- At the end of the day, this is the most important metric. Conversion rates should be 3 to 6 percent of total prospects contacted at a minimum.

- Make the CTA clear. Try being very specific with the day and time for a call.

- If a prospect responds "not interested," pick up the phone and call them. You'll get a ton of useful feedback to improve your messaging.[8]

The average cold email response rate is 1 percent.[9] The average success rate for a cold call is 1.48 percent.[10] Those rates of failure are unsustainable if an expensive human is laboriously executing the process. Success is increased dramatically by "warming" emails and calls with researched targeting and personalization. Technology is the key to being effective at scale both on the phone and with email. Jason

Bay says: "We created the Reply Method to help remove the mystery of what to say when you're prospecting."[11] Here is a summary of the REPLY methodology:

- **Relevant results.** Prospects expect to see relevant results you've created for similar companies with similar challenges.

- **Empathy.** Prospects want to feel understood. They expect that you know about their job, their responsibilities, and the challenges they're having.

- **Personalization.** Prospects are inundated with terrible outreach these days. They expect personalized communication that shows your outreach was intended specifically for them.

- **Laser-focus.** Prospects deal with more distractions than ever on a daily basis. They expect brief, succinct communication.

- **You-oriented (buyer-oriented).** Prospects don't care about you, your product or service, or your company. Make them the hero.[12]

TQ BOOSTER:

SalesSource released a touch pattern analysis that is not to be missed. Study it here: https://salessource.com/resources/4-must-have-touch-patterns-for-new-account-based-sales-development-teams/.

Read this carefully: we believe 30 percent of field sales roles are going extinct with resources being moved to inside sales. The reason is that field sellers are consistently failing, with 60 to 80 percent missing targets being the norm. Inside sales roles are half the cost, and investing in them with supporting technology creates much better revenue outcomes.

Lars Nilsson and Travis Henry prophesize:

The inside sales world is evolving. Fast. Covid has hyper-accelerated the move from outside sales to inside sales. With these changes, it's more important than ever to make sure your touch pattern is dialed. Every touch matters a ton. We've spent decades watching the trends. Implementing.

Testing. Tweaking. Re-implementing. . . . We suggest twelve touches for tier one. Sixteen touches for tier two. Eighteen for warm inbound and twenty for hot inbound.[13]

Outbound is an exercise in workflows and machine logic. The key is to nail the messaging at every touchpoint and master the technology that drives everything. Let's dive into the psychology of how you sell. Ernie Santeralli says: "Negative reverse selling is a 'reverse psychology' selling technique that helps to direct a conversation and test your prospect's resolve. It's done by asking questions and making statements contrary to the goal of closing a sale."[14] An example being: "Ms. Prospect, I'm sensing you're not interested in driving {{wildly desirable goal}} for {company}?" If all fails, hail Mary the ball by sending something unexpected. When you "close the file" they'll often bite, which is not dissimilar to strip lining a marlin while fishing, letting line out. Kreuzberger's "close our file" email is worth reviewing. Essentially you say, "Look, John, I had a meeting with my manager today and I need to close out your file unless I know where you stand on this evaluation."

This is wild, we know, yet you must be bold if you are to be successful. Not arrogant, but a true believer in the value you provide and not desperate in any way. Be willing to help them "qualify out" if it's just going to be a waste of your time.

TQ TAKEAWAY

A note on breakup emails: Mean them. Actually break up. It's all fun and games to reference a crocodile eating the prospect, but it's better to use reverse selling, a la Sandler, than be desperate or needy. Treasure your time and drive the conversation about why they should care, rather than about what you do and how it works.

We must start with the *why* in our messaging, as Simon Sinek teaches. Golden Circle messaging is where the rubber meets the road (see Figure 6.4). An important distinction for sellers is that it must be about "why they should care," not "why we do what we do." The cardinal rule of all messaging is to speak to both heart and head in honoring the "law of self-interest."

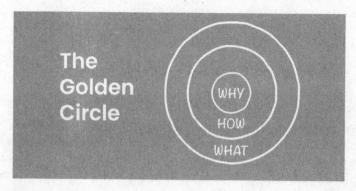

Figure 6.4
Image courtesy of simonsinek.com

Also recognize that every individual touch or single message must work in and of itself. If you focus on one LinkedIn message, does it properly represent the entire campaign? The whole is greater than the sum of its parts. The reason is executive short attention spans—they often only finally open one touch, like number seven. You only get one chance to create that first impression, so that single message must stand on its own. You can have touches that reference other touches, but make it like a hit Netflix show that you binge-watch: they always nail the preview to keep you hooked.

Here is sage sales copywriting advice from Shakespeare, da Vinci, and Einstein: 1) "Brevity is the soul of wit." 2) "Simplicity is the ultimate sophistication." If you only apply these two quotes by Shakespeare and da Vinci you will absolutely dominate sales. How hard are they? Near impossible. Yet this is what you must master to fuel your sales automation machine, both for written and verbal sales communication. Einstein's caveat: 3) "Everything should be made as simple as possible, but no simpler."

> **TQ BOOSTER**
>
> Become certified on as many platforms in this book that you can. XANT, SalesLoft, Outreach, and Groove all have universities, online training, and FAQs that go beyond the original onboarding sessions. Get certified on Salesforce Trailheads for Sales Operations (free resources abound!). Get under the hood of these platforms and certify yourself to future-proof your career.

Wesley Pennock is a coder by trade and the engineer whisperer for sales. He trains product founders and CTOs on sales techniques. He says: "The future of sales is a salesperson who speaks engineering, plain and simple. If you cannot understand what your product is doing at a technical level you cannot sell it!"[15]

Imagine if the CTO speaks CRO and the CRO speaks CTO, common understanding of fully automating, scoring, optimizing, and iterating agile development fashion across all marketing and sales functions. They could run hyper-lean supersonically like the scene in *Minority Report*, but with a CEO running all marketing and sales from a single VR cockpit with a holographic interface driving quantum computing.

Imagine a day when sequencers simply personalize for you. Tell it the personalization factors, it pulls in the data points from social profiles, and whips up the syntax and insertions via curly brackets with custom parameters that correspond, and stack ranks the most relevant based on broad analytics. It can dynamically choose whether to insert "common connection" and/or "head-count growth" and/or "funding event." It can quantify the propensity of success of blended personalization factors based on historical campaign analysis. You could even start to see autonomous campaigns using deep learning AI that gets smarter as they are run.

> **TQ BOOSTER**
>
> Google "Outplay 30 Sales Teams Share Their Sales Sequences." It's an enlightening real-world playbook.

Visual Prospecting—Pictures That Tell Stories

Eighty percent of communication on a phone is tone, so why aren't we working on *how* we say things and not just on *what* we say? Eighty percent of what we are responding to in a cold email are the feelings, emotions, and images (especially) implied by the writing. Oto.ai provides voice intelligence and can analyze emotion and tone during calls for next level automated coaching.

In essence, all phone training should focus on tone and all outbound email should focus on imagery (without actually emailing images in first emails that could cause blocking by spam filters). If you think of Amy Cuddy's TED Talk on power posing, and also Art Sobczak's concepts in *Smart Calling*, they encourage sellers to stand when they speak. Confidence is signaled universally through positive body language and tone. On the phone, you only have tone—what you're saying is within a window of marginal improvement, but one seller can have a C grade script and crush your A+ script if she actually sounds confident. Everyone can tell if it's BS because neuroscience and brain evolution makes us wizards at this discernment task.

Build immediate trust to set the recipient of communication at ease. How do you do that? Things like down-tones, pace, and so on. We could write an entire separate book on phone techniques (after ten thousand hours). But in the sequence specifically, how do you convey confidence? Directness is something to A/B test. Think about DISC personality profiles; high-D "Dominance" (decisionmaker!) wants you to get straight to the point as a pattern interrupt. Put the business case in two sentences. No pleasantries or "Hope you're doing well." Imagine a two-floor elevator ride with Mark Cuban. What would you say?

Crystal Knows can tell you someone's DISC profile instantly because the Crystal AI analyzes millions of data points to assess personality operating style. It enables you to nail the conversation as they want and need. "Hey, Sally, Acme got a 57 percent increase in productivity by applying this [differentiated facet of our solution]. Imagine how that could help [your co.] quantum leap the current process and output. . . . When's a good time to talk?"

Being direct is confident, and many high-D drivers who generally would never answer a cold email will respond extremely well to this kind of thing, even out of an automation layer. Yet beyond psychometric profiling, knowing their learning style (visual, auditory, or kinesthetic) is insanely effective—learn to tell compelling stories with pictures.

This is where we began to develop a novel method of selling for tech companies where we put a competitive landscape diagram into a Venn diagram. We would then screenshot it and put it in a sequence. The results were astounding.

This works because a picture is worth sixty thousand words based on how the human brain processes imagery versus text. We were once blown away by a herculean slide deck from our CRO with incredible depth and analysis. We were struggling to stay engaged but slide 263 jolted us awake with an image. We started to build bespoke Venn diagrams based on it that pertained to the competitive technology landscape. The title of the email was usually "Growth," while the body was, "What are your thoughts on the implications of this diagram?" That's it. Amazing responses. The Chief Digital Officer (CDO) of McDonald's responded in a single email with the Venn in the body. The Home Depot VP, on the first send, cold-called my phone and asked me to pitch him. I was dumbfounded. Brevity and visual relevance was breaking through.

Eighty percent of email is visual, so you should use CloudApp and make mini feature explainer GIFs with wow or aha factor to capture the essence of your tech differentiation. Remember, you are trying to use visuals to pique interest. There's a whole new school of selling built around diagrams that is very effective. While sequencing, make sure you consider inline explainer GIFs, Venn and Blast diagrams, comp analysis infographics, and anything visually short and sweet that will spike opens.

TQ TAKEAWAY

Visuals need to be used on email two or three at the earliest, because you first must ensure that you get through the spam filter before you start manually adding or programming imagery.

There are a ton of ways to implement visual prospecting using HTML scripting to customize and automate the visuals in every single email sent outbound pulling in logos and assets from the prospect's sites. Imagine the logos change each time, based on a check of the website. It can be very space age, but remember, use images only on the second or third touch to clear the spam filters. When done properly, you can achieve almost 3X opportunity creation rate!

We recommend using video from Vidyard, Loom, and BombBomb, building out explainer GIFs, screen grabbing diagrams, and inserting things like a Venn. A powerful video is a live recording of you navigating their website on the screen with your talking head in the bottom corner pointing out flaws or opportunities! Give them the point of view of a customer navigating their site and how it could be improved in ways that make them money.

CloupApp is awesome for this! We humans are visual creatures and decide to buy on emotion and justify on logic. Images fuel inspiration, awe, and emotion, which makes your message come to life in technicolor. This makes everything you're doing even stickier. The company Potion is using AI to dynamically change what's written on the whiteboard in the video per message. Instead of recording two hundred times, you just do it once! To make it even more sci-fi, it will even attempt to change what your mouth says. Deepfake video production is getting very good, very fast . . . you could have your own replicant avatar selling for you while you're snoozing. Your talking head with whiteboard text appearing as you speak. Could the ultimate empathy profession of teaching be at risk, just like selling?

You can even use apps such as REFACE to make your face realistically appear on other video content. It supports the deepfake premise, but imagine putting your customer's face on an Iron Man video action sequence and sending it to the prospect with: *Hey Tom, you can be the Iron Man of the soft drink manufacturing business with our optimization solution. When can we talk?* You would literally be making the customer the hero of the story with massive emotional cut-through. Search on Google or YouTube for "REFACE" and check it out.

Outreach and Salesforce both have simple functionality for importing screenshots. If you have a business intelligence (BI) system with a screenshot-able insight per prospect, take all the shots you need. Then rename the files to simple app or company names, put them in a folder, upload to a Google drive, then each one has an image code you put into a spreadsheet. The CSV file can then be pulled into Outreach and other platforms. Read that again: you can do it; it's not hard, and you'll look like a genius with your Luddite boss.

Another visual prospecting technique to add to your personalization toolkit is to annotate images from the prospect's LinkedIn profile or other social channels. If you're a Mac user, the slickest tool for this is Skitch (by Evernote). It lets you efficiently snap a targeted screenshot using crosshairs. In under a minute you can add your own text, arrows, or drawings.

Another example is using a LinkedIn cover photo with the background image, which is prime real estate from which to build personalized, visual prospecting outreach. A person's ego is wrapped up in their cover photo: it's a form of self-authored content, which Becc Holland's research tells us is the most potent premise on which to build personalization.

Frequency and Recency

Figuring out how frequently to phone, message, or email prospects is a subject for an entire book unto itself. Figure 6.5 summarizes the principle of lower frequency outreach the more senior the person being contacted.

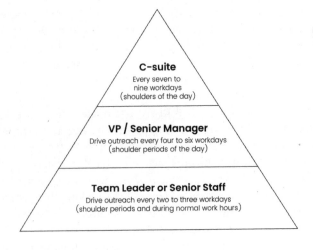

Figure 6.5

TQ BOOSTER

Search YouTube for "Becc Holland and Josh Braun and How to Personalize at Scale." This video is one of the best coaching videos you will ever see on personalization and automation of sales outreach. Note: if you do just one TQ Booster in this book . . . this is it. Becc is a legend.

We have some axioms around this to share along addressing questions of header, subject line length, body copy, and the best context of sequenced emails.

All sequencer emails need to look natural and real, not like automated spam, on a mobile device. Send one to yourself, some customers you trust, and colleagues internally to confirm this. Examples of automation problems include curly bracket fails, double-line-spacing, purple text, and weird formatting where personalization is inserted.

You need to do tight timelines on sequences; otherwise the prospect can feel like they've been inadvertently added to a newsletter they didn't opt into and that they're being spammed to death. As we will see, there is much dark art in the construction of campaigns but let's start with this most basic example in Figure 6.6. The philosophy in this example is to warm them up with email and social before making the call in the fourth sequence, which occurs in week two of the campaign.

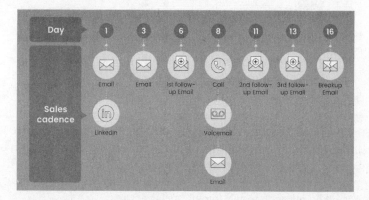

Figure 6.6

Source data for image: Freshworks.com "Example of a Good Cadence"

Figure 6.7 is another example from Max Altschuler at Outreach illustrating a sequence with a manual email and phone call on day one, and then a LinkedIn InMail on day two. This 'high touch sequence' is an example rather than prescribed best practice. Every business needs to define what works best for them in their markets.

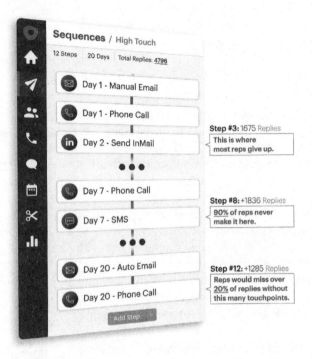

Figure 6.7

The workflows above may be okay for marketing-led campaigns or when selling high-volume, transaction-low value products; but emails on their own are just too easy to ignore and people sometimes don't look at LinkedIn for a week. This is why it is best to employ combinations of concurrent outreach to pattern-interrupt the buyer; and this is the premise of *COMBO Prospecting* with the phone as the tip of the spear supported by other channels (email, social, etc.).

COMBOs are essential because they pattern-interrupt people's propensity to just ignore anyone they don't know, and especially anything that looks like marketing or sales spambulum. Here is how it works. Their phone rings but you're not in their contacts. They ignore or dump the call. Back to skimming their email. *Ding! Hmmm, they left a voicemail; I wonder who it was.* They listen to the voicemail and hear your dulcet tones. "Hi, Mike, it's Justin. I'll shoot you an email. Looking forward to speaking." No, pitch. *Hmmm, I wonder what he wants? Ding!* Your email hits their inbox. Almost always, they will open it. This scenario is a triple—phone, voice-mail, email. If you just did one of those things and each touch was spaced apart, they would just do what they usually do . . . ignore.

Our previous examples included multiple channels, but you'll notice much stronger sequences in the following from Remington Rawlings, where he designs COMBO triples early within structured sequences.

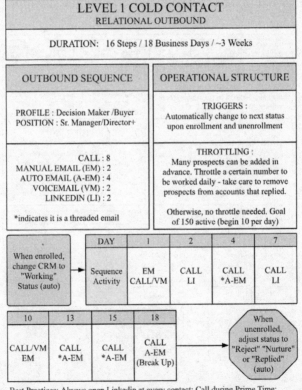

LEVEL 1 COLD CONTACT
RELATIONAL OUTBOUND

DURATION: 16 Steps / 18 Business Days / ~3 Weeks

OUTBOUND SEQUENCE	OPERATIONAL STRUCTURE
PROFILE : Decision Maker /Buyer POSITION : Sr. Manager/Director+	TRIGGERS : Automatically change to next status upon enrollment and unenrollment
CALL : 8 MANUAL EMAIL (EM) : 2 AUTO EMAIL (A-EM) : 4 VOICEMAIL (VM) : 2 LINKEDIN (LI) : 2 *indicates it is a threaded email	THROTTLING : Many prospects can be added in advance. Throttle a certain number to be worked daily - take care to remove prospects from accounts that replied. Otherwise, no throttle needed. Goal of 150 active (begin 10 per day)

When enrolled, change CRM to "Working" Status (auto)	DAY	1	2	4	7
	Sequence Activity	EM CALL/VM	CALL LI	CALL *A-EM	CALL LI

10	13	15	18	When unenrolled, adjust status to "Reject" "Nurture" or "Replied" (auto)
CALL/VM EM	CALL *A-EM	CALL *A-EM	CALL A-EM (Break Up)	

Best Practices: Always open Linkedin at every contact; Call during Prime Time; Protect SDR Dial Time; Customize every message with a small investment

Figure 6.8

> ## TQ TAKEAWAY
> If you have to look at them in LinkedIn as part of your process for sending an email, send them an InMail or maybe a connection request. You're there anyway so hit them up. If they look back at you in LinkedIn, treat it as a trigger event and call them.

Figure 6.8 (previous page) is for target contacts where there is relationship history. Figure 6.9 applies to cold contacts.

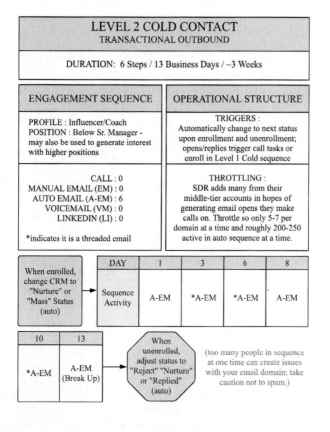

Figure 6.9

The transactional versus relational sequences show the difference in approach that can be taken to create disciplined effectiveness across a large team when prospecting while also allowing the flexibility of personalization for a rep as they start the sequences. All of these cadenced sequences are best enabled within your SEP. Higher priority would be relational inbound or outbound, with lower priority being transactional inbound or outbound.

Inbound is less rejection-laden due to the prospect having attended an event, downloaded a white paper, requested a demo or quote, and so on. Yet inbound leads still demand persistence in order to secure engagement. Figure 6.10 is for an inbound lead where there is no prior relationship, and it is therefore transactional in nature.

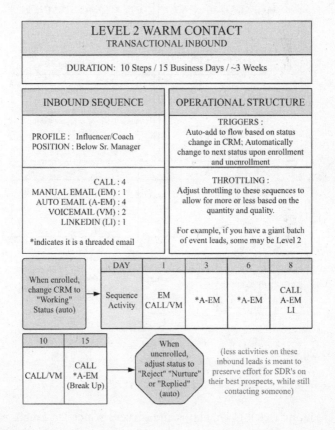

Figure 6.10

Figure 6.11 relates to what he describes as "In Conversations" or a sequence used to qualify a prospect. It illustrates how the SDR can stop worrying about keeping track of all the people who replied to an automated email or answered a phone call, which can cause the prospect to drop out of their previous sequence. The "In Conversations" sequence instead allows a rep to do whatever tasks are most important for that person every few days because tasks are automatically served up to them.

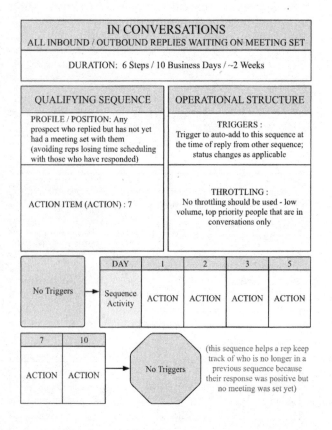

Figure 6.11

Let's jump back into email tips and success principles. Emails should never contain HTML or spammy links. The signature pane alone is a big problem for most senders because it triggers the spam filter and negatively impacts sender score. Never put *Sales* as your title. Again, avoid images and links in early emails . . . your first goal is to get past the spam filters.

In deploying automation, you are seeking these outcomes: *No, Not interested, Remove,* or *Refer,* and even the amazing *Yes.* If you are not assertive enough with the frequency of the sequence, they'll sit on the fence forever with it. False hope and *maybe* is the killer of sales. A real *no* liberates you to focus where you can actually help someone else.

More on pattern-interrupts later, but that's why you want to execute all outbound at the times of day most likely to achieve engagement (see Figure 6.12). Yesware analyzed nearly fifty million emails going out on their platform and discovered that higher response rates occur during the shoulders of the day. It's the same for using the phone, but be careful invading people's personal or family time with calls. Obviously the post-COVID work from home (WFH) environment changes the best times to call with far less commuting time in the buyer's life.

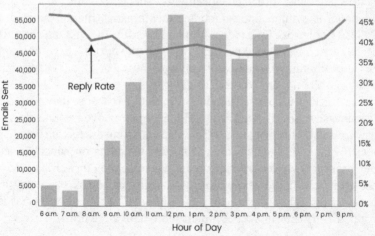

Figure 6.12

Pixel Tracking and Ruleset 3

We were once using pixel tracking within a primitive sequence in Yesware. The prospect kept opening our email and we'd call him, leave a voicemail, and send another email. Weeks went by and one day we saw him open the email seven times. We called and left a message. Then an email reply came almost immediately: "Nice data-driven response." This massive, famous company had entered the buying window and we did the deal in under a month. We've seen this result multiple times.

When you're firing with major semi-automated or fully automated sequences in Outreach, SalesLoft, or other platforms, you need to set an automatic task trigger any time someone opens an email more than three times. Three times is an open; four times means they checked it out twice. Over five times, it's likely been forwarded around inside the company. This is a huge reason to go COMBO on them with a triple (phone, email, and voicemail or text). We had special sequences at massive scale just for all the replies based on sentiment. Usually, replies to sequences are manageable one by one.

The point here is that you need to be watching the pixel-firing as a major signal of buyer intent just as you should be watching who comes in and views your page on LinkedIn. Add "profile views" as a trigger and back them into your cadences, invite them to become a first-degree connection, and make sure to do LinkedIn voicemail drops and video drops. Videomail is a huge thing—embrace it. Morgan J. Ingram created a 10:30:10 framework for a video drop on LinkedIn. The first ten seconds can be spent on a piece of personal research, the next thirty seconds on the value prop, and the final ten seconds on the call to action. That's what to put into a LinkedIn voicemail or video drop.

Pixel tracking is not used by some corporations because they consider it too invasive. But it's been around for a long time. We first saw it with Yesware and Cirrus Insight; also ToutApp and Groove. Revenue Grid has been tracking engagement for years, even including on which device your prospects viewed your email and whether they forwarded it to a colleague. You should be monitoring all your email opens every day. In Outreach and SalesLoft you can set a "Ruleset 3," which means a task is dropped every time a prospect opens more than three times.

Systems such as ClearSlide, Brandcast, Showpad, and DocSend are useful because they let you know how much time prospects are spending on various areas of your PowerPoint. DocSend has a heat-seeking missile in that you can set the forwarding to require inputting an email. Imagine you send the VP your deck and she forwards it to five people—with DocSend, they'd each input their email. What's remarkable here is that they're willing to do it and you can therefore sniff out the power base. We have seen presentations forwarded within their organization to four continents and out to third-party consultancies we had no idea were in the mix. It's really wild putting a tracker on the power base in an organization.

Personalization, Relevance, and Timing

As Bryan Franklin says: "Learn to hold the paradox." Here's one: "Personalization isn't always relevant. But strong relevancy is usually highly personalized."

—Matthew Kloss

Kloss says: "If one personalizes or hyper personalizes without relevance, sales messaging loses its fluidity and meaning, making the seller come off as awkward, unknowledgeable, or creepy. I've seen some crazy examples of this."[16] He is right. We've seen lots of personalization that misses the mark or alienates the buyer by referencing non–business related attributes. Beware pulling personalization from Facebook into business context unless being truly authentic. LinkedIn and a company's website is a safe place to source personalization.

Jeremy Donovan and Alea Hokison say, in their brilliant book, *Leading Sales Development*, "Personalization of at least 20 percent of email content yields a nearly 2X increase in reply rate."[17] The very best obsess on personalization.

Max Altschuler, Mark Kosoglow, and Manny Medina wrote in their book, *Sales Engagement*, "At scale, minuscule increases in reply rates and conversions translate into massive increases in pipeline dollars (a marginal increase of 1 percent to your reply rate over approximately six months [250 emails per week] is sixty-two additional conversations)."[18]

Despite the advancements, there are no technologies that can do what a human being can do. We've injected all manner of personalization into thirty-five custom fields and asked for more fields. The farthest we've pushed it is:

1. Mention stack-ranked common connection.

2. Mention school in common.

3. Mention company size.

4. Demographic, psychographic, technographic injection on a sequence.

As a human, you can quote an article, come up with a nuanced reason the common connection matters, and infer meaning from an annual report or business case in a similar vertical. Machines simply aren't there yet and human creativity knows no bounds.

Yet what we mainly see in personalization are epic fails with ham-fisted sellers fumbling the ball. Hi ((first.name))—the dreaded curly bracket fail that's comedic fodder in so many LinkedIn post feeds when it happens. All sellers need basic coding and data-wrangling skills, along with the mindset of an engineer in driving effective outreach at scale harnessing the bots.

The best way to personalize currently is to segment your prospect base ABM/ABSD style. Lars Nilsson is an expert. He recommends you bucket them into personas and then build campaigns relevant per persona. Use personalization injection snippets for tier-one accounts so each rep can pause for the most valuable connections to inject that most relevant manually curated snippet. Snippets are saved, snackable text bites you can place in Outreach to inject into messaging. We've even seen entire kill sheets and battle cards (competitive matrixes) injectable as snippets. Run a sequence to each persona by vertical or simply a sequence per vertical with different data in each for unique prospects. If you are selling to CPG CIOs, that's one sequence—then e-comm, then tech, then media, then industrial. Each would have a sequence with a case study or relevant application of the tech per vertical. As a sub-personalization, you could break into specific personas within each vertical.

The future of personalization is the ability to inject common connections, alumni affiliation, common groups, or any element of a LinkedIn profile into a custom Outreach/SalesLoft field 1:1. You send a thousand emails and each email surfaces the perfect common connections. Imagine if we all know Max Altschuler. The issue is, he would be the referenced common connection for each email so you need smart suppression and exclusion to stack rank personalization factors. This is the stuff technology can be trained to do.

The counter thesis is the art of obfuscation or confusion: cryptic messages, connection requests without personalization. Jake Dunlap of Skaled can confirm a 40-percent accept rate with no message attached so it's effective either way.[19] Keep in mind having a big network (as a thought leader) with lots of connections in common improves acceptance rates. Pique curiosity and interest. The mystery close. Cliffhanger! Leave them wanting more. Create desire and intrigue. There are only seven movie plots and it's an airport paperback novel approach, but you still need to A/B test it.

Nova.ai can pull from five or six personalization options including school, city, interview, or press release. It then puts it into a usable snippet, and then plugs it into an Outreach play as the first sentence. One of the best parts is sentiment analysis for replies. So one campaign might generate high replies but it's full of negative replies. This compared with another that has lower replies but higher positive intent in the replies. It's true that *any* reply can be good but you need a formula for analysis of all the eventual outcomes of those replies, and factor that into A/B testing.

Nadir Mansor, founder & CEO at GR8 INSIGHT, has built a technology that integrates with the majority of the sales enablement tools and CRMs. It is primarily aimed at supporting more personalized outreach at scale by providing research with relevant, actionable, and primary-sourced insight on the companies and contacts via an extension on the side of an SDR's daily cold calling and email tasks. The snippets technology allows for entire messaging to be customized at scale in an automated way with a simple click, enabling a fully personalized outreach per prospect in less than thirty seconds. The technology also allows for ranking of emails based on ICP by analyzing on behalf of the vendor the level of relevancy between it and the prospective contact. Value proposition here being focus and execution in boosting SDR and sales operations' top- and bottom-line conversion rates.[20]

Guillaume Moubeche at lemlist believes that personalization only works if it's based on detailed research:

> You can write great intro lines and customized value propositions but they only land if you go in full Sherlock Holmes mode to show them you know them right up front. You can use LinkedIn and Facebook groups, and YouTube for intro lines. For example, you can check out a video of them on YouTube and start your email like this: *"Just watched your video about X. I loved your angle on Y."* It's critical to make it sound natural and genuine, rather than write a meaningless and shallow compliment. This is called the 'tiramisu cold email strategy'. If I'm trying to sell to you, I can go on Indeed.com and look for your sales job posts to understand your team's objectives. I'd then transform that info into a personalized value proposition to excite you about using cold emails, not lemlist per se.[21]

TQ TAKEAWAY

In order to cut like a laser with outbound, limit the number of customizations per email (humans don't write like that). Also focus on a specific proof-point for that industry, and make sure you sample test and quality assure any new sequence by having a trained evaluator actually read and QA a representative sample of emails before you start blasting. You'll know you are doing well if people respond as they do when you text them with a great idea.

Relevancy, Humor, and Brevity

Humor makes you truly human but be careful because it won't always land successfully, especially when you're not delivering in person with your cheesy grin. For written communication, go for dead short, direct hit on relevancy, and quirky, wacky, ridiculous. Having a sense of humor will help you in extraordinary ways in life. There is usually a funny side of most situations, especially rejection.

We can remember an entire thread based on *Tango and Cash* and a year or two with lots of Ryan Gosling and *Great Gatsby* GIFs. Only you can let your unique freak flag fly so be yourself because everyone else is taken. Remember the Shepherd's Lament and greatest jazz standard of all time, "There will never be another yew!" More later, but relevant humor that lands with the audience is tough.

Just sending a baby harp seal probably sets appointments on novelty but gets old fast, as does asking if they fell in a hole and need a shovel, or if they've been abducted by aliens. When we talk about how emails get read, it's worth looking at the F curve of eye tracking studies. Executives snack your content. They read in a strange F shape darting their eyes up and down the page. Content is best in snackable bits. We broke three-paragraph emails down to three sentences and open/response rates went through the roof. We took a bunch of existing sequences and compacted them into spears, and brevity alone caused all metrics to shoot up, especially because it also positively impacted deliverability.

Again, be careful you don't have a bunch of messy links in your signature and remove any HTML from emails. There's a setting in Outreach where, rather than sending as HTML and plain text, you can just send it as hard-coded plain. Do that. Remember not to include images until the second or third send to make sure they are interacting with the content, signaling to the spam filter algos that it's decent mail. We're being repetitive for good reason: so many sellers get this wrong.

Richard Harris suggests taking titles out of your email signature unless you are at the same title or above, but especially for SDR and AEs. This is controversial for many, but why would I give someone any reason to dislike me more than they already do? Naysayers will suggest we are being ashamed of the profession. In actuality, it's the opposite. We are proud of what we do, so much so that our self-worth around a title is irrelevant to the discussion. Here is what Richard does: *Richard (415-596-1234)* vs. *Richard Harris, Sales Development Rep.*

Some advanced sequencers should have domain suppression on large sends. If your entire team is independently going after AT&T and nine emails come from three SDR/AEs, the spam array could catch it and ding your domain. Be savvy about how you segment. Be careful how many you hit per day in an account and with how you use email automation technology.

Greg Meyer at Data Czar has a definite view on this: "Yes, Outreach has a sequence setting (limiting daily email sends to that sequence), a user setting (limiting daily sends to that sequence). To limit overusing a single domain, there is a global setting to limit how many emails can be sent to a domain during a single day. We recommend that to limit overlap you use named accounts so that the chance of crossover on a given company between SDRs/AEs is smaller."[22]

Guillaume Moubeche contributes: "Personalized images made people more open to using humor. I feel they fear to play with emojis in emails, let alone joke with VPs of companies because they think it makes them sound unprofessional. But, at the end of the day, we're all human and we all like to laugh."[23] True . . . if what you send is actually funny.

Guillaume believes that Starbucks misspells names intentionally because they know you're more likely to take a photo and share your "new" name on social. He borrows this technique and as an example sends a personalized image with the {{firstName}} tag instead of the actual name of the prospect.

Below the image, he then writes: *Just kidding {{firstName}} [with their name written properly].* A joke on his unpronounceable name follows and that's gold. This was one of his best-performing cold emails. Plus, all images and tags were automatically updated, without him having to do anything! It also makes fun of the way so many sellers jumped on the fad of sending a coffee shop picture with the prospect's name on one of the cups—that approach was novel for about ninety days and then got tired and worked against sellers as buyers saw it too often.

To state the obvious, humor is tricky, so be careful. Stay away from politics, religion, radical social issues, environmental dogma, race, gender . . . most things, actually. We live in the age of supercharged virtue-signaling where many stand on the pinnacle of Maslow's hierarchy of needs—judging others and puffing themselves up with morally superior virtuosity. Being perpetually outraged is the new normal, and those pesky salespeople are a great target. Best strategy, just make fun of yourself.

CHAPTER SEVEN

Automating Everything

Applications including Tray.io, Workato, Zapier, Syncari, Automate.io, and IFTT (If This Then That) can help you link systems together via APIs and web services to automate a bunch of stuff. We had the opportunity to work with Data Czar and offshore VA resources to get some impossibly tedious manual lead processes done overnight while we slept. We have friends in India that pride themselves on delivering 98 percent accuracy of data quality. How can they do that? Painstakingly verifying each record via stuff like Hunter.io and Data Czar.

Nick Bonfiglio, founder of Syncari (former EVP, Product at Marketo), speaks about the future of data automation as not just triggers but being able to sync your entire data model and schema in real time. He believes: "Data automation is not just trigger, fire, and forget app-to-app integrations but being able to sync a unified data model from connected systems, in realtime."[1]

According to Greg Meyer: "Hunter does not verify; it provides pattern matching on likely email and identifies failed emails. Email verification is an art not a science and you generally know whether it's working based on response rate, not necessarily on inbox rate. You could be getting inboxed and silently spam filtered."[2]

Almost every sales process should be painstakingly prototyped manually to then be automated. Teams offshore execute tasks affordably and at scale and most data sources that you utilize—and we've tested them—are about 20 to 30 percent inaccurate despite the claims of vendors. This makes sense because stakeholders in many industries are changing jobs ever more frequently. The preferred sales intelligence tool for recruiters globally is LinkedIn Recruiter, with Lusha for personal email and cellphone numbers. LeadIQ has strong cell data, SalesIntel in the US, as well as Cognism in EMEA.

It's important to mention MixMax here for workflow automation to streamline workflows such as follow-ups to cold emails, calendaring, and automating replies. Email templates can be customized, standardized, and automated. With neat organization of templates and analytics, you can optimize performance of email-driven objection handling faster.

Sam Feldotto contributes:

> SDRs spend far too much time researching prospects and not enough time on the actual outreach. The average SDR makes about $70,000 per year, which ends up over $100,000 in cost once you factor in managers, technology, taxes, benefits, etc. That SDR is costing their company about $50 per hour to manually research prospects, which usually requires very little experience. If each SDR on a team of ten spends fifteen hours each week researching, their company is paying $374,400 per year for manual research. For a fraction of that cost, they could hire an entire team of research assistants in the Philippines to help perform that manual research. The SDRs can take that data and integrate it into their process in a way that enables them to replicate and automate highly targeted outreach without spending hours each day on the manual research itself. Not only will they be more effective with their outreach because they will have far more time to actually sell, but it will quite literally save their company hundreds of thousands each year that can be reallocated to increase team effectiveness through investments in new technologies or training.[3]

LinkedIn Sales Navigator and Boolean Search

The bottom line is that Sales Navigator has many advanced capabilities that you won't get trained on by LinkedIn. There are Easter eggs galore in it. Most users don't even notice that you can leave voicemail drops from a little hidden microphone icon in the native LinkedIn app. You can also record and leave direct videos from the LinkedIn app. You can tag up to six custom tags on your lead list in Navigator and re-sort the list almost like a CRM. You could tag prospects you've previously reached out to and there are six tags you can re-customize.

You can do Boolean searches by keywords and go further with OR operators: "VP of Sales" OR "Sales Ops" OR "Revenue Operations" and there's even a filter to see which prospects also follow your company.

Wouldn't it be helpful to prospect decisionmakers who already have an affinity for your company?

If you don't understand Boolean search, and if you cannot build one yourself outside the wizard in Sales Navigator, your TQ as a sales professional is too low. Without Boolean search skills you are operating at kindergarten grade when your competitors are executing at university levels! Launch Google and build a Boolean search. Practice your skills with AND, OR, and NOT. Filter, refine, find what you really need to succeed.

Here are the basics that you can apply in Google and in the free version of LinkedIn if you do not have Sales Navigator. In LinkedIn, Boolean searches rely on specific modifiers to help you find results more closely related to the types of profiles you need to find. You can build search strings in the Keywords, Title, Name, and Company fields. The modifiers you can include in Recruiter are quotes, parenthesis, AND, OR, and NOT. Here is a summary with specific examples.

Quotes. If you would like to search for an exact phrase, you can enclose the phrase within quotation marks. You can use these in addition to other modifiers. Examples include:

- "product manager"

- "account representative"

- "executive assistant"

Parenthetical. If you would like to do a complex search, you can combine terms and modifiers. This will find both software engineers and software architects. Examples include:

- software AND (engineer OR architect)

- (instructional designer OR instructional design) e-learning

- (human resources) AND "customer service"

AND. If you would like to search for profiles that include two terms, you can separate those terms with the upper-case word AND. However, you don't have to use AND. If you enter two terms, it will assume that there is an AND between them. Examples include:

- software AND engineer

- "product manager"

- "account representative"

- "executive assistant"

- "customer service" and hospitality

- "instructional design" AND "e-learning"

OR. If you would like to broaden your search to find profiles that include one or more terms, you can separate those terms with the upper-case word OR. Examples include:

- "Pitney Bowes" OR "Hewlett-Packard"

- Helpdesk OR "Help Desk" OR "Technical Support"

- "Vice President" OR VP OR "V.P." OR SVP OR EVP

- J2EE OR "Java Enterprise Edition" OR JEE OR JEE5

- "account executive" OR "account exec" OR "account manager" OR "sales executive" OR "sales manager" OR "sales representative"

NOT. If you would like to do a search but exclude a particular term, type that term with an upper-case NOT immediately before it. Your search results will exclude any profile containing that term. Examples include:

- NOT director

- (Google OR Salesforce) NOT LinkedIn

- director NOT executive NOT vp NOT "Vice President"

TQ BOOSTER

Search YouTube for "Using Booleans on LinkedIn Sales Navigator—Advanced Training" AND "Lead Cookie."

The LinkedIn wizards and interface make it easy, but as a professional you need to understand the underlying logic that is being applied. Your future career depends on combining the human aspects of selling with high TQ in the areas of search, workflow, integration, and blending the stack. Let's keep exploring the LinkedIn UI.

InMail is vastly underutilized. You receive limited email credits per month, but every time someone replies to an InMail you get a credit back. We've unlocked meetings with the C-suite with InMails, but be aware there is often a time delay. Most people give up on InMail too soon yet it can outperform email by 4X. Utilize all your InMail credits every month, trust in the process, and you will see conversions into meeting a few weeks out. The time delay on InMail is bizarre, but we think it's because so many executive assistants are tasked with blocking vendors to protect the time of their boss. Many C-suite executives jump into their LinkedIn account only a few times a week. Sunday evening is a prime time for them doing this.

Another underused feature is TeamLink. Essentially, within enterprise LinkedIn, there's a feature that allows you to see anyone in your company who is connected to anyone in the target prospect's company globally. We've had some outrageously good meetings set up this way. We were once sitting in Chinatown prospecting a top consumer electronics company and saw that an engineer at our team had previously worked with engineers at the prospective company at a prior company. It resulted in some powerful inside coaching that informed our outreach and we nailed the meeting into the C-suite.

Another feature in Navigator few know about is Shared Lists. You can build a Targeted Lead List or Account List in Navigator and share it with your SDR or AE and vice versa. The impact is huge as you're working the same laser-focused ABSD list and compare notes on who you know, connections in common, and TeamLinks.

Sales Engagement Platforms (SEPs)

The big four in this category are Outreach, SalesLoft, Groove, and XANT. They matter because it's not just about building out a sequence of emails to "set it and forget." Top of funnel selling is very dynamic and iterative. If you spam your entire TAM too quickly, you could burn out the known universe. In limited niches you might have two hundred top targets or fewer than two thousand contacts total.

Technology is not just about mass automation with A/B testing, it is also for laser-focused effectiveness.

In 2020, Manny Medina, CEO of Outreach, released Kaia the smart AI assistant. It was their biggest announcement in five years: "Outreach Kaia provides real-time transcription and can surface the right information when a rep needs it. Imagine being on a call, and a prospect asks you how X competitor is different. Outreach Kaia will automatically surface your battle card. A prospect asks for a specific followup action: Outreach Kaia will make a note for the rep and automatically add it to the meeting summary."[4]

Outreach, SalesLoft, and XANT are all moving into AI and ML in different ways. XANT (formerly InsideSales.com and raised $250 million from Silicon Slopes) is squarely attacking the market with a business process management approach. XANT is a play on *cognizant*, aspiring to future software that can actually think. Their goal is to inform the rep on the next touch, next action, right channel, and have a statistical way to back it up with anonymized big data. Outside of this innovation, it's a two-horse race—Outreach owns startup culture and SalesLoft has made its way across the entire long tail.

Aaron Janmohamed at XANT writes: "To accelerate improvement in your team's effectiveness, you need to adopt the practice of aiming before shooting (aiming being targeting customers and shooting being the deployment of a proven and data-informed engagement strategy tuned to the right customer). Unlocking insights from collective buyer behaviors allows you to refine your approach to meet buyers where they're at."[5]

To do it in Playbooks is fairly straightforward. There are a couple of ways to approach it in product today. Salesforce introduced their high velocity sales (HVS), which starts with sales cadences to enable the creation of customized pre-built activity sequences to help guide new and veteran inside sales reps through the prospecting process. Those sales cadences then populate a rep's work queue, a prioritized task list inside the console. That way, a rep knows exactly what next step to take with which customer, in order to build the strongest pipeline. Add to this email templates and native dialer, and sales reps can send an email or place a call with a single click. Outside Salesforce, here are other examples.

A/B test plays: Create an A version and a B version of a play and keep everything the same except for one variable (such as using a different email template, call script, switching the order of an email and phone step, adding or subtracting a step, etc.). Or you can A/B test with robots (automation engine) on separate sets of leads (such as A leads and B leads).

Always include in-app activity reporting even if relying on bi-directional sync with your CRM as a way of preserving data integrity in the primary system of record. This way, you ensure everyone has access to all the execution data from playbooks and you can measure A/B test effectiveness from native reports.

Someone living in a platform like Outreach for a year will outperform a brand-new user hands down. There is a significant learning curve for effective adoption and usage. We know this because we've often struggled to find all the settings and imports ourselves while watching others execute as fast as lightning. They had high TQ! There it is again, the inescapable factor. Old dogs who can learn new tricks will be hugely valuable . . . wisdom and effectiveness.

Revenue Grid takes a more decentralized approach. Sales leaders can tweak and bend the system to include anything and everything with a sleek, surface-level UI that encompasses analytics and reminders for every team member. Leaders have dashboards that display constantly up-to-date information and next moves for everything from prospects to opportunities to the team's own reps. Reps get "signals" that are both proactive and reactive, and automated playbook reminders and alerts based on real-time events.

Parallel Assisted Dialing (PADs)—a la ConnectAndSell

If your business connects once in every twenty-four dials using a team in India or the Philippines making thousands of dials and switching in the live contacts, it almost seems like automation of a different stripe. It can be a viable strategy if both your target addressable market (TAM) and ICP (ideal customer profile) within that TAM are big enough, and if you have a reliable data source for direct numbers.

Parallel Assisted Dialers (PADs) automate outbound dialing with thousands of calls being placed concurrently and then hot-switched imperceptibly to a live seller. Chris Beall from ConnectAndSell is the leading mind on this and says: "It's easier today for sales reps to find information about potentially relevant people, but research based on publicly available data still consumes valuable conversation time. The optimal mix appears to be:

- Lists created centrally by specialists as per the go-to-market market strategy.

- Lists then pooled by campaign with reps plugging into conversations on demand.

- While waiting for the next conversation (approximately four minutes) each rep makes and sends personalized follow-up video/email/social."[6]

Chris is the Batman of outbound and continues: "This mix maximizes conversation time—actually selling—and conditions future conversations for success. The target is thirty-plus relevant conversations per full day per seller. This works for SDRs (full day) and AEs (whenever not in discovery, demo, deal ideation, closing, contract, training). And fits the new WFH (work from home) world we live in by filling the day with selling (fun) and not rabbit holes (research without outbound)."

The jarring part is once you go from four live conversations to forty, you discover your reps often aren't capable of carrying the conversation, overcoming objections, peeling the onion on discovery, and so on. Your sales process could literally break because you are too successful in breaking through. It's an easy fix: upskill the phone training of your reps and have them drill the calls with each other. Suddenly getting all this live fire is like a return to 2007.

Ryan Reisert, from Reisert Consulting, says: "The beauty of forty conversations today means you advance ten days for every one day. Daily coaching and feedback means you fix broken systems way before a 'twenty-seven day magic sequence' yields insight on how to improve opens!"[7]

ConnectLeader's approach is a more holistic way of doing outbound marketing. There are always target accounts in your target addressable market (TAM) that are receptive to the right message at a certain time. The more specialized the messaging and timing, the higher the quality but lower the quantity. In order to cover your TAM, you can't pick quality or quantity; you have to do both. And in order to predictably reach enough quantity of accounts with high enough quality of messaging, you likely need myriad stories to tell supporting the variables and triggers.

FrontSpin has integrated their Powerdialer with their Playbooks (their sales engagement tool) to maximize the number of conversations between reps and prospects. This integration increases the number of live conversations per rep between 2X and 3X.

Dialing upstarts like Orum are distinctive in that they are software-only platforms. This opens up a whole world of possibilities around data intelligence and performance optimization. Additionally, Orum has integrated with cadence management systems such as Outreach and SalesLoft and the systems work well together. The technical and business background of the Orum team, coming from Stripe, Mozilla, and Rubrik, means there's real future innovation and development. If we mimic what reps are doing in a given day, they are creating to-do lists to prioritize. Orum allows them to click a button to have those to-dos auto-complete.

Amir Reiter, CEO of CloudTask, illustrates the category value: "If like me your time is better spent on having conversations with future partners and customers versus navigating your way through dialing and listening to voicemails, Orum and technology services like ConnectAndSell are the way to go."[8]

Route, Ruin, Multiply—Scramble Their Thinking

Here is a secret formula we've innovated for live fire on the phones since developing it in 2007. Back in the early days of SaaS, seven out of ten prospects picked up the phone. So if you are able to use Orum, ConnectAndSell, or ConnectLeader and go from five live conversations per day to twenty or even forty, you'll need to know what to say. Loosely, here's how it is done. The concept is ROUTE, RUIN, MULTIPLY.

The first question to ask is not: "Did I catch you at a bad time?" This has been worn out by constant use since it was recommended in *Predictable Revenue* by Aaron Ross. In fact, Gong tested that as a baseline for opening and "How have you been?" far outperformed it.

Here is an example of how we would open. "Hey, Susy, it's Justin from Acme Corp. Who's in charge of your mobile strategy?" [ROUTE]. They usually answer and then say who they currently use. "Oh, you already use competitor X." Now you need to RUIN by asking what's not working well for them without being disparaging . . . then shut up! If they expound on the incumbent competitor, that's fine. "What if we could augment/enhance/super-charge, etc. the effectiveness of your current solution by plugging us in to it?" [MULTIPLY].

This simple framework works because you call the person in charge of data and ask, "Who's in charge of your data strategy?" Natural reaction is the prospect is forced to take ownership and self-identify. This by-passes the trigger reflex to hang up the phone or intone "not interested." It's hyper-short and low overhead.

Laborious manual live dialing is going the way of the dodo bird so use parallel assisted dialing. If you are manually dialing, read *COMBO Prospecting*, which is heavily focused on blended touches with the phone at the center.

Data, Data, Data!

We've worked with nearly all the available data sources including ZoomInfo (which acquired DiscoverOrg, which had acquired RainKing), LeadIQ, Adapt.io, SalesIntel.io, and Seamless.ai, Data.com, Lusha, and Triggr.ai. All these systems strive for accurate data for calling and email-ing. They all claim secret IP and ethical methods in how they operate. You need them because without accurate data you're dead in the water.

Aaron Janmohamed at XANT says: "The fuel powering our Playbooks, including its scoring and prioritization engines, is collective data. One key answer to data going bad so quickly is to capture and harness real-time engagement and outcome data, refreshed constantly from across a network of buyers and sellers."[9]

We recommend you test all the sources that intrigue you and let the best performer win. All data needs to enrich your CRM system source of truth. You can purchase intent data from Bombora, leverage techno-graphic data from HG Insights, Triggr.ai, or Orb Intelligence. The list is endless. The magic is in how you use it. By injecting technographics from HG Insights and Triggr.ai, you can find companies in a specific vertical that have incumbents in their stack that you complement or replace. Mintigo AI (now Anaplan Predictive Insights) offers FIT modeling and intent data across first-party and third-party sites, to find other accounts that match your ICP—with Bombora further supplementing intent data if needed.

Lars Nilsson says: "At Cloudera, we used our own technology to join 'intent data' provided by Bombora with data from our Salesforce CRM. With several visualizations and tables at our disposal, we can detect if our accounts are 'surging' in interest in topics we care about and our target personas care about. If a prospect account is surging on Cloudera, Hadoop, or Big Data, you better believe we prioritize going after that account. Conversely, if a customer account has a surging interest in our competitors, our account team will take action to sniff out if something is amiss within [the account.]"[10]

Greg Meyer contributes: "Intent data from Bombora is a signal that appears from a network of affiliated publisher sites to indicate interest on a topic based on third-party white paper downloads at a company. A good way to access this information is through ZoomInfo, which aggregates this signal into a *scoop*."[11]

On the rep level, you might use intent data at a small company as a strong signal that a company is researching a topic. Max Altschuler, commenting on an Outreach feature, says: "Leveraging intent data to contact the right person, at the right time, with the right message is powerful. The integration automatically creates Outreach tasks for reps to engage with the accounts showing the highest intent."[12]

At a large company the value of "signals" may not be as strong because big companies have lots of people who research many topics. There is a lot of noise rather than intent. A similar deduction is true of technology signals—they can be a weak indicator but helpful in understanding the overall landscape of the company and whether they identify as a "Microsoft shop," a "Google shop," an "open-source shop," an "AWS shop," and so on.

At the leader level, you can use a combination of technology and hierarchy information, along with ZoomInfo Scoops and data on funding, and so on to inform the way you build your ideal customer profile (ICP) and customer segmentation strategy. Triggr.ai and HG Insights provide a technographic signal on the usage of technology within a company. It's a good directional signal, especially if you are prospecting based on usage of a family of technologies or similar. You can also access a version of this data through ZoomInfo or purchase it directly from HG Insights.

Orb Intelligence was a provider of company-level hierarchical information. They have recently been purchased by D&B. You would use company-level hierarchical information to identify companies and subsidiaries if your account model includes ownership of company subsidiaries. Obtaining an accurate list is difficult and you need a rock-solid email data source. If 20 to 30 percent of your data is bad, you'll have ultra-low open rates as a false negative. ClearBit and Lusha are great tools for locating email addresses. Even do reverse lookups using Rapportive. Data abounds! The trick with data is to find the right pool in which to swim rather than drown in an ocean.

You can pull custom data from Salesforce fields into custom fields in Outreach. This could include store counts, company size, imputed ROI—the possibilities are endless. One company had an ROI calculation per prospect so they just pulled that data into personalization for relevant prospects. According to Greg Meyer: "You need to match field values and not everything can be imported in, but in general this can work." He goes on to say: "Outreach defaults users to thirty-five custom prospect fields and thirty-five custom account fields. Users can request the addition of more custom prospect fields; however, additional custom account fields can be requested."[13]

LinkedIn Sales Navigator is the gold standard of lead searches. Overlay LeadIQ and then push into sequences inside Outreach, SalesLoft, or Outplay. If you can afford it, take the lists and pay for a manual verification process offshore to drive accuracy above 90 percent. Ryan Reisert says: "If you have budget for a rep you have budget for this . . . anything less than perfect validated data costs you more in labor writing an email or making dials than it will to human-validate. . . . At fifty emails and fifty dials a day you're paying $75,000 for a fully loaded rep which equates to nearly $10 per activity. Validation is less than $1 per contact. Do the math and it's typically the biggest contributor to waste in TOFU—GIGO."[14]

TQ TAKEAWAY

When you're executing Booleans, seek a manageable number under 3,000 or even 1,500 down to 500 leads. Bridge Group studies highlight that a great SDR can handle on average 200 accounts per month and be effective.

A thousand contacts per week is a strong number to run sequencing on if you're applying the hygiene and personalization practices spoken about, but if this is too generic, Greg Meyer from Data Czar provides a specific example:

> Let's say you want to get to technical leaders who work for high-growth companies. First you need a list of high-growth companies (you can use CrunchBase for funding information); then you find a list of leaders based on title (be careful though, a vice president at a bank is different than a vice president at Amazon.com). Then, look for commonalities (they have a keyword listed for a technology, they went to a school you did, they worked with someone you did) and build your filters to screen for these attributes. You don't want to use all of them at once—that would seem creepy—but you do want to highlight something that makes the reader feel you've done your research.[15]

LEAiDS.com can contribute because many intent data suppliers only provide the company that's showing buying intent. If you want more detailed information, and want to know who the individuals are within that company doing research, then tools like LEAiDS.com augment with the next-level data. LEAiDS combines behavioral targeting data, identifying who is in the market for what you sell, with the full contact record, so you can reach out to the right person at the right moment in the buyer's journey.

We've worked in the mobile marketing and advertising industry, and business intelligence systems like Apptopia and MightySignal were hugely helpful. They have SDK emulators that look at the ways an API fires to understand which SDKs are inside the mobile app build. The way we innovated using this for targeting was to assume clients were on twelve-month SaaS contracts, and pulling a report of all the SDKs of a direct competitor installed nine months ago. This imputed a three-month buying window and we could stack rank based on popularity or monthly active user count, plus who was most likely to renew. We share this case study as you could impute buying windows using install with several BI systems including MixRank. A genius SDR even took the trend analyses, turned them into mini websites, and injected them into Outreach custom fields.

What's the future of data platforms? With the ZoomInfo IPO in 2020, consolidation has gone berserk. Capital raising in the sales tech stack category is also rampant. Amidst all the offerings, when we think about gaps in what data providers offer, the glaring holes are normalization, enrichment, hygiene, and the ability to smoothly ingest that signal into sales engagement platforms via .csv export/import automation. Right now it requires human offshore VA work to build paper prototypes of these highly manual processes. You could automate them by having your developers write scripts or utilizing Tray.io or Zapier. Some companies such as Adapt.io are resting their data and sequencer on the same code base, which is a tough challenge to master for data accuracy and sales engagement power all in one. Other upstarts, including Outplay, are building a faster, leaner mousetrap to the Big 4 sales engagement players.

We asked Greg Meyer how he solves this now and in the future:

Today we would do the following: 1) identify the fields used to trigger enrichment (for lead usually email or email plus company name, for account, name and website and country), 2) decide which fields we want to bring in from enrichment if successful, and build a "holding area" on the object or on a supplemental object to compare data received from enrichment to data currently on the object. For example, if you received a lead from an event and the lead indicated that their phone number was 212-555-1212 in the US, you might want to compare that to a phone number you receive from that phone number using enrichment. If you have a list of known bogus phone numbers, you might know that the lead gave you an intentionally incorrect number. On the other hand, you might receive a fresher phone number from the lead than you do from enrichment.

So step one is to decide how to take some or all fields from enrichment and to make that process triggered by a button click. Step two is to build something into your lead process that prevents routing until you have a minimum viable lead. This might mean you wait to route a lead until it is enriched. Step three is to automate and standardize the collection of data— the best bet there is to identify your most common sources and standardize the delivery of that information. Whether API, CSV, or ETL, you need to know that you are getting a certain type of information in a known schema so you can transform it or import it.

When it comes to what data providers could do to make that data more digestible, ultimately they will need to identify, per each item of data they collect, the source and date of that data, as well as the confidence they have in the accuracy. For example, you might have a record with a First Name, Job Title, Email, Phone number, and Company name where the most recent data is the email and company name because the person changed jobs. Exposing the confidence and source of each data point will be key to increasing transparency and trust for data providers.[16]

Greg Meyer is one of the best minds on the planet and we can see the power of having the right data to drive effective outreach, whether it be for marketing or sales teams.

Tommy Liantonio from LiftCertain is building device graphs for B2B targeting so you can understand which visitors come to your site. His tech will allow you to use paid media and DSP (Demand Side Platform) style programmatic advertising to grab B2B prospects and the highest intent leads. When you think about LinkedIn Marketing Solutions and the acquisition of Drawbridge to enhance AI-driven advertising targeting, you can understand another strong play for B2B marketers and sales leaders beyond integrating intent data is to place paid media ads that are hyper-targeted to B2B buyers.

If your marketing team is going long on SEO, SEM, and native ads within B2B on the site and external ad network within LinkedIn Audience Network, shouldn't the sales and marketing orgs be on the same page to do hyper B2B targeting with a proprietary device graph system like Tommy's? Only 7 percent of B2B sales leaders are doing paid media targeting. Consider the insane power of knowing exactly who hits your website, identifying strong attribution, and grabbing look-alikes across the far reaches of the web, matching them up for identity resolution to your customer or prospect database!

Mark Chaffey, cofounder and CEO of Hackajob, is thinking outside the box by blending everything together. According to Mark: "We're running SDR Outbound via SalesLoft using email, call, LinkedIn plus Video. We add to this retargeting (across LinkedIn, Facebook and Instagram) while contacts are in cadence. It's exciting to see the combo of outbound and inbound ads in the same workflow! We're leveraging ActiveCampaign in Salesforce with smart rules that automatically trigger paid media campaigns when someone moves into cadence inside SalesLoft. They see the ad and automatically get moved into the SalesLoft cadence. It's mind-blowing."[17]

The Ethics of Data Sourcing

Public information on the internet is the insanely powerful database for sales and marketing to use, rather than relying exclusively on internal

CRM or marketing automation system data sets. This is because augmented data is essential for meeting customer expectations with personalization and the right context in engagement.

The best sellers already research before engaging, but humans are inefficient at filtering big data sets, reading, copying, and pasting information. Automated data capture is already augmenting systems, and it is common practice. Every modern business is embracing technology to improve efficiency.

Automation of data enrichment is important because customers and potential clients expect us to engage them on the basis that we 1) truly know them, 2) personalize their experience, and 3) anticipate their needs. Researching before engagement has never been more important and AI can provide efficiency gains by machine reading public data to provide contextualized summaries and personalization coaching for sellers. Machine reading (scraping) simply does what a real human does, just faster and more accurately, in accessing public-facing webpages and publicly available data.

In recent years there was a battle that raged where LinkedIn sought to restrict access to members' public data. Facebook is also leading the resistance despite their actions arguably being in breach of antitrust laws as they seek to eliminate competition and leverage their monopolistic market dominance. The issue is that users have given their permission for certain information about them to be made available to the public, but the terms of use of the platform provider prohibits any machine reading of that data.

LinkedIn engaged in a watershed legal case against hiQ who (along with thousands of others) were machine reading public-facing data. LinkedIn believed that scraping violated the Computer Fraud and Abuse Act (CFAA), a 1986 law that makes computer hacking a crime. After LinkedIn issued a cease-and-desist order, hiQ sued, asking courts to rule that its activities did not, in fact, violate the CFAA or constitute hacking.

The result? David defeated Goliath; hiQ won the initial case in late 2017 with US District Judge Edward M. Chen in San Francisco granting a preliminary injunction giving hiQ access to LinkedIn. In his twenty-five-page opinion, Judge Chen said that the 1986 CFAA was not intended to outlaw the collection of online public information. But Microsoft had acquired LinkedIn and they appealed, knowing their very deep pockets and armies of lawyers could very well win the second battle.

Orin Kerr is a legal scholar at George Washington University who was disturbed by the Microsoft/LinkedIn position and said: "You can't publish to the world and then say no, you can't look at it."[18] Microsoft/LinkedIn lost the appeal and the hiQ victory validated the position that public data is *public* data.

Here is what we believe concerning access to LinkedIn data:

- The law is unclear on the legalities of machine-automated reading/scraping. The Computer Fraud and Abuse Act (CFAA) from 1986 needs to be clarified in the context of a modern world where people choose to publish public data on social platforms, blogs, and websites. In a world where machines increasingly assist people, public data should be freely accessible regardless of whether it's done by low-cost data entry humans working offshore or automated machine reading.

- LinkedIn's terms of use expressly prohibit machine reading/scraping of public-facing data, but this is anti-competitive within the framework of US antitrust laws. It is the members' data that those members want publicly and freely available, rather than for LinkedIn to monetize exclusively via LinkedIn Recruiter, LinkedIn Sales Navigator, LinkedIn Advertising, and their Talent Insights product.[19]

- Thousands of companies do machine-automated web browsing, including Google and LinkedIn themselves. It's how they and everyone else index the web and enrich their own data to efficiently provide insights to their users.

- If LinkedIn users choose to have their information publicly available, why should LinkedIn have the right to prevent that information from being read in any form? The public and an individual user is protected by GDPR legislation, and from January 2020 in California, the California Consumer Privacy Act (CCPA). Other countries and jurisdictions have their own derivations to protect the public along with anti-spam legislation. All things considered, interests are reasonably balanced.

- The overriding principle is to use public data for good and avoid spamming. Relevancy and personalization is the key while also making it easy for anyone to opt out of your sequences or sales efforts.

All data intelligence companies (ZoomInfo, Lusha, Hunter, Data Czar, Triggr, SalesIntel, etc.) need to be compliant with GDPR and other frameworks. All companies, your own included, need to have a data privacy officer who is responsible for ensuring that:

1. The user opt-in to terms and conditions acknowledges data privacy and anti-spam requirements in the jurisdictions in which they operate.

2. You externally source only publicly available data and store all data in a compliant manner.

3. You make it easy for any member of the public to request to be forgotten (removed) from the database.

The world is changing fast and laws need to keep up. According to Victor Antonio and James Glenn-Anderson who wrote the book *Sales Ex Machina*: "The evolution of machines and machine intelligence can augment sellers to help them find answers faster, retrieve information quickly, and fulfill requests with simple voice or text commands. Think of virtual assistants that can answer questions via text or voice recognition systems that can find the information or content you need."[20]

The beauty of machine learning is its ability to pull in a constellation of data points and begin to predict or draw conclusions about the ideal buyer. Technology can go beyond merely harvesting data but also sift through it to find the signals amid the noise and then equip sellers to drive highly relevant and personalized outreach.

TQ TAKEAWAY

Public data is exactly that—public. Be committed, however, to using only data that is sourced ethically, and ensure anyone can be removed from your database or sequence upon request. Make sure you have policies and systems to make that easy to execute.

CHAPTER EIGHT

Working Your Systems

Reply Management and Sentiment Analysis

All responses are inherently positive. It's a paradox. If someone has no interest whatsoever, they won't even take the time to respond negatively. When you start to send dozens of sequences, you will begin to generate a sufficient amount of replies to start managing and studying the responses.

Replies are the modern objection or rebuttal. Often, before you even start booking meetings in a cadence, you'll start to surface replies. Some are just simple FAQs, some indicate intent and buying impetus, others are just standard objections and hurdles to the sale.

One of the biggest things you can do if you secure a referral in a reply is to show "proof of life" to the person you are referred to. Do this with a screenshot of the referral message or just forward it to the appropriate person to showcase that "wow, yeah, the CIO actually did recommend this person." Anytime we're referred, either directly or indirectly, we reference the referrer and state that they "suggested we talk."

Answer every single reply, negative or positive, and make sure you operate rapidly because speed of response makes a difference. Response times can be A/B tested because replies come in around the clock. It's a big task to position virtual assistants (VAs) on multiple time zones to deftly and quickly handle replies even if the responses are canned from a template sheet you build.

Ryan Reisert has a view on this: "Marketing should be doing all the building and testing work in sequencers (or a growth expert like Krishan at Apollo) and your SDRs simply execute the work by making dials, sending personalized videos, etc."[1]

Technology such as LeadGnome can sort through bounces, update your database, update "out of office" cell phones, and also sort replies to your reps. SiftRock was acquired by Drift and is now Drift Email, which routes qualified email replies to the right people on your team to book more meetings and drive more pipeline from your email marketing programs. It also automatically updates your marketing automation platform and CRM—keeping your database up-to-date when people change jobs or unsubscribe, and adding any new contacts found in those replies.

Revenue Grid takes nurturing automation seriously—the tool allows you to create automation rules, especially for account nurturing. Revenue Grid will automatically stop a sequence for all leads from the same account when one person from that account engages with you in some way; or a prospect from that account has been mentioned in an email; or your fellow SDR just secured a meeting with them. The same goes for a multitude of scenarios, like stopping a sequence if your lead just changed ownership in Salesforce.

Outreach's data science team has innovated in leaps and bounds, leveraging machine learning for Outreach Amplify. Here are some examples:

- **Email Reply Detection.** Automate a pause and resend based on dates in autoresponders.

- **Phone Number Extraction.** Compile the numbers quickly from email signatures to notify update of the CRM record.

- **Contact Referral Extraction.** Automate referrals into fresh sequences.

- **Guided A/B Testing.** Outreach feedback on the validity and prevent poor tests.

- **Email Intent Classification.** The classic example is high replies with bad sentiment versus low with positive. Enables you to ferret this out more quickly to optimize.

Social Signals to Influence Calling

When we're monitoring and optimizing large-scale outbound campaigns, we always look for something we've dubbed "signs of life." Has the prospect interacted with me or my content in any way that is a positive signal? If so, I'll take action such as reply inside that thread (nudge), triple (call, email, vmail, or text), or quad by adding text or WhatsApp message to the triple.

We need to give Jack Kosakowski of the Creation Agency some credit for getting us thinking along these lines. Many years ago, he did a video about calling a prospect who viewed his LinkedIn and we initially thought, *Wow, that's so invasive. It's just a profile view.*[2] Truth is, you're either serious about engagement or not: treat the view of your profile like a trigger event. We've taken that philosophy and morphed it into a whole social signals modus operandi.

If someone comments on a status update and they are relevant, call and sequence them. If someone views your profile, send a sequence to them. If you notice someone commenting passionately, even on any random thread, use that as a signal to initiate outreach to them around that topic. It's all contextualized reasons to engage . . . strike while the iron is hot!

Social platforms, especially LinkedIn, are gold mines for finding context for your outreach. You will also regularly find diamonds. Play back someone's own words from their article or post. You can comment on their posts or articles to bring yourself into their orbit as they see your name and face. Give before you seek to get—harness the law of reciprocity. When you contact them later, to sell, there is nothing cold about it.

TQ TAKEAWAY

Never "connect and sell" on social platforms. First connect and provide some form of value (share their article, provide positive commentary, give them a genuine white paper or industry report relevant to them and not about you). The same rules of etiquette that apply in meeting someone at a physical social event also apply online. You would never introduce yourself and jump into your pitch. Warm the relationship first.

Stunts to Set Meetings

We once sent a shoe to get a foot in the door. We've sent out a substantial amount of FedEx envelopes next day at $35 a pop to get 100 percent deliverability. A company we worked in sent cakes to its competitor's clients and drones without the control to be redeemed if they took a meeting. The world leader in these stunts is the inimitable Stu Heinecke. He calls this the art and science of contact marketing.

Consider using Sendoso to send physical goods with your theme. Gong.io executed a memorable lantern campaign where they sent all the lapsed prospects a lantern that said: "Sorry to see you go dark." Ryan Reisert says: "Even though Amazon is faster, cheaper, and more reliable, you really should really think outside the box." Get them a jersey from their favorite college team with their name on it. Donate to their local charity. This will take some social sleuthing to find the perfect gift.

Solutions such as Sendoso will allow you to send twenty-five to fifty coffee cards with analytics to the top openers of your sequence. Now you tie light gifting and automation together with analytics on both ends. Work with your CMO on a guerrilla marketing approach to super novel, differentiated swag. At one company, we laser-etched our logo into a Bluetooth-enabled Marshall mini amp speaker. Another time, we gave CXOs a custom-painted skateboard. Accompany these physical objects with an appropriate witty, funny sequence and you're off to the races!

TQ TAKEAWAY

Blend physical world tactics with digital engagement. Old school and new school combined is the best approach in personalization. Harness the power of your marketing team and their budget to break through with new sales.

We covered trigger events in detail earlier, but it's worth restating here. Find everyone who has ever purchased from the company, look them up, and throw them in a cadence in which you will be creative beyond the obvious of: "Hey, I see we worked with you at XYZ company—how can we help you in the new [or current] role?" Then build a harder list where the stakeholder's past role was an existing customer. You want to map the champions of your product or solution into the power base because they either moved companies to get promoted or were promoted from within. They are familiar and have an affinity with your solution and can be an internal champion for your product where they land.

Craig Elias focuses on three types of trigger events: awareness, bad supplier, and job changes. The vast majority of Outreach or SalesLoft sequences are awareness messages or specious ROI claims such as: "Drive revenue by 234 percent!" Prospects are immune to such claims, and no matter how much awareness and education laced with excitement you blast, you can't move a market this way.

Craig claims the average CXO makes buying decisions early in their new role, shaking up the status quo when they join the new organization. Get in early. We've mainly leveraged trigger event selling by performing a won sales analysis that also maps stakeholders as they move around utilizing a tool such as Sales Navigator. We also believe in grabbing the deadwood and finding the people wherever they are now. Turnover rates are so high you probably have the same potential buyers in fertile new companies.

Look for new leaders in the role as an impetus to reach out. This is the most powerful trigger because new people are hired to effect change. Lead with a quote or highlight how one of their competitors is managing change. Remember to focus on a pain or fear statement to pique interest but do it in a positive way. If they're new enough, they'll actually be interested because they haven't become complacent yet.

Strength of Weak Ties

Reid Hoffman's book *The Startup of You* is an awesome manual on an entrepreneurial approach to everyone's evolving life. One of the wild things he explains is why LinkedIn was built the way it was with first, second, third, and cascading degrees of concentric circles. He explains, much like Adam Grant, that the fewer ties you have and the more isolated you are, the lower opportunity you have in life.[3]

Someone works at the same company for twenty years; shouldn't they be rewarded with not only tenure but access to more opportunity? The truth is that it creates a silo, making it harder to move to other networks that could have more lucrative or abundant opportunities.

There is actually a bizarre strength to having lots of weak ties that overlap you into myriad other social networks. You need what's called "nodes," or the super-connectors on the network. These folks can make introductions into other streams of the economic graph. LinkedIn themselves said at a big conference: "Tony Hughes is a node in the network for sales leadership globally. If you're in sales, you should connect with him to enhance your own brand and improve search results if you use a free LinkedIn account."[4]

In our view, a node in the human network is someone with a strong personal brand evidenced by integrity and real thought leadership, plus high quality and high quantity of direct connections and following.

TQ BOOSTER

Find the nodes in your target market and connect with them. It's easy to ask your clients who they admire and respect, and then connect to those people so that you are no longer an outsider.

Referrals and Trusted Relationships

The best sale you can ever make stems from a warm referral. You are five times more likely to open an opportunity referred to you by a trusted common relationship. This is because referrals start a new relationship with a degree of trust.

Referrals also shorten sales cycles, improve win rates, reduce the presence of competition, and are the lowest-cost source of new leads. We simply need to ask the right way and at the right time. Anytime a client expresses happiness with our level of service or satisfaction with our product or solution, it is an opportunity to ask for a referral. But avoid using the word "referral," as it sounds too much like a seller wanting permission to pitch and pressure their contact. No one likes being sold to, but everyone likes to buy. No one wants to provide referrals to a seller, but everyone wants others they know to benefit from their own experience.

When seeking a referral, simply use phrases like these:

- Thanks for saying that! Who else do you think we could help?

- Thanks for the feedback! Who else struggles now with what we've solved together?

- Thanks! Who else should I be talking to in the organization?

You will notice here that we identify and then act on the trigger event of "expressed happiness with our service" to source a new contact that we can engage. Always pick your moment to ask for a referral and do it in a way that shows the right intent of *who else can we help*? Rather than *who do you know I can sell to*? "Commission breath" repulses everyone. Instead, the intent you're seeking to convey is that your current customer is the hero of the story, and you want to share that story with others in their network.

Maintain control rather than ask them to provide a formal email introduction. Simply say: "Would it be okay if I let them know that we spoke?" Then ask for the contact details. Alternately, you can find the person on LinkedIn or use sales intelligence tools to source contact information. When we contact the new potential buyer on the phone, we simply introduce ourselves briefly and then say, "John thought we should speak," or "Mary thought I could potentially help," or "Fatima thought we should get together." You simply use the referral for personalization at the beginning of your conversation narrative and then position a double-edged point of view about how they could potentially improve results.

When the potential buyer asks for more information, you reference the results being achieved by the person who provided the referral. It could be something like: "John has managed to reduce widget defect rates by 23 percent and it's saved his company $876,000 in year one. How's your calendar to find a time to explore whether you could drive similar results?"

The key point here is that a referral—a common trusted relationship endorsing you—is the most powerful way to open because there is a level of trust. Trigger events and referrals together are like a sales superpower because they transform sales results and they make the sales process much easier than cold calling or sending generic emails.

There are so many different applications of referrals and a big piece of this dovetails back into reply management with emails. Every reply is an opportunity to write a script that says: "If you're not the appropriate person for this, who should I speak with?" Outreach software automatically extracts the additional addresses out of auto-responders (like out-of-office notifications) and may even automatically add them to the sequence (not at the time of writing but this is surely coming). If you receive a *no* or *not interested*, run a referral script. If you get a bunch of referrals off a sequence, use personalization to reference the stakeholder who referred. This can be set up with relative ease in Outreach.

Ryan Reisert says: "Everyone talks about referrals but then nobody knows how to actually ask or when to ask. They seem to believe you must already be working together and have long-term results. I ask for referrals on cold calls. It's a topic that is mentioned all the time but there are not great documented examples."[5] Here is an example of a reply to *not interested*: "Thanks for coming back and letting us know you're not in the window right now for this . . . who do you know who might be focused on solving {{problem you solve}} now?"

TQ BOOSTER

Remember these key points because they will fuel opportunity pipeline creation and your sales success:

- Trigger events create context for outreach to new potential buyers.
- Referrals enable us to open a new relationship with a level of trust.
- Combining triggers and referrals amplifies the probability of sales success.
- Technology can automate the monitoring of trigger events.
- We see what we look for and we receive what we ask for—be aware and be bold.

Again, here is our greatest tactical secret for referrals . . . prove you were referred. Screenshot the message inside LinkedIn and send it inline in the email. "Lucy said we should talk." Insert the screenshot that proves it. Even in social, capture an image and show you were referred by sending the screenshot inside LinkedIn. In emails, forward the referral thread to the target. This is crucial to convert because buyers think many sellers lie.

When you think about combining timeless truths in selling with modern methods of execution, this section on referrals may be the most important part of this book. Think about the math. When you look at the funding climate of outbound automation companies and the proliferation of technology vendors, it's a Cambrian explosion. What does that mean for P&L holders with a real budget? They could start receiving hundreds of emails per day, even thousands when you count all the likes, tweets, DMs, InMails, snailmails, and VMs. So what's the best path in? The answer is warm introductions or referrals from a trusted source.

Quick stats: According to LinkedIn, buyers are five times more likely to engage with a seller if they approach via a warm relationship in common.[6] Going all the way back to Dale Carnegie, 91 percent of customers would be willing to give a referral but only 11 percent of sales reps actually ask. We think this statistical horror has gotten even worse eighty years later. Imagine if LinkedIn opened up their API and you could programmatically scale TeamLinks. It could work and not be spammy because it's based on actual second-degree relationships with your own colleagues into the prospective buyer's company.

The company that figures out how to programmatically scale warm referrals will be a billion-dollar unicorn. Cosell.io looks promising. One of the keys in a great referral is being willing to ghostwrite the referral for the referrer to make it easier and frictionless for them. So if this piece is automated at scale and with personalization, we may have a hit record on our hands.

Rich Toland is the master of warm introductions, and he is working for Relationship Science on this problem. The company uses a novel approach, which includes proprietary research, data science at scale, and algorithms to find hidden warm paths of introduction with impossible-to-reach powerful prospects even outside LinkedIn. Here is an example. Instead of going into the meeting with the CXO whose profile is locked down and you can't see common connections, you'd now arrive and say: "Hey, Rachel, I see you've served on the board with our CFO. You were both in the military, and our private equity backer co-invested in a joint venture on another board that you're on." There's actually so much data outside social media that's publicly available that it creates enough big data to be crunchable and is a quality solvable problem. The biggest problem in building ML models for B2B is that the data sets are far too small. However, once you take ten million or more hard-to-find C-levels hiding from social media and map all the overlapping data points, it becomes a really interesting problem for data science.

The acquisition of Slack by Salesforce in December 2020 was a genius move for more than the obvious reasons. Private B2B Slack channels are beginning to vet the buyer and seller in *pay to play* environments where CXOs join to learn about trends and insights. Vendors pay but can't sell; they must instead share use cases. This model has legs where LinkedIn has become too noisy. Some now describe LinkedIn as the narcissistic echo chamber of annoying sellers, and the depreciation of LinkedIn Groups has already caused an exodus into private Slack Groups. The future of B2B is paid micro communities within platforms such as Slack, Patreon, or Discord where membership criteria controls the quality of the vendors placed in front of the CXO.

TQ BOOSTER

Join think tanks, collectives, and societies that help you cross-sell with other sales leaders in your vertical by knowledge-sharing to become smarter about revenue strategy. That includes Revenue Collective, Sales Enablement Society, WizOps, Sales IQ, RevGenius, SalesStack.io, SDRevolution, SDReady, and Modern Sales Pros (MSP).

ICP and TAM to Nail Product/Market Fit

Every business, marketer, and salesperson needs to target potential customers based on product/market fit. This is important because we all operate with a finite number of hours within which we can apply the right activities with the right people. Finding alignment within windows of need or opportunity is far more effective than hoping that luck can overcome the law of low averages.

Knowing your ICP is how you identify and size your TAM (Total/Target Addressable Market), and then knowing your buyer personas and engaging based on trigger events or trusted relationships is how you maximize sales results. Combine them all together and you can be a top performer. Let's explore the elements of an ideal customer profile. They are:

1. Firmographics

2. Technographics

3. Psychographics

Firmographics

Firmographics are also known as corporate demographics. The first attributes to identify under firmographics are geography and industry vertical. For example: local government on the West Coast, or tier-1 accounting practices in Singapore, or manufacturing companies in Bangalore. This is important because potential buyers want to know that you've delivered for others in their industry or region. You will also have industries that you specialize in and have a competitive advantage, and regions where you have strong reference customers and the necessary resources to deliver.

Once you've gated your search based on geography and vertical, you then filter and look for potential alignment based on additional criteria such as their revenue, size, and number of employees in roles relevant to your products, services, or solutions. You should also include financial year-end dates and budget cycles.

> ### TQ TAKEAWAY
> Firmographics are to businesses and organizations what demographics are to people. You are identifying organization attributes that indicate a potential fit for what you sell.

Technographics

What technologies do they use? Analyze your customer base and identify common technical attributes and telltale signs of probability for a successful sales campaign to win them. Which competitors do you ideally replace or augment and what is the commercial status of those relationships concerning contract expiration or renewal dates?

For example, many Sitecore (Web CMS) customers also use Salesforce (CRM), and many Taleo customer also use Alteryx. New Voice Media has a telephony platform that integrates into Salesforce, and New Voice Media should segment and target based on companies known to be Salesforce users and then further segment and prioritize based on other attributes. Even if you don't sell technology, there will be interesting common stacks within your best customers…look for others who have the same attributes.

> **TQ TAKEAWAY**
> Techographics are the technical or technology attributes that indicate product/market fit or higher propensity to buy. You can automate the detection of many technologies using headless browser technologies such as Clearbit, Triggr, InsideView, and others.

Psychographics

Psychographics explain how the leadership in an organization thinks, feels, and acts. Psychographics provide insights into what they value and what motivates them to buy. Psychographics also identify the mindset of a business or the mode of operations—whether they are growing, in a steady state, or in a crisis. These modes of operation have a huge impact on an organization's appetite for change.

If an organization is growing fast, then they will be open to change if it improves efficiency. Monitor the number and types of roles they are hiring and whether they are expanding into new geographies or making acquisitions. Is their share price rising strongly? Are they making announcements about new client wins or new products and innovations being launched?

Customers in growth mode are seeking to improve efficiency, grow revenue, expand markets, drive loyalty, and so on. Growth often indicates openness to change and a willingness to invest in improving operations and financial performance. Organizations in maintenance or survival mode are reluctant to embrace change unless it reduces costs or improves cash flow.

> **TQ TAKEAWAY**
> Your best customers and new prospects have a growth mindset. Monitor trigger events that highlight growth with hiring new roles, launching new products, making acquisitions, or announcing expansion or positive results.

ICP is about identifying the attributes of organizations with the highest likelihood of engaging with you in conversations about changing away from your competitor or away from the status quo. ICPs help you define your TAM (Total/Target Addressable Market). When it comes to TAM, many sellers are either wildly optimistic and vague, on one hand, or too narrow and restrictive on the other. That is where the "known universe" problem of sales development automation hits, because you cannot effectively scale your effort. If you are reaching out to just CMOs, there might be two hundred in the Fortune 1000. Now those two hundred are being spammed with outreach by up to seven thousand companies in the Lumascape. Think about it—it's not just your competitors seeking an audience with the CMO at a particular prospect; it's *everyone* competing for their available spend on any number of problems and priorities.

Take your time to define your ICP. Build at least three to five buyer personas and title cloud arrays. Hone in on the stories of similar customers for each persona. Understand the challenges, trends, and drivers in their industry. Understand typical corporate buying motives. Opening is the most difficult phase of selling and sets the agenda for everything that follows. Deft use of ICP and buyer personas is therefore essential as it informs your messaging to make your sequences sing.

If you are selling into the enterprise or driving ABS or ABM strategies, Eric Quanstrom has sage advice:

> Think through an account penetration strategy specifically through divisions/departments—and title clusters—of potential decision influencers at a target company.
>
> Many SDRs and companies get lost in the trap of focusing on only decisionmakers when the reality of the consensus sale means that anywhere from five to ten or more are realistic targets to start conversations with. Having the ability to go up and down a given department to start conversations is one of the best ways to adhere to an ideal customer profile. It also gives you the opportunity to leverage referrals and responses moving through that org chart in order to triangulate your value proposition for the most relevant audience. Most SDR campaigns suffer from skimming strategies—rarely from immersive, ABM-centric penetration of even mid-sized (but especially enterprise) target companies.[7]

> **TQ TAKEAWAY**
>
> Brutal honesty about product/market fit is essential. You must solve a serious problem for the customer and with a strong business case that nails the commercial value of change in working with you and your solution. Always target accurately before you execute.

Buyer Personas

A buyer persona is a summary of the archetype buyer role to whom you sell. You need these for all the roles you frequently engage in a sales cycle, especially in the C-suite where they make the decisions to either let you cross the moat or instead raise the drawbridge. According to Marylou Tyler: "Being able to reduce sales cycles and increase conversion rates depends on knowing who the buyers are, what they care about, what results they are looking for, and how they communicate."[8]

ICP and buyer personas go hand in hand but they serve different purposes. The easiest way to remember this is to think of the ICP as the description of a customer organization that is a good fit for what you sell, whereas the buyer persona is a summary with baseline messaging for an individual buyer or influencer who works at your ICP.

A buyer persona needs to capture demographics, goals, and objectives in how they are measured in their role. It also needs to capture key areas of focus, challenges and problems, sources of influence, phrases that resonate, objections to anticipate, and proof of results we enable (reference customers). Most importantly: Why change, why now, and why with you? Your best reference clients would be included along with an influence map and trigger events.

Figure 8.1 is page one of a three-page buyer persona template created and used by Sales IQ, which is an eLearning and sales enablement business selling to the head of sales. They drink their own champagne in how they operate. If you do their online Create Pipeline program, you get to use their ICP, buyer persona, and other templates. The examples below are used by them internally.

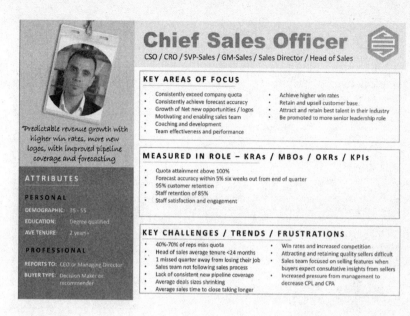

Chief Sales Officer

CSO / CRO / SVP-Sales / GM-Sales / Sales Director / Head of Sales

Predictable revenue growth with higher win rates, more new logos, with improved pipeline coverage and forecasting

ATTRIBUTES

PERSONAL

DEMOGRAPHIC: 35 - 55
EDUCATION: Degree qualified
AVE TENURE: 2 years+

PROFESSIONAL

REPORTS TO: CEO or Managing Director
BUYER TYPE: Decision Maker or recommender

KEY AREAS OF FOCUS

- Consistently exceed company quota
- Consistently achieve forecast accuracy
- Growth of Net new opportunities / logos
- Motivating and enabling sales team
- Coaching and development
- Team effectiveness and performance

- Achieve higher win rates
- Retain and upsell customer base
- Attract and retain best talent in their industry
- Be promoted to more senior leadership role

MEASURED IN ROLE – KRAs / MBOs / OKRs / KPIs

- Quota attainment above 100%
- Forecast accuracy within 5% six weeks out from end of quarter
- 95% customer retention
- Staff retention of 85%
- Staff satisfaction and engagement

KEY CHALLENGES / TRENDS / FRUSTRATIONS

- 40%-70% of reps miss quota
- Head of sales average tenure <24 months
- 1 missed quarter away from losing their job
- Sales team not following sales process
- Lack of consistent new pipeline coverage
- Average deals sizes shrinking
- Average sales time to close taking longer

- Win rates and increased competition
- Attracting and retaining quality sellers difficult
- Sales team focused on selling features when buyers expect consultative insights from sellers
- Increased pressure from management to decrease CPL and CPA

Figure 8.1

Importantly, the buyer persona must highlight how the person is typically measured in their role. This fits within the category of professional objectives, which are valuable because they enable us to align with their personal objectives. Independent of what you are selling, you need to be aware of the goals and priorities of your potential buyer. Objectives go by many names, including goals, critical initiatives, key performance indicators (KPIs), key result areas (KRAs), management by objectives (MBOs), and more. If you speak to how they are measured in their role . . . then you've set a winning agenda.

Page two of the buyer persona, Figure 8.2, is where baseline messaging or "value narrative" is articulated in the form of "why change, why now, why us?" Also included is guidance on potential pushbacks or objections to anticipate, and words and phrases that usually resonate with the person in that role.

Chief Sales Officer
De-risk hitting targets with consistent self-generated pipeline coverage

WHY CHANGE?

De-risk hitting aggressive targets in a tough market and with more sales reps hitting quota from stronger pipeline coverage. Enable teams for self-generate sales pipeline in a way that you can hold them to account. Improve new deal win rates with elevated engagement into the c-suite. Reduce churn, improve loyalty and increase sales productivity.

WHY NOW?

Recession means inbound lead volume have dropped and sellers struggling to stay motivated and effective working remotely in a tough market. All sellers must elevate engagement into the c-suite and lift their game in order to succeed today. Act now to de-risk annual targets.

WHY US?

Best methodology + platform + coaches. Proven success in delivering for B2B sales leaders and teams supporting current methodologies without confusion. The approach is from the best minds on the planet for B2B sales pipeline creation (Tony Hughes) and has delivered 2X-4X pipeline around the world for companies such as ...

OBJECTIONS TO ANTICIPATE

- No budget for training
- No time to look at this
- Already have an internal sales enablement team
- Training doesn't work
- Already have a methodology
- Currently planning

WORDS THAT RESONATE

- Proactive pipeline creation
- Hold salespeople to account for outbound activity
- Accurate forecasting
- Decrease cost per lead and cost per client acquisition
- 4x pipeline coverage
- More sellers hitting target
- De-risk hitting targets

Figure 8.2

The third page of their template, Figure 8.3, is where you draw a typical influence map and identify trigger events to monitor. Completing one of these accurately is no simple task. Interview your existing clients, and research the role on Google by searching "CXO KPIs." The Sales IQ sample here uses circles of influence, but you could choose to have an org chart–style hierarchical view.

Chief Sales Officer
Influence Map and Trigger Events

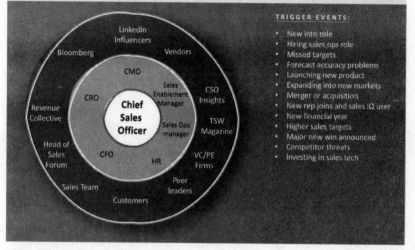

Figure 8.3

A well-constructed buyer persona provides a baseline value narrative that informs the types of messages and conversations you should drive. It is a cheat sheet for engagement and enables new sellers to ramp fast. It allows everyone to be on the same page for marketing and during every sales engagement. Importantly, it also drives you to make sure your messaging is all about their opportunity to improve results in their role rather than you droning on about what you do and how it works.

TQ TAKEAWAY

You have almost no chance of being effective at sales or marketing if you do not have clarity and understanding of your ICP and buyer personas. These two documents should be the fulcrum between sales and marketing collaboration. You're not enabled as a seller without killer ICP and buyer persona documentation.

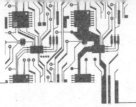

CHAPTER NINE

Powering Up

Outsourced SDR Consultancies

Miles Veth of Veth Group and Mike Scher at Frontline Selling have great offerings. They will go through exercises on ICP and buyer personas plus messaging with you and set meetings with a combination of humans, proprietary tech, and, well, they just do it right. Chris Marin, cofounder at Convertist, offers the following questions to vet the right outsourced sales development vendor:

- How much commitment in terms of time/resources is required to make this successful?

- What ideas do they have to bake into the campaign, to make it successful?

- How long would it take to "ramp up" and hit a steady weekly lead velocity?

- Have they targeted similar ideal prospects in the past?

- Which companies in the space have they successfully booked appointments with before?

- Can they offer case studies/success stories with other customers targeting a similar industry and buyer roles?[1]

Sam Feldotto, who spent multiple years running sales and marketing for an outsourced SDR agency, SalesReply, adds: "The ugly truth about outsourcing, though, is that many outsourced SDR companies are great at smoke and mirrors and know less about sales development than your average SDR manager. It's easy to say you'll get certain results, but executing and meeting those expectations is an entirely different story. When considering who the right outsourced partner for you is going to be, it's far more important to dig into the processes they use and the people on their team that will be executing than it is to look at easily inflatable numbers like their open rates or how many meetings they claim they'll get. While those numbers are important to an extent, understanding how they plan to do that is far more indicative of what their true results may look like."[2]

We have worked with many appointment-setting agencies, and we've virtually built one with clever tech and humans working in India. We think the thing to remember is you get back out what you invest and put in. Almost seven years ago, a stealth mode entity came to our company with a plan to set us twelve appointments per day in the Fortune 1000, and at the peak, they actually did. That's kind of how we got involved in all this fascination with sequencers and automated sales development (ASD). We've worked for and with Salesforce and sold Pardot marketing automation, used Marketo at a company, and then driven their ABM module. We've been heavily involved in marketing and mobile marketing automation technology for a long time. In 2020, Jon Miller's Engagio, one of the cofounders of Marketo, was acquired by Demandbase. The sophistication of drip marketing, inbound lead scoring, and marketing automation is shifting to outbound sales automation. Soon, paid media B2B advertising will follow suit as the leaders continue to acquire and consolidate these platforms just as LinkedIn acquired Drawbridge (targeting/reach) and Marketo acquired ToutApp as its SEP.

We've experimented with early programming Gmail scripts to do various things. This has included using ToutApp and Yesware, and then Groove before running scaled campaigns on Outreach and SalesLoft. In more recent times, we've worked closely with XANT and have been fascinated by machine learning algorithms that get smarter. Artificial intelligence in decisioning must be an integral part of every element of these stacks—not just a hypothetical road map feature.

In working with any agency taking on your end-to-end lead generation requirements, make them show you how they use their sequencer and personalized messaging like a scalpel rather than a Gatling gun. Whether you are enabling your own SDRs or working with an outsourced SDR agency, to be effective you must have laser focus on crafting the value messaging and narrative supported by a UVP/USP per persona. It all needs to be validated by scientifically granular A/B testing of the campaigns before scaling up.

> ## TQ TAKEAWAY
> You cannot outsource a mess and hope for the external party to magically solve your problem. Do the hard work with ICP, buyer personas, TAM, and messaging before talking to an agency, then challenge them to add value and prove they can deliver results without damaging your brand.

Inbound Meets Outbound Techniques

If you have enough funds, go full-blown SEM (Search Engine Marketing) meets SEO (Search Engine Optimization) and game the algorithm to get your company listed on the front page of Google for your main keyword families. Maybe even on a competitor keyword, or if you blitz PR and are innovative or viral enough, you may suddenly get an avalanche of inbound leads.

To be ready for this, you must have a chatbot front of site. That chat should be dynamic so that if it's during business hours, reps can chime in live, or after hours consider outsourcing to players such as Chat Metrics who specialize in creating sales qualified leads (SQLs) and booked meetings or demos 24/7. The very best chatbots actually respond and banter to hand off to live humans. Amir Reiter at CloudTask has a whole squad that can do this in Medellin, Colombia.

True story. A man once walked into a California car dealer and asked for Wendy. "We don't have a Wendy working for us." Incredulous, he responded, "Yes, you do. She told me you have a blue demo model on special. I work in sales, too, and I want her to get the commission if I buy; she was very helpful." The receptionist excused herself to go check with the sales manager who appeared a few minutes later. "I'm so sorry if this is a problem . . . um, Wendy is our website chatbot. Can I show you the car?" The customer was speechless, then shook his head and smiled. "I feel like an idiot. You better give me a good deal."

The future is a virtual assistance bot that books your meetings, confirms appointments, prompts you on outstanding tasks, and more. Salesforce Einstein happily communicates through the assumed identity of Siri, Cortana, or Google Voice to warn about deal risks, provide a forecast, or act as a virtual sales coach to recommend the best next steps to progress and close a deal based on data-driven insights.

The key point here is that technology can help you flood inbound as you surge wide to tens of thousands of targets outbound. It can work to inevitably produce an equal and opposite reaction with replies, form-fills, webinar, and demo requests—you name it. Make sure you have a gifted MDR (marketing development rep) who is filtering through all of this for MQLs to SQLs distributed appropriately. If not, run a round-robin system so it's fair where the leads come back or align to the territory. In many organizations an SDR or SDR team is creating a halo effect over the country and then transferring to reps as befits the patch.

According to Sam Feldotto: "One of the dumbest things that smart companies do is treat inbound and outbound like they have different objectives. They don't. They're both trying to get opportunities created with a lead. So why do marketing teams make leads fill out a form and then sift it through their cluttered CRM in hopes that a SDR will be able to catch it, reach out to the lead, start a conversation, qualify the lead, and then pass it to an AE? Most of that sounds just like outbound, but only with more steps and more room for the lead to slip through the cracks."[3]

It's true. If a buyer is coming inbound on your website and doesn't get a prompt response, how do you think that reflects on your organization as a whole? For far too long companies have let inbound leads slip through the cracks, only to call them up at the end of the quarter when they are scraping the bottom of the barrel.

Feldotto continues: "Coming inbound should be a simple and pleasant process for your leads. Consider setting up your inbound machine to book meetings directly with SDRs. Rather than having the lead fill out a form and wait for a response, direct them to a calendar after they fill out the form so they can book a meeting immediately after. Now, the SDR doesn't have to worry about the lead slipping through the cracks or doing unnecessary back-and-forths, and instead has a time on their calendar to speak with the prospect, qualify them, and book a follow-up call right then and there with the appropriate AE if they think it's worth moving forward."

Multi-threading and *COMBO Prospecting*

There is a cohort of decisionmakers (individuals and groups) in every deal. *The Challenger Customer*, follow-up to *The Challenger Sale* by Brent Adamson and Matthew Dixon, talked about the inherent cemented dysfunction if you convince all the stakeholders to buy via challenging them but then you get gridlock because everyone is on their own island of locked-in stubborn opinion.[4] How do you combat this in the age of consensus? The answer is concurrent multi-threading and talking the language of leaders (desired outcomes and compelling business case). You need to be reaching out top-down, bottom-up, and middle-out . . . all at the same time to avoid being blocked by someone who feels they have the power to say *no*. You are seeking momentum with a referral delegated down or a referral lateral to anywhere.

The best way to build out cadences is to create a spreadsheet of all your top accounts and then a minimum of five to eight stakeholders each with a verified email from Adapt.io, Lusha, LeadIQ, RocketReach, Triggr, ZoomInfo, Seamless, and so on. Never load just one stakeholder from each company into the sequence. Map the power base and the influence map.

Go wider and deeper to multi-thread. Even if one stakeholder says *remove me from your database*, you can still gain traction with their colleagues.

This is excellent advice from XANT: Gartner (2020) has it at ten-plus people in some enterprise segments. "Additional People" maps reps to additional people they should engage who may influence a deal, even if they're not in CRM. If I as a rep reach out to John Doe at company XYZ, Playbooks Buyer Intelligence will recognize, from its collective data, if there are other people who other reps interact with at company XYZ and who may be part of the buying group based on previous purchasing decisions, and recommend you enroll them into Plays. More development is coming, but the notion of Buyer Maps is an exciting area of innovation.

The principle is to avoid being seen as a spammer and take the time to personalize a letter to a CIO or CFO. You could even print it out, hand-sign it, and send it via fax or FedEx. *Selling to VITO* is an excellent book by Tony Parinello: VITO stands for Very Important Top Officer. If you blitz her with eight touches over fourteen days, you're probably dead to her. So consider manually sequencing to the very top tier or injecting highly relevant snippets. These would be hyper-personalized with verbiage tailored to that title and industry.[5] Patricia McLaren, cofounder of RevShoppe, calls this "manual intervention."[6]

Frequency of outreach should also be tempered based on the seniority of the role being contacted. *COMBO Prospecting* is a slew of tactics derived from boxing as a metaphor—which in sales is similar to Gary Vee's jab jab jab, right hook. The whole idea is to enter into your sequences with the phone while also peppering away in digital channels. So send a few automated emails but between each, attempt a call, leave a voicemail, and hit them up in digital channels concurrently by adding email, phone SMS/text, or other direct messaging platforms. As Brigid Archibald, Asia-Pacific head of SAP Qualtrics, says: "Try *every* way of reaching someone until you find the way that works for them."[7]

The key here is to pattern-interrupt them away from ignoring strangers or sellers. If the prospect opens your email, give a call, leave a voicemail, send a one-off reply inside an Outreach sequence. We call that move a nudge. If you see high opens on emails, always call and nudge. The way you need to feel is like this: *Give me a valid no or give me a conversation, but don't ignore me. I'm not going away—I have a worthwhile point of view on how you could potentially improve results in your role.*

When it comes to how many people you should be targeting in an organization and whether you should start at the top, the bottom, or build out from the middle, here is our very definite advice. Call everyone at the same time and gain traction with multiple executives before someone seeks to block you. It's a good thing if they ask each other about your messages and emails . . . someone needs to get back to you.

Organizational Waterfalls

Most organizations are not flat and holacratic (look it up—great word to know for anyone in enterprise sales). Instead, even amid convoluted matrix mayhem, they are typically pyramidal or hierarchical by nature. You can make these power moves work for you. Water falls downhill because of gravity. It's the same way when you're being delegated down from VITO.

The Bryan Kreuzberger "Waterfall Technique" is where you send one email that references three other people and send the same email flipping the names of those three people to the other three people (see Figure 9.1). It's complex to pull off with a sequencer but we've actually done it. It causes a forwarding frenzy where everyone tries to get the email off their desk, hot potato style. Ultimately, the game of musical chairs stops and you reach the decisionmaker you are looking for.

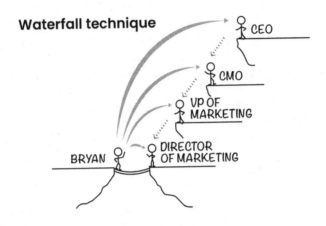

Figure 9.1

Source: breakthroughemail.com ©Bryan Kreuzberger 2020

Kreuzberger crafted the "Appropriate Person" subject line, which became more popular than the Save PBS! chain letter. The fundamental problem with a template that everyone uses is . . . everyone uses it and it becomes ineffective. Yes, you can still close big deals if you follow the tenets of anchoring high at the C-level and then push for meetings at the next top layer.

If you get delegated down, report back to the senior person you started with. Multi-threading to all stakeholders who form consensus for change is essential, but we must avoid being blocked by a mid-level "seymour syndrome" operative who loves to comparatively analyze all the vendors but has no decisionmaking power. Some technology companies sell seat-based SaaS software and give dozens of demos just to build consensus at the user level. No matter which way you go—top-down, bottom-up, middle-out—take the findings and feedback up to the leadership.

Pareto Principle—Applications of 80/20 Power Laws

The truth of the matter is that just as laws of physics tell us gravity is real, Pareto laws tell us that 80 percent of every system is waste. So when you are setting-up sequences, 80 percent of the results are going to come from 20 percent of the outbound. We literally encourage you to build ten variants and pick a couple of winners, then riff and A/B test those subject lines and body copy.

You must test and refine early running of a sequence to ensure it's performing well. Do not attempt to make the campaign symmetrical—there will be a lot of waste before you can identify a clear winner. Once you see the winning streak, write a few parallel sequences and riff off them to drive results. You need to set up your outbound approach so you literally are prospecting while you sleep. Once you set these sequences you can work 20 percent of the time and achieve three to five times more output from that work. It's about thinking like a chess master fifty moves ahead.

One of the biggest problems is the accelerated full pipeline of senior AEs. This is where Mike Weinberg breaks the day into thirds. One-third of time each dedicated to prospect the top, the middle, and the bottom of the funnel. If you are isolating the 20 percent of time within those segments to sequence design and deploy outbound automation accurately, it will free up your day to focus on high-value activities. You are basically automating the very top of the funnel, just handling replies and focusing your day on progressing the middle and lower funnel. The calls you make are all warm and with greater yield.

Outreach, SalesLoft, and XANT all operate like adding a couple of SDRs if you work on your TQ and master the messaging and systems. Otherwise, just like Sales Navigator, these things become AFL: another frickin' login. Most sales tech is like an expensive gym membership . . .

you pay every month and hardly ever use it. By mastering Sales TQ you move rapidly and are not bewildered by the tools. Sales Navigator becomes quick targeting, business intelligence, job changes, and pre-call research. Your sequencer becomes a bedrock for awareness marketing that starts to drive new opportunity creation, even worldwide.

Multi-tasking and Outsourcing to Offshore VAs

You can go to upwork.com and other platforms to test many VAs. Your best bet is to poll your network and see who they recommend. At great scale we've seen contract folks working in Medellin, South Africa, Berlin, Thailand, India, the Philippines, and on and on. Ultimately a few of these talented people became the most reliable and accurate so we've hired them repeatedly.

We initially scoffed at hiring VAs, a la the Tim Ferriss "four-hour workweek" model, because we thought it was just too good to be true. From calendaring, to list building, to pre-call research, there's almost nothing tedious you are doing now that you can't farm out easily. Even if your boss won't pay for it, put your hand in your own pocket! Start behaving like you are running a territory franchise and think like a businessperson rather than a salaried rep. This approach gives you real competitive advantage and pays for itself in additional commissions . . . or in just keeping your job. If you wake up in the morning with a hundred, or even a thousand, perfect contacts and your competitor takes days or weeks to send a sequence with a 30 percent bounce rate, you have a time edge and penetration advantage . . . game over, you win.

Screen several VA candidates at once and give them manageable projects that you yourself can nail. Never seek to outsource a mess . . . you'll just have a more expensive catastrophe. Make sure you can do it and define it accurately, and that you can coach them and manage the process and metrics. You can locate experts offshore with an entire appointment-setting operation as sophisticated as account-based sales (ABS) opportunity generation. It is essential that they can tie all the systems together such as Sales Navigator (social) + data + sequencer + phone, and execute in ways that are consistent with your own style and brand for seamless handoffs.

Scheduling Sorcery

Chili Piper is hands down, far and away, the most effective scheduling software for sellers. We've tested Calendly and the "flake rate" went from three out of ten to as high as five of ten meetings evaporating. Calendly has added email reminders to improve the stick rate and is worth testing in case it works well for you. Chili Piper, however, has an uber-friendly UI/UX and the reminders it auto-sends can push flake rates down to as low as one out of ten. That's incredible and you should experiment with it, too, even if you have Calendly, kronologic, or something else within your native sequencer scheduling technology.

The only alternative is to have a human (you, your SDR, or VA) send emails or call prospects to remind them the day before. That's painstakingly laborious but important, especially when traveling extensively for meetings that could waste significant time and money with a no-show. Calendar automation is powerful but beware the potential buyer feeling like they are part of your sausage machine of booking meetings . . . it's a turn-off for buyers who do not yet know you.

Jason Oakley, Director of Product Marketing at Chili Piper, says:

> Sequencing tools offer basic scheduling capabilities that allow reps to share booking links in emails. This is useful for booking their own meetings or booking on behalf of others, like an SDR to AE handoff. Chili Piper ups the ante in two ways. The first is our intelligent lead distribution, which can automatically qualify and route a lead to the correct sales rep. In the case of a handoff, this makes it a no-brainer for SDRs and a one-click booking experience for prospects. The second major difference is our Inbound Concierge, which sits behind a company's inbound web form and instantly allows leads to book a meeting or start a live call with the correct sales rep.[8]

Honorable mention here to X.ai with excellent technology for scheduling a ton of personal meetings. Your assistant's names are Amy or Andrew Ingram. Get it . . . A.I. CEO and founder Dennis Mortensen is a visionary who has a passion for creating real AI. He's been at this for years and isn't slowing down.

The major sequencers have built calendaring solutions in-house. Automated calendar rescheduling is a killer feature from Outreach.io. Systems are getting so smart, they can automatically manage out-of-office replies, pausing the prospect in sequence and then restarting again at the appropriate date. It can ingest emails in auto-responders and add those back to a relevant sequence.

Pattern Interrupts—a la COMBO

Imagine writing to someone in a very formal role, "Hey, Jim!" Or imagine starting a sentence on the verb. Instead of "I was looking at your profile," you could take poetic license and say: "Looking at your profile and . . ." Maybe tell a joke up front, crunch all the text together into one glob or a grammar interrupt. Send Justin Bieber lyrics. Odd titles. Upside-down or weird font. Shawn Sease did two blue dots in the subject line. Be creative. We suggest you hold a brainstorming session to come up with the best pattern interrupts. What's the most unexpected thing you can think of and then A/B split test it as an opener or subject line. The trick is to make everything truly human while being brief and on point with what the buyer cares about rather than banging on about yourself, your company, and your market-leading, award-winning, innovative (and other verbiage) *solutions*.

Ryan Reisert says: "This type of stuff is the real money maker—the automation is going to be managed by a bot with one human architect in the future—how can I as the human stand out?"[9] The answer is to be creative but not cheesy. Use conversationally ubiquitous phrasing to be familiar and sound like a peer. *Hope you're doing well! Fifteen minutes?* Ask for a twelve-minute or twenty-two-minute slot. Every email should go left brained / right brained. Facts and stories, logic and emotion. Grab your CEO's email or LinkedIn inbox and study the subject lines. Your head will explode in the sea of sameness. Dare to be different linguistically. Cognitive dissonance is real. If content is bizarre, it will get read . . . just don't damage your brand!

TQ TAKEAWAY

Don't look like everyone else with the content you create! Apply the principles in this book rather than copying the phrasing.

Non-hunger Principled Disinterest

One of the things that will shoot you in the foot the most is having a salesy tone. So when you're cold calling, emailing, texting, or reaching out on LinkedIn, you always need to communicate from a position of strength. You must not sound needy, hungry, or desperate . . . no commission breath! Write confident sequences that state the story, the right- and left-brain factors, and ROI claims that seem reasonable and can be proved.[10]

Non-hunger is also known as the Law of Principled Disinterest. This comes with a paradox: you can come across as arrogant or uninterested. Conversely, the more interest you show in closing a deal, the more repulsed the prospect will be with your demeanor. Jeb Blount calls this "the universal law of need." It's the idea that when you need a deal too badly, you're going to have sales breath, which is a repellent to prospects.

How do you manage the paradox between non-hunger and engagement? The best salespeople are not desperate but genuinely curious. They seek to be interested rather than needy. They have no desire to pitch anything until the buyer is in the zone. Genuinely curious people have an advantage when prospecting because questioning is in their DNA, and they don't have to fake it. Barry Rein advocates selling through curiosity, and he is famous for being paid on future revenue performance by his customers.

The egomaniac blabbermouth never gets to the root cause, so they are incapable of being able to propose the right solution. However, curious people with the right values go through hell to understand another person's business. They actively listen to cultivate curiosity on both sides, and this is fundamentally important.

Non-hunger and curiosity, combined with a love of customers and enjoyment in making a difference, prevents sales burnout. But to do it at scale you need high TQ in harnessing "the machine" to slave away for you so your energy is available for empathy and creativity. If you leverage intelligent automation for top of funnel and other repetitive tasks, you can then focus on where there is alignment rather than pressure for a close. These values beat negative attempts at Machiavellian manipulation or brute force tactics.

Hunting big game takes courage and an extremely sharp spear. In sales you also need a willingness to walk away and exhibit gravitas in how you carry the conversation, remaining dead calm while operating at the highest echelons. You cannot be hungry, needy, or pushy—nor lose your cool when anyone accuses you of spamming them. It's also crucial at all times to be driving the necessarily high levels of effective activity that open doors for you to create value in conversations, listening proactively, and remaining detached from the outcome of the deal.

Neighborhood Techniques and Ghost-Driving for Your CXO

This strategy was outlined in the *COMBO Prospecting* book and is especially powerful prior to any distancing barriers from a virus crisis where everyone is suddenly fully remote. In normal times, with events, conferences, and company parties du jour, you can create a sequence around an event. Load your best prospects there from all over the world, and do three to five touches asking about their attendance at the event, whether you should add them to the VIP party, and who else are they bringing.

In the new normal of remote working and online conferences, we're challenging all CEOs to launch virtual events where the livechat influences the content in real time. Hopefully Zoom and others will innovate something excellent because we think sponsors will still pay and B2B attendees will derive a ton of value. Innovative ideas around Zoom calls include turning the background into sponsorship images and advertising. One innovative startup is working on building iframes to pull in intel on the prospect, including CRM data, trigger events, social signals, notes—even battle cards.

Here is a wild idea that we've done to great effect. Become the trusted expert with your own CXO. Don't be intimidated; it's not as scary as you think. Here is how to execute once you have the keys to their LinkedIn account. Focus outreach around events where your CXO can appear. It reduces friction when a CXO is inviting a prospect to another relevant conference or thought leadership dinner or event. This is infinitely better than trying to land discovery calls where the C-level prospect feels that they're going to get cornered by a seller.

Especially powerful is to ghost-drive your CEO's LinkedIn account around a specific event that they are going to attend. Here is why it makes sense. An outside sales call costs up to six times more than an inside sales call. On this note, many startups heed the siren song of hiring guys in suits to close enterprise deals ASAP. They instead just increase their cash burn but without the commensurate revenue, and they start hemorrhaging money. Typically, they then fire the squadron before the first red ink dries on the contract for a mere trial or pilot.

A savvy sales professional can make themselves indispensable if they are the CEO's trusted ghost-driver. So here is how you can fireproof yourself to be the very last player booted off the island! You use LinkedIn InMails and emails from the CEO's accounts to set up "neighborhood" meetings for them with you in attendance. These focus on a conference or industry event that's coming up or a planned trip to a particular city. Ideally, you and your CEO go as a team to the meetings. If the CEO can't attend, then you, ghosting as the CEO, simply hand off the meeting to yourself "due to unforeseen circumstances" just before the scheduled date.

When it comes to targeting for this strategy, those with TQ use software to triangulate potential clients in a geographical area or likely to be interested in a particular forum or event. Data.com can be searched by city and state for a relevant list of prospects. RainKing also has a GPS-like heat map element that you can use to schedule a bunch of meetings around a nominated city with similar prospects. Even Sales Navigator, with its friendly Boolean search interface, enables you to identify the executives in a particular region. Proximity-based, event-based, neighborhood techniques work extremely well leveraging cadence software normally used to sell tickets to conferences. Just ask David Dulany of Tenbound!

Be the EA of your own CEO by calling and emailing the executive assistants of a targeted list. Ask if they can find thirty minutes for your boss and theirs. "Hi, Daisy. My boss, the CEO, is in town Thursday speaking at a conference, and he asked me to tee up a meeting with your boss because he has some research he thought would be of interest to Bill. How is his calendar for dinner or breakfast on Wednesday? If that's no good, how about twenty minutes for them to talk over coffee?" Simply being in their area dramatically ups the probability of a meeting. You're already there, so they don't have to feel guilty about committing you to your travel costs.

Neighborhood techniques work flawlessly for conferences post-pandemic too. Special thanks to Scott Britton who came up with the best conference idea: Call every single prospect attending or on the list of speakers. Then, either for yourself or your CXO, book a meeting room across the street at a premium hotel and secure back-to-back meetings there. In general, neighborhooding and setting meetings with like-minded people attending events is a good strategy. Throwing events while at conferences is also very powerful. Create a VIP dinner with extra seats, and as C-levels roll through your booth that day, get fifty business cards and then text them all about the dinner. You should be able to fill a dinner party of twenty that way.

Use your own CEO and CXO team to help you elevate everything you do. Be known internally as the stately honey badger who can build pipeline like no other in the history of the world. But also be known as someone who operates with intelligent stealth, finesse, gravitas, and business acumen. Be seen as someone who talks the language of customers and who understands the language of business leaders—achieving financial results, important outcomes, managing risk of change, and reliably delivering on a rock-solid business case.

In short, you are the one and only person worthy of the login and password of the CXO's LinkedIn account. This is because you are intelligent, well read, have command of the English language—you're not slippy in how u right [yes, that was deliberate but we've seen worse]. You humbly enhance their brand, work with pre-agreed templates and scripts, build out their network with high-quality contacts, and leverage their own time to drive growth in their business.

TQ TAKEAWAY

You cannot execute a CXO ghost-driving strategy if you can't write credibly. It requires trust and competence as you are handling their precious personal brand.

We've been riffing on this concept for years and the examples in the previous section are real. If your own CEO will allow you to drive their LinkedIn profile, the first wild thing you will discover is that even they struggle to secure meetings with new people. It's rough for a vendor, even at the top! As you ghost-drive your CEO's profile, remember almost all CEOs have an executive assistant inside their social email account and business social profile. What you are doing is an aboveboard practice as long as you are authorized and executing as instructed or agreed.

Provocative perspective on this from Ryan Reisert: "Personally, this is why I believe text on all channels will die; because of no trust. My email accounts are fake aliases and now the same is happening on social . . . it's very sad."[11] We agree and this is why the phone must remain central to elevating engagement. Conversation first, ideally with an introduction from a common trusted relationship, will be the fastest path to engagement. Ryan goes on: "Conversation with the actual person, not an alias, is what is needed."

Be intelligently bold and brave in approaching those in your company's C-suite. Have a proposed plan and scripts that you will work with so their brand, profile, and network are enhanced, not damaged, as you tee it up on their platform. Make sure you communicate in their voice and never do anything that could damage their precious brand or reputation.

Targeting and Pragmatic Research

There are people who advocate you just dial semi-blind and engage in conversations—"Screw the technology, I differentiate by being human and old school." We think this is a poor use of time and leaves money on the table. A little bit of research into the quality of your list is the key—data, data, data! We know that a quality list of targets and a B– message will set qualified meetings all day. Pushing to the dead wrong targets, even with an A+ message, does not have a snowball's chance in hell!

If your target buyers suffer from seasickness, they're never buying your yacht. This all comes back to PMF (product/market fit) defining ICP (ideal customer profile), even before defining buyer personas. "Let me try to sell you this amphibious vehicle kit for your car." Nope, no interest in buying a kit to take your car out in the harbor. "Okay, I'll give you a 50 percent discount." Hmm, still don't want to drive your car in the ocean. There are so many interpretations of this parable for the good, bad, and the ugly of how many seek to sell.

Instead, go figure out your exact ICP and buyer personas based on real product/market fit. Then use BI (business intelligence) platforms such as LinkedIn Sales Navigator, InsideView, ZoomInfo (Scoops), SalesIntel.io, Triggr, and Bombora to identify the people who actually have a reasonable to high propensity to buy. Demand Matrix is a data as a service and can do some serious stack ranking. For example, if you sold Hubspot and were given a list of every CEO, CMO, and CIO who was just appointed into a new company, and the previous companies they worked at were all raving fans of Hubspot . . . then you would have very happy hunting with insane success and low rejection.

To effectively and rapidly personalize on the good target list, take a batch of fifty names from your master sequence and decide that you will do the necessary research to "show 'em you know 'em" and record a personalized LinkedIn video. CheetahIQ and Owler are great tools for this.

Mention a few custom things about their profile that meaningfully stood out. Joe Benjamin adds: "In order to show them you know them, LinkedIn is a good starting point but you'll want to go wider to find something that will show you've done your homework and aren't another salesperson taking the traditional research path. Look for podcast appearances which can be full of interesting and valuable personal insights. If they use Twitter, you'd be negligent not to review their account. Using a tool like CheetahIQ allows you to quickly do this for multiple prospects at the same company with one click."[12]

The secret to good personalization is doing things that a machine won't be able to do anytime soon. Another technique is what is called hyper-personalization—directly quoting them, picking something idiosyncratic that really shows research. You may choose to focus on a virtue or attribute from their LinkedIn recommendations. Jeremey Donovan highlights the importance of tying your personalization back to the product for added firepower. A quirky one you could use, but maybe too gimmicky, is to load a prospect's LinkedIn profile if they are a first-degree connection and hit the *contact* button (in a web browser not the mobile app); it will show the date you were connected. You could open the message with: "Wow, John, we have 1,234 common connections and connected on April 7, 2012 . . ."

Bucketing the rest of the pool into personas by vertical or title is key and then delivering compelling messaging or value narratives to these folks. You shouldn't spend all day on personalization, but you get spam all day so you know how ridiculous it feels when you can tell, flat out, *This seller has no idea and is just being lazy or clumsy with rubbish personalization. Their referral approach is like it modeled on a chain-letter pyramid scheme. They've never really looked at my profile. They've probably just automated my name into some rogue mindless sequence.* We receive this rubbish all the time—people offering to help us create leads or learn how to use LinkedIn! Even InMails offering to help us with leads for our (nonexistent) dentistry or plumbing businesses.

We need to tip our hats to Josh Braun. His concept of making deposits before withdrawals is profound. You'd share the eBook to enable them before asking for time. This is far more powerful right now than just a social proofpoint and an ask. He has pioneered "illumination questions," which help to uncover latent pain. We love his concept of "sword versus superpower," and he's been gracious to let us reference his work here. He writes on illumination questions by asking: "How do you loosen your prospect's grip on the status quo? You shine a light on a problem that can harm your prospect or a missed opportunity."

Here are some examples from Josh:

- "Mary—are you aware that you can import all your Dropbox files into Google drive with one click?" That illumination question would get me to think differently about Dropbox because it eliminates the force that's holding me back from switching.

- "How do you know what your best closers are doing differently?" That's a great question for the sales leader if you were selling Chorus.

- "What are you doing to ensure that every cold call connect converts into a booked meeting?" That would be a great question if you were a sales coach.[13]

Luigi Prestinenzi from Sales IQ often asks business leaders or the VP of Sales similar questions: "What's the average cost per lead from marketing versus sales self-generated by reps?" He follows up with: "What's the conversion rate from each channel?" Then the knock-out combination: "How many of your reps are on target year-to-date?" A thoughtful pause: "Hmm . . . what's the gap costing you in revenue and what's the impact of not fixing this for you and the business?" The business case for change has been illuminated.[14]

You don't want to be the sword writer—all about feature, function, benefits. You must instead highlight the *why*, or as Patty McLaren calls it, "the unicorns in the sky"—the superpower, ROI business case, compelling reason for investing in change.

According to Guillaume Moubeche: "When sending cold emails, the first twenty seconds of their attention is key. Tailored personalization will motivate prospects to let their guard down, and it's not always time-consuming to set it up."[15] Great advice, but we think no email should take more than twenty seconds to read . . . period! The right video can hook interest to then go longer.

Here is an example from Guillaume: "If I'm cold emailing, I'll use the personalized video thumbnail strategy (search for it on YouTube to see). Add their company logo and first name onto the image to create a unique thumbnail for each prospect. Result? A click rate of 86 percent, plus the image grabs their eyeballs in an instant. Once they click, they get transferred to a dynamic landing page that's also personalized using the same tags. Furthermore, it reduces friction if I'm trying to book meetings because my Calendly is embedded right below the video."[16]

The above example takes minutes, instead of hours, to connect the dots. Guillaume Moubeche is an intelligent innovator in this space and the strategy was one of the main reasons why lemlist was able to hit the $1 million ARR milestone in less than two years as a startup.

Semi-Automation to Automation

The truth of the matter for complex enterprise selling is that semi-automation is the best we can achieve right now. There's much fake AI with rule-based automation behind the facade. A vast amount of companies are pulling off the appearance of full automation with a Mechanical Turk function offshore.

Fun fact: The Mechanical Turk was a fake chess-playing machine built in the eighteenth century by Wolfgang von Kempelen. It appeared to be masterful at chess, winning most of the games it played during demonstrations around Europe and the Americas for years. It defeated many challengers including Napoleon Bonaparte and Benjamin Franklin! Yet the Mechanical Turk was in fact a mechanical illusion that allowed a human chess master hiding inside to operate the machine. It looked like AI but was just an extension of a real human.

We are still at a level of technology where the human being needs to program the sequences and mash up the tech stack with insane levels of nous to be effective. Imagine a new bold era where the machine, almost like Siri meets Google Duplex Assistant, picks the target accounts, parses the relevant case studies, writes the personalized emails per persona, and then generates the back-and-forth to close the meeting. This could even happen at the speed of high frequency share trading, encrypted blockchain, in binary computer language—human intervention wouldn't even be involved. We helped build a beta version of this and it was a true thrill ride but even harder and more expensive (millions) than it sounds!

The ultimate expression of this will be beyond Turing, with machines replacing humans for the very top of funnel. It can happen with simple use-cases. Remember the story of the man who walked into the California car dealer, thinking he had been interacting on their website with a real person? The chatbot merely says: "Hi, how can I help you?" The buyer says: "I'm looking for a blue model XYZ if you have one in stock and can give me the best price." The chatbot does inventory lookup and says: "We actually have three in stock. One is a demonstrator and we could do a deal on it . . . it's loaded with all the options. When would you like to come in and have a look?" The buyer asks about opening hours and the chatbot responds with the address and asks what time of day works best. The buyer replies: "Saturday morning works," and the chatbot says, "Great, would you like to also test drive the car when you come in? . . . I'll make sure it's ready for you." The missing step with the real example is that the chatbot should then confirm and say, "I'm not at this dealership but ask for Tina when you get here; I'll make sure she has all your information and looks after you." The appointment with the dealer is confirmed and a real human, Tina, is all set for a warmed-up conversation with the buyer when they arrive on the lot.

More on the future of selling later, but if you want more proof of the fact that Tomorrowland is already here, go to YouTube and search "Google Duplex 2018 AND Sundar Pichai." It made a huge splash in 2018 and then went quiet. But make no mistake, much is happening in the background for a reemergence that blows people's minds with what Google Assistant can do with live, intelligent, humanlike voice conversations. Google Text-to-Speech can also convert written content or scripts into speech using hundreds of different voices across thirty languages.

Their Wavenet capability replicates the nuances of human intonation with colloquialisms, inflection, pauses, *ums* and *ahs*. The AI can sound like it comes from the outback of Australia or the Ozarks, or from New York, San Diego, or the west end of London. In 2020, Google Assistant had more than five hundred million users in ninety different countries speaking more and more languages. It can even master the New Zealand "Kiwi" accent with a complete absence of vowels where *six*, *sex*, and *sox* sound exactly the same.

Where does the SDR and AE go in this "*Blade Runner* meets *Minority Report 2049*" scenario? Actually, a return to innocence: The best sellers are leveraging technology to achieve more real human-to-human (H2H) interactions. They are returning to discussion, discovery, qualification, probing all the things that make inside sellers great and future AEs. Gosh, it sounds like just a little history repeating . . . but not for too much longer. Can you feel the winds of change?

Building Sequences:
Messaging Meets Cadence Across Channels

There are three jarring realities about the linguistics of the very best outbound touch patterns—they lack formatting, are hyper-short, and are very conversational. This is a style we adapted called "compacted" or "spears," as opposed to massive bullet-pointed, marketing-looking pablum, that sadly, most outbound sales teams are sending out of sales engagement platforms. Here is our advice.

Strive for hyper-short subject lines with just one to three words with one being an action word. Strive for three to five sentences maximum in the email, with a CTA as the third. Use pattern interrupts and make what you say stick out. Be novel in word choice. Be assumptive without being arrogant. Make the personalization about the relevant pain rather than vanilla demographic, psychographic, or technographic information. Preview these on your friend's or colleague's mobile device. Remember, just like copywriting, the purpose of the first sentence is to get to the next. You usually only get the subject line and preview text on iPhone or Android so structure accordingly for that limited view. Experiment with cadence frequency—we recommend even every twenty-four business hours; then it doesn't feel like marketing.

Program your touch patterns to "press in" so you actually receive a response—*No, Remove, Refer, Not interested,* or even a *Yes.* Referrals are gold. If you see any outreach achieve more than three or four views (with pixel tracking), then *triple* them—call, email, vmail in less than ninety seconds. We believe in narrative arcs and clusters, so the first subject and resultant two bumps pertain to one value narrative or theme. The next cluster, another theme. You can A/B test all of this. Essentially you have three or four topics bursting out in a main email with two bumps in Outlook or Gmail.

Chip away at prevailing myths. Challenge convention. Pique interest. Using *thank you* increases reply rates by 20 percent so use it. There are pattern interrupts throughout, combinations of words and formatting you're not expecting. Apply your human creativity, quirky idioms, and unique personality with the machine . . . yes, you must be the ghost in the machine when it comes to automation.

Sales Ops and When Sequencers Go Wrong

There is a new category emerging: sales ops for SEPs (sales engagement platforms), sometimes just called sequencers. These platforms are so powerful, just setting them up for more than fifty sellers requires specialized governance, data sharing, profiles, and all sorts of back-end settings depending on which CRM and data sources you're using. De-duping and DNC become tricky, especially if sellers are cross-pollinating and uploading their own lists out of umpteen data platforms.

Ben Sardella, cofounder of Datanyze (acquired by ZoomInfo) and OutboundWorks, started an amazing new company that provides sales ops for Outreach and SalesLoft customers, helping with sequence design and outbound strategy plus tactics. These platforms are becoming very sophisticated.

A big issue for all sales automation is data governance on prospects, whether it's handling GDPR/CCPA compliance to something as simple as suppression lists, or handling DNC and permissions across your system of record (CRM) and system of engagement (SEP) including Outreach, SalesLoft, and XANT. There's much to be gained by having an experienced sales ops expert internally or a consulting firm to dial this in and be ready to intervene instantly when needed.

You need to be able to "stop the line" and rejig at a moment's notice. Stopping the line is a reference to a manufacturing environment where you ask assembly line workers to stop the line if there is breakage, defect, or injury. In the context of a sequencer, this might happen if you are using language in your emails that suddenly becomes inappropriate due to world events. For example, think of jokes or language that references disasters (e.g., "a tsunami of responses to our offer" or "it's going viral") and how that text looks during a real tsunami or pandemic.

Greg Meyer highlights that when stopping the line, think about how you would handle redirecting people who are in the middle of a sequence. The key point here is: never let the bots run wild or have the automation run the asylum. Always be ready to insert human judgment and governance at short notice. No sequence should ever be "set and forget." Always be A/B testing, refining, remediating, and learning for the next campaign.

TQ BOOSTER

Have a person in command of what's happening and ensure they can jump in to instantly stop the line and rejig the messaging and tooling. Check out RevShoppe.com for expert advice and support with sales engagement platforms—big shout-out to cofounders Jason Vargas, Patricia McLaren, and Josh O'Brien.

Prospecting with Exotic B2C Platforms

Platforms like Instagram, WhatsApp, Snapchat, Facebook Messenger, Skype, and more abound. According to Brendan Short: "Platforms change but the methodology stays the same."[17] People wonder how it's humanly possible to simultaneously manage so many activities and achieve cut-through with key people. The answer is WhatsApp. This platform is nearly 100 percent adopted in Tel Aviv and Asian markets. Many leaders have migrated their inner circle communication to it. It's lightning fast, encrypted, and always works flawlessly. You even sometimes get it for free on Delta and other airlines.

You can port your WhatsApp into a web client and it acts almost like Meebo (the 2007 chat aggregator that let you manage all chat platforms) where anyone in the world is always available there. For mid-funnel progression to bottom-funnel closing, we highly recommend WhatsApp. Text messaging is very strong for top of funnel opening and also the very bottom of the funnel closing. Leaders love brevity, and any app that forces others to be brief is favored.

Use all the channels of engagement until the prospect self-identifies their preference. There's a more recent app called Cameo where you can pay a fee to have a celebrity record a personalized message. Imagine sending notes to prospects from Snoop Dogg, our favorite Real Housewife, or Bob Saget? Hilarious, and maybe something you could consider if playing with the fire of humor.

Fast reply rates to inbound inquiries make all the difference, so consider platforms such as XANT that can round-robin leads to the team so that potential revenue does not die on the vine.

When to Text Message a Prospect

Some people believe you should only use text messaging once the prospect knows you and has expressed interest. They advocate text messages only in the mid to low funnel phase, positing that it's creepy and illegal to text at the top funnel. But a phone is a business tool and text messages are a common method of business communication. Include text messages if you are determined to break through, but be aware of the many rules and regulations in your market. If you're networking with them, ask for their number and send a text or WhatsApp message.

> ### TQ TAKEAWAY
> If you've been in deal review and legal for ages, by all means move your communications into WhatsApp and text to poke the bear and drive momentum in the deal. It's more intimate and the response rate approaches 100 percent. Read that again.

We met a CRO who is developing all his business over text and he claimed response rates at nearly 100 percent. Once you have gotten past the creepy factor of meeting the prospect, you have carte blanche to start directly messaging them.

What's stopping you from texting everyone in the mid to lower funnel? It might seem like a very bold move, but it cuts through in a way that email just can't. We see sellers passively hide behind email and that's a mistake. If a prospect has expressed interest, feel free to move things forward with a text. You'll be amazed at the increased efficiency. Outreach, SalesLoft, and XANT all have text options (you can schedule sends right out of the platform!) but you must be very careful and meticulous with that channel—you don't want to get it wrong, and an opt-in is required.

Exotic B2C platforms must be explored by all reps even if it seems risky. That includes Facebook Messenger, WeChat (Asia), Snap, even TikTok (content strategy). By the time you read this, they will probably be growing like gremlins so experiment with them all across the entire funnel to see if you can crack them. Jake Dunlap of Skaled has had B2B success with content on Instagram. This is similar to Gary Vee. Can you imagine using Instagram DMs to B2B prospects?

In the not-too-distant future, private Slack Communities will emerge where vendors pay an entry fee or per interaction to be paired with the optimal decisionmakers. The host mediator (could be an AI) will play matchmaker. We will move into a post-email world in the not-too-distant future.

The Role of Twitter

LinkedIn has a set of hashtags, so if you hashtag early enough in your LinkedIn update it will push to Twitter and then ride the same hashtag streams there. It's a useful growth hack for content publishing. Then, on your Twitter, set your about link to your LinkedIn URL. So as you post and push to Twitter, some things pick up and go viral on hashtags and suddenly you get a steady flow of inbound connection requests coming back in from your popularity on Twitter and they have a way better hashtag system. Best part is, LinkedIn has no speed limit (or throttle) on inbound invitations. Yahtzee!

Hashtags are used to monitor topics, organizations, or people you wish to follow, but using @ instead of # in front of their Twitter handle sends a direct message (DM) . . . just like the old days of beepers, then SMS messages, and now modern-day messaging platforms such as WhatsApp, Facebook, and so on.

Twitter is most powerful for monitoring the activity of any target prospect and quickly creating engagement or awareness so that your outreach is anything but cold. Treat Twitter as a trigger event monitoring platform and then use it to direct-message them, just like sending an SMS (text message) to their phone or WhatsApp message. Make their mobile device ding, beep, and buzz so they cannot ignore you.

Developing Hyper-Specialized Sales and Lead Generation Functions

Back in the 2010s, business focused on specializing sales team roles for the Henry Ford production line of selling. An SDR should focus on sourcing new leads, and AEs should work opportunities to close deals, often working with technical pre-sales specialists. Parsing out the SDR/AE functions especially made sense for teams targeting mid-size or enterprise deals.

As this model evolved, it became clear that SDRs should focus on engagement rather than building lists. We saw the introduction of the LDR role, or the lead development representative, to focus on building account lists for SDRs. The LDR would become the trusted resource for teams to build, cross-check, and clean up lists for each SDR to prospect. For many, LDRs also parsed inbound touches or weak MQLs. Others create entry-level roles focused on segmented data-wrangling.

A clear trend emerged. Once a given function spent a considerable amount of time working on a task, efficiencies started to surface by turning that task into a function in itself. This is not only because context switching from separate tasks takes a toll on the brain, requiring a few minutes to adjust to the new task each time, but because everyone has a unique set of strengths and weaknesses.

Chris Marin, cofounder of Convertist, went even further to specialize teams to focus on their strengths. After hiring over a hundred SDRs, he noticed that great phone-based conversationalists did not always write with the prose of Steinbeck. Similarly, excellent email copywriters did not always speak with the oration skills of Morgan Freeman. So they slowly began carving out *dedicated* functions for their team. This included roles focused on list development, outbound email copywriting, inbound email handling, task routing, social media engagement, and phone-based engagement. This required significant work and customization but resulted in a lead-generation engine that drove more business for their customers than before.

To develop hyper-specialized sales and lead generation roles, you need a set of KPIs for each role consistent with how SDRs are evaluated on their qualified leads and AEs on quota attainment. For instance, list development representatives have a daily volume of email, dial, and social data points they need to curate. Phone-based SDRs are expected to dial through a predetermined number of leads, have a number of positive conversations, and meet their appointment-setting lead commit. You cannot manage what you don't measure—the challenge is to implement CRM in a way that enables everyone's processes and proactive management, rather than people gaming the metrics or feeling confronted with a cacophony of data vomit that no one could possibly wade through.

Each role should have a series of assessments that gauge their readiness for a successful start on day one. Additionally, remember you should never have a single point of failure with any one of these functions. Build redundancies around each role. Once you have someone who is excellent at executing in a role, find someone else and train them so they're every bit as good with the coaching of that person. Ensure that reporting for each role is based on the input activities that feed into objectives, which in turn create the final outputs or results.

It's a giant mistake to "manage by results" instead of managing the activities. Also ensure frequent check-ins, role-plays and coaching. These are all essential for maintaining motivation and improving competence.

CHAPTER TEN

Driving Sales Success

Metrics to Measure

According to Greg Meyer at Data Czar: "Look at account level, not person level, metrics and response rate per account per campaign. A simple way to think about this is to look at the number of people you had to contact at that company to secure a meeting, and the elapsed time between the first email/task and the meeting. By doing this you'll eliminate some of the noise you see in a sequencer around emails sent, 'out of office' replies, polite 'not interested but thanks' messages. Reply rate is a vanity metric just like open rate. It's a leading indicator of response and interest but not necessarily an indicator of positive sentiment."[1]

For a manager, the main point is that you want action-based outcomes from your SDRs. "This week I talked to twelve decisionmakers at three target companies and so far landed one meeting." No one cares if you sent more than a thousand emails that ended up in people's inbox or filters and were unread. They do care if you have successfully secured a *yes* or a *no* from a qualified buyer.

According to Ryan Reisert: "The metric of the future is 'daily completions working TAM, Total Addressable Market, period."[2] Brendan Short, another million-plus email sender, has advocated for a new set of metrics to track SDR efficiency. He has formulas measuring conversion rates against contacts and accounts (see Figure 10.1).[3]

$$\text{Outbound Account Conversion} = \frac{\text{\# Qualified Appointments Set Per Month}}{\text{\# Accounts Touched Per Month}}$$

$$\text{Outbound Contact Conversion} = \frac{\text{\# Qualified Appointments Set Per Month}}{\text{\# Contacts Touched Per Month}}$$

Figure 10.1

Source: Brendan Short, "The Most Important Outbound Metric That No One is Talking About."

Brendan, a thought leader in the emerging field of RevOps, says: "Outbound sales teams use more complex systems called funnel metrics. I've tracked these two metrics at dozens of companies and, generally speaking, here's what I've found." Figure 10.2 tells the story.

$$\text{Outbound Account Conversion} = \frac{15}{50} = 30\%$$

$$\text{Outbound Contact Conversion} = \frac{15}{1{,}250} = 1.2\%$$

Figure 10.2

Source: Brendan Short, "The Most Important Outbound Metric That No One is Talking About."

Brendan emphasizes that the key thing to consider in these numbers is outbound account conversion. OAC rate varies depending on the size of companies you're targeting. And thus the number of companies you can reach out to on a monthly basis. That said, If you're within 1.5 to 10 percent, you're in a great place. When it comes to outbound contact conversion (OCC), if you're within 0.5 to 2.5 percent for your OCC rate, you're in a great place.

Creating a Career Path as an Expert Opener

Some people actually just sell better at the very top, bringing the fish by the boat or actually hooking so others can excel pulling them in. The point is that you have openers and closers. Aaron Ross, who wrote *Predictable Revenue*, spawned the modern SDR-AE industrial complex in chronicling the Salesforce business model where they broke up the opportunity creation sales process like Henry Ford to have people specialize in different stages. We would argue the commitment for time is the first commitment and the way it is achieved sets the agenda and tone for everything that follows. To again quote Anthony Iannarino: "Opening is the new closing."

Yet this is contradictory because there really is no such thing as an opener and a closer. The truth is that you cannot become a great closer without first mastering the science and art of opening. You cannot be a great opener if you cannot close for an initial commitment of time, and qualification, and discovery information—that's the way the paradox all fits together. The same is true of hunters and farmers, with each role needing to perform both functions for sustained success. Metaphors abound in sales but if you master the art of opening in any season, crisis, economy, and by any channel, you will always have well-paid work and move up and away from the "opening only" career track.

This is where we respect voices such as Collin Cadmus and Tito Bohrt who have been rallying the collective VC community to compensate top funnel practitioners better because the gig can be twice as hard if not ten times harder than the role of progressing and closing deals. This is because it's so rejection-laden that it's just like being a "hungry dog on the back of a meat truck" operating at 10X flame-throwing Grant Cardone levels.

The big money in new sales is at the account executive layer. To get there faster, convince your manager to let you run the inbound leads, or some trial stage opportunities, or any deals under an agreed threshold. Just get some at bats on doing discovery and qualification. Convert some of these free trials into paying customers, crush your job, and then they'll make you into the next AE.

Average tenure for inside sales roles is less than eighteen months, so they know they have to promote you or lose you. Closing sales is just the act of securing another commitment, the commitment to buy it, which is not too dissimilar to closing on the first commitment, which is the agreement to give you their time and information for discovery and qualification. There is no such thing as a good opener and a good closer. If you can't close for time, you can't close a seven-figure multi-year contract through an F1000 procurement department.

Smart SDRs who become great can replace lazy AE field reps who don't use the new tech and sit around waiting for a truckload of leads to be backed up to their desk. Many AEs are just pedestrian account managers closing the occasional new deal . . . enough not to get fired but not enough to be successful. Mike Weinberg said it best: "You can't teach a zookeeper to go hunt game."

It is essential, however, to do your apprenticeship and not to jump too early. Sam Feldotto says: "Too often though, SDRs will be promoted after a few months of proving themselves in the SDR role, but don't have the ability to be effective as an AE, and they set themselves up for failure. Seventy-eight percent of SDRs that are promoted to AEs don't hit quota at all their first year."[4]

Our advice is *not* to take an AE role in order to escape prospecting and rejection. Only take the role to step up into being a full-cycle sales leader, where you feed yourself and coach others for top of funnel effectiveness. Once you've mastered the full cycle of sales, you can go and run a company or become the next Elon Musk entrepreneur. Make no mistake, opening the right new relationships with opportunities that convert to mutual benefit and profitable revenue is where the magic happens for commercial success.

Sam Feldotto continues with solid advice about not jumping too soon: "How do you think that looks on their resume if they get fired from their first closing role? Now they're trying to get another AE role but have eighteen months total experience, nine of them as an SDR and nine as an underperforming AE that got fired. From there, it's a hard uphill battle and can lead to them taking jobs they aren't passionate about and missing out on jobs they were. Smart SDRs will stick around a bit longer in that role to learn the ins and outs of the entire sales cycle. They'll use their 'boredom' in the role to channel personal growth by shadowing their AEs and learning everything that they can so that when they do get promoted, they aren't another statistic."

Advice to AEs and SDRs Working Together

One honest CEO told their reps on the first day: "The best it gets with leads from SDRs and marketing is about 40 to 60 percent. You'll need to farm accounts and hunt on your own to make your numbers. Treat leads as a bonus." Any salesperson who claims they can sell but cannot fill their own funnel with qualified opportunities is deluding themselves. Real sales professionals act as their own SDRs. They time-block and allocate prime time for executing outbound activity daily. They automate the never-ending search for trigger events. They are highly attuned to recognizing referral opportunities and asking for introductions in ways that maintain control and maximize results.

In some organizations, the SDRs and field reps will set up separate outreach cadences or collaborate very closely. Well-run businesses link the SDR layer with marketing to make sure the engine operates smoothly.

AEs should meet with their SDR at least weekly to review the cadences inside Outreach or SalesLoft, and so on. Look over the metrics, reanalyze the messaging, personalization, and verbiage, think through new experiments and things to retest. Do you have a new case study that better fits a persona? Is copy feeling a little wonky or long? Anything confusing or conflated? Too much jargon, cliches, or sales speak?

Get to know how everyone works and create a rhythm in how data is wrangled, CRM hygiene is managed, and handoffs are done seamlessly. Set clear expectations about the information needed from the other person at each stage. Understand both writing and communication styles.

SDRs should always respond quickly to all the outbound replies and assiduously follow up to make sure they are sending the AE the names of "high opens" and referrals so the AE can triple them (call, vmail, email in under ninety seconds). If voicemail is not a thing in your market, such as in India, use other channels such as WhatsApp text and voice, or LinkedIn voice for an audio message. Remember, the minimum for a COMBO is a triple that makes their pocket device buzz and ding multiple times within ninety seconds.

If you're very savvy with sequencers, you should have a login to Outreach and do nudges, as defined by highly viewed sequences where you can interject a quick ping to ask for the meeting. Salesforce has introduced High Velocity Sales (HVS) to rival SalesLoft and Outreach natively within their platform, and it is powered by Einstein AI for recommended best next steps. Harness the tech to bump, nudge, and keep the pipeline fires burning. Do it all from your systems of record and create CRM notes so you know what everyone is doing at all times ... don't tread on each other's toes

We encourage AEs to take an active role in collaboratively building the optimal shared lists (best in Google Sheets to then import into CRM or cadence platforms) and sequences. Go through an ICP and buyer personas exercise and work very diligently on picking the right lead lists in Sales Navigator, Triggr, Zoom, and so on. For the SDR, once you've set some initial appointments or received replies, share with your AE. Both should create a reciprocal value exchange around the best subject lines, body copy, frequency, case studies, explainer GIFs, stories, buyer personas—everything you can think of together. You need a dedicated Slack, Chatter, or other channel on what's working specifically within your cadences.

Sometimes, SDRs roll up under marketing, which is ideal if a strong portion of the day is fielding inbounds. This is where qualification is a must so you don't waste the AE's time. Platforms such as Clari can help you score your opportunities against your qualification acronym du jour. The marketing team can help you on the back end by securing opt-in for newsletters and running drip campaigns and lead scoring out of Pardot, Marketo, or Hubspot. Those long-nurtured leads become grist for the mill of outbound much like mining the deadwood pile—the opportunities you marked closed/lost.

In Sales Navigator you can share lead lists with another member on the team. Shared Accounts and Targeted Lead Lists are so powerful to cowork the social patch! Simple innovation, very deep practical application, and high ROI.

How to Be a Full-Cycle Seller— No SDR Required

Kristin Hersant, VP of Marketing at Groove, suggests the key themes for full-cycle sellers are:

1. Effective time management (strategies for not letting your prospecting funnel drop when you're actively working deals). It's also imperative to make sure you're always checking in with your book of business, which can be automated and personalized at scale.

2. Automate everything you can—meeting scheduling, email/call/meeting logging, outbound dialing, so you can rededicate 20 to 60 percent of your week to actually selling and relationship-building.

3. Use a sales engagement platform like Groove to always keep

Salesforce up to date in the background, without ever having to leave the places that they live—inbox, LinkedIn Sales Navigator, or mobile phone.

4. Full-stack sellers are all about building meaningful relationships, which is why automation requires the ability to write meaningful, personalized emails at scale. To craft meaningful 1:1 communications, you need a platform to surface real-time information from the CRM system in the inbox so you don't have to waste time switching between applications to figure out what to write.[5]

Groove worked with a multibillion-dollar financial institution whose field sales reps were resisting using the company's CRM system. By providing them with a simple user interface that "just worked," the entire team was able to rededicate their data entry day to relationship-building and closing more deals. Groove "gave them their Fridays back."

Remote Work and Closing Business Purely over Zoom

Zoom skyrocketed in 2020 and will innovate so much more. Imagine moving from a 2D to a 3D space utilizing VR, AR, or holography technology. It will be possible to create deepfake AI to put on a snap filter, Bitmoji, or simulate a MeMoji. You could call up a friend as Madonna, Snoop Dogg, or the president. Seriously, the videoconference category is rife for disruption post-pandemic to let its proverbial hair down.

Chris Beall believes that one phone conversation is worth 240 email interactions. The neuroscience concerning image-processing versus text reveals a single image is worth 60,000 words. We also know that propensity to close a deal goes up by 30 percent when you can see the prospect's face, and that was proved by early GoToMeeting and WebEx research.[6]

So what does this have to do with closing massive deals remotely? It is possible to do effective enterprise selling while *inside* and *remote*. Everyone was forced to do this in 2020 when the whole world was suddenly on sequester. There was no field selling.

To get tactical, dominating big-ticket selling with Zoom is about multi-threading, holding many calls top-down, bottom-up, and middle-out across the multitude of decisionmakers and influencers. But the future of virtual selling effectiveness is brought on by more three-dimensional information going into the communications itself.

Building your TQ means becoming masterful with myriad virtual meeting platforms as you avoid monotone presentations, share your screen seamlessly, switch from gallery to speaker view, drive engagement by asking questions of individuals, jump into Jamboards, Miro or Mural virtual whiteboards—all to collaborate. Learn all the platforms and which browser works best plus install the client software on your laptop including Zoom, Skype, Webex, GoToMeeting, BlueJeans, Hangouts, Jabber, Teams, Rainbow, and more.

Beyond all this, it astounds us when we consider how many sellers just have no idea about the basics when it comes to selling virtually. Problems include having an unrecognizable face because the lighting is wrong, rubbish audio with a hopeless microphone, variable annoying audio levels, looking up a person's nostrils, double chin, and ceiling as they talk down to us. We could go on, and failures in this area are enough to get someone fired.

TQ TAKEAWAY

Make sure you have lighting behind your screen/camera instead of behind your head. Invest in a quality microphone and avoid headsets with a mic that captures heavy breathing like you're a phone sex worker. Stand to lift your energy and have the screen/camera up at face height so you're not looking down on them. Create a professional environment at home with appropriate background and invest in the best bandwidth available. If you want to use a virtual background image, then invest in a green screen so you don't have parts of your body chroming away like you're Casper the friendly sales ghost. Frame your head in the middle of the screen and look them in the camera so for them it is like you're looking them in the eye. Record sessions and play the video back to critique and coach yourself on body language, tone of voice, eye contact, engagement, and so on. For goodness' sake, don't be online like an amateur.

How to Be a Hummingbird, Honey Badger, and Machine Multi-Tasker

Urgency is a myth conveyed by real-time operating. We've tested this by being dead calm but rapid fire replying to every Slack, text, chat, email, you name it. Ironically, nothing on a smartphone ever buzzes with the hundreds and hundreds of thousands of followers and connections we have in LinkedIn. It's a case of checking for alerts to never miss a thing.

A few secrets to our thinking here. We look at pipelines as becoming more urgent the further they progress because of the decay rates that create downward pressure—time kills deals and stalling in a stage is the kiss of death. You need to hammer the mid to low pipe with the same tenacity as the top of funnel. We like to humorously refer to this as prospecting your own pipe. This is not dissimilar to using Sales Navigator Boolean searches on your own first-degree network to slice and dice the best segments as your LinkedIn network becomes large.

ABP = always be prospecting, always be sending out sequences, always be operating asynchronously. It's like a lobster trawler—just draw that net 24/7 and eventually, maybe even 9:00 p.m. on a Saturday, you will hit pay dirt and set the meeting. Technology allows us to relax while appearing to be always on and hyper-responsive, even superhuman. This is especially true for account managers and CSMs.

Account Management and Customer Success Roles

Account-based selling (ABS) and the customer success manager (CSM) roles are massively important in a recession because new clients are even tougher to acquire than in good times. Treasure the installed base to retain and grow them. Every dollar you spend well on retention and growth will give you the best ROI available. This is because the cost of new revenue from existing clients is massively lower than the slaughter field of new logo acquisition.

We invested time with Zack Gasaway, who manages CSMs, and gained insights that can transform results, especially with sales engagement tools scaling efficiency while increasing average revenue per customer and reducing churn. The following captures his wisdom.[7]

When you're managing a client, you're responsible for troubleshooting issues, finding areas of opportunity, leveraging long-term partnerships, often while being measured on satisfaction and promoter scores using metrics such as NPS. The best customers are experts on your product or service, and an extension of your sales team. The CSM's goal is simple yet complex: maximize growth, maturity, and satisfaction for their entire book of business. The task of proactively reaching out, scheduling review calls, and using day-to-day creative problem-solving can make it overwhelming to manage and even more so as your book gets bigger.

The KPIs for a CSM often include coverage of accounts, connected calls, renewals and new revenue, contract terms, and most important, net churn. That's a lot to wrap your mind around, so where does automation and sequencing come into play for account management? The ability to keep tabs, monitor triggers, schedule calls, analyze account behavior, communicate updates, and monitor for risks and opportunities is essential.

Zack is right and we believe all CSMs and account managers must be hunter-farmers. You can't be a "vegetarian hunter" poking around in the dirt for beets when your company needs pelts on the wall to feed the tribe. SEPs and automation can be just as essential for effective account management as for new logo sales.

Sales engagement platforms such as Outreach, SalesLoft, and others are exploding because they enable multi-touchpoint, custom sequences or cadences that can be tailored and delivered with strong relevance. Unlike with new account prospecting, ABM and ABS to existing clients can be fueled by rich CRM data. According to Zack: "You can filter and email your entire book of accounts with a touch of a button. You can even create custom email templates that make it feel less automated while including a scheduler link to book some time with you."

Selling into existing accounts means you're already past the spam filters and blockers. You can go full throttle to help your client derive greater value form the existing relationship, which is something the CFO and head of procurement is seeking to drive. Be bold and step up! Zack says: "I can't tell you the amount of times I've created a simple email template that I sent out to all of my not connected accounts to just see calls getting booked while I'm able to focus my time on other things. Right there, both of those controllable KPIs are ticked with a few clicks of a button!"

Zack has thrived by creating filters and triggers for all his priority accounts, and then using SEP platforms to send tailored sequences. Right person, right time, right message—minimal effort because of automation . . . boom! All this matters because 90 percent of the battle as a

CSM or account manager is just in turning up at the right time for that highly relevant conversation. Monitoring trigger events and automating engagement is key. Farm and sell, sell and farm—it's a virtuous cycle of sustainability and thriving in your role.

TQ BOOSTER

Role-based trigger events are insanely powerful for CSMs and account managers. Create opportunities in CRM when supporters leave and move elsewhere. Build relationships with key new people joining your customer's organization, before your competitor follows them in. New senior people usually seek to drive change. Read the trigger events section of this book again!

Yet go beyond automated emails introducing the new account manager and inviting a meeting to be scheduled. Go beyond the table stakes of triggers. Elevate engagement by aligning with the client's OKRs (objectives and key results). Know their big audacious goals, and their strategies and initiatives or projects designed to achieve the results. Align with what matters to them and then take a point of view about how they go even further with results, achieve them even earlier, and reduce their risk. Every client wants more value from you as an incumbent relationship.

Successful CSMs are not "professional visitors" but instead are trusted consultative partners, aligning with the customer's strategy and priorities. They automate to proactively manage risk and identify opportunities in the existing base regardless of new accounts being added by the sales team. You must leverage technology to map and manage relationships and also apply business acumen to elevate engagement and create value for both your employer and customer. Also consider platforms such as Ultimate.ai that automates up to 80 percent of customer support interactions to free account managers to focus on high-value activities.

Relationship Intelligence Graphs

Relationships have always mattered, and they always will in enterprise selling where there is complexity and risk. The key is to identify the signal amidst the noise and nodes within the network. In the world of enterprise selling, most people look to a CRM system and their LinkedIn network to assess relationship coverage. Yet most CRM systems are choked with inaccurate data and weak or dead connections rather than strong, active relationships. Similarly, most first-degree connections within LinkedIn do not represent actual trusted relationships. This is because people are often aggressively seeking to build followers and connections for status and to open up the LinkedIn database for search.

The reality is that being connected on LinkedIn does not mean there is a relationship of any value. Behind the façade of LinkedIn, actual *engagement* with the platform is decreasing, with leaders and buyers regarding the platform as the spammy domain of sellers. A CEO we know once described LinkedIn as "the world's biggest spam generation machine," complaining that it clogs his mental inbox. He resented the time LinkedIn consumed just to identify the small amount of content and communication he regarded as being of any real value.

The world is drowning in data, and yet businesses continue to thirst for the insights and relationship coverage required to power success. Everyone in sales is looking for the commercial nodes in relationship networks that create success, yet they are prevented from seeing what they need because the sheer volume of data is overwhelming. The key to success is human relationships powered by AI that leverages big data and analytics.

In complex enterprise selling and account management, success depends on knowing "proof of life" in relationships and mapping the real economic and political power base within and between organizations. This is game-changing capability: What if there was a way to automatically identify the real relationship and influence graph between enterprises? Imagine if you could easily visualize the nodes of influence against commercial opportunity and risk situations. Could relationship analytics be the X-factor in customer relationship management and the superpower of CRM systems that incorporate the capability at scale in an ethical and legally compliant manner?

Revenue Grid took on the same problem, especially for cases when customers have a higher-than-average number of people involved in communication—and subsequently, a decision to buy from you. People such as CTOs, security officers, members of innovation teams, admins, and the rest of the influencers, validators, and even decisionmakers may be absent from your CRM records. Revenue Grid lives in your email, calendar, and messengers, and therefore knows who is really involved in a deal, from both sides. The tool also shows just how strong each connection is, on top of the surprise of who actually knows who.

TrustSphere is a company that is transforming business results through the use of relationship analytics. Manish Goel, CEO and co-founder at TrustSphere, is excited about how relationship analytics can take customer success to the next level by leveraging the collective intelligence available to an organization from their own communication and collaboration systems. According to Manish: "The collective Social Capital of an organization is one of the most under-utilized and under-valued assets an organization has. It is rarely systematically leveraged, particularly by large enterprises."[8]

TrustSphere uses both real-time and archived data, including email, instant messaging, and business social platforms, as data sources that contain real two-way communication data between individuals and organizations. TrustSphere automates relationship intelligence with LinksWithin, which finds common relationships with people from both organizations beyond LinkedIn. It also enriches CRM data by automatically finding all the relationships from communication systems to enrich CRM around actual engagement. Finally, TrustSphere provides data-driven staff transition information to accelerate new seller onboarding so that new sellers or account managers come up to speed with an existing account. Their Transition Report highlights the most important and relevant client relationships, which a new relationship manager should prioritize when they first take over an account. It's like a heat map of the client account. This accelerates revenue realization by around 70 percent as well as customer satisfaction, minimizing the impact of the transition.

The automation of relationship intelligence through relationship analytics is also important because it can rapidly and reliably detect powerful trigger events that signal both opportunity and threat within an account. This is because new senior people often seek to drive change, and the sooner we cover these relationships, the more likely we are to successfully influence the person and organization.

Interaction platforms and communication channels are the real system of record for identifying relationship coverage. The best companies will integrate relationship analytics into their customer success strategy and CRM systems to drive next level effectiveness with their people and deliver accelerated growth.

Sales Enablement and Coaching

Platforms such as SalesHood and LinkedIn Learning can help reps to upskill, but knowledge alone is not what drives change. The world is awash with self-proclaimed sales experts talking into the camera and offering a downloadable eBook—but that is not what changes behavior or results. Sales IQ is our favorite because they identify the very best methodology for a problem domain, and deliver "knowledge with application" at scale, honoring best practices in adult learning and with real-world coaching for accountability and refinement for result. We have an interest in Sales IQ with our content on the platform. Engagement, application, and accountability are keys to effective sales enablement. When it comes to developing TQ, you must immerse yourself in the tools within your stack.

SEPs, Outreach, SalesLoft, and XANT all have certification programs. For CRMs, Salesforce has legendarily good Trailheads for eLearning with communities of practice that create raving expert advocates. Get yourself certified in every tool you use and participate in the operational pieces of setup and governance. You need to know where all the buttons are, integrations and advanced features. Be technically curious, figure out how to use snippets, rulesets, and custom fields, placeholders, merge fields, and templates. Success is about the ability to create a mashup tech stack for your own highly targeted purposes. Maybe you think this is beneath you? Consider the following true story.

Legendary pilot Richard de Crespigny converted from 747s to the A380. He knew that Boeing versus Airbus computer flight law was radically different and chose to learn everything he could about how the systems operated. Richard went beyond normal certification and delved into A380 system logic to truly understand what was happening beyond the UI in the cockpit. His TQ, and the culture within Qantas and teamwork on the flight deck, saved hundreds of lives when the world's biggest commercial airliner suffered a catastrophic mechanical failure. Flying can be described as thousands of hours of boredom punctuated by moments of terror, and when things go wrong, it takes IQ, EQ, and TQ for humans with machines to succeed.

TQ BOOSTER

Buy and read Richard de Crespigny's books *QF32* and *FLY!* Also Google "QF32 Tony Hughes" for articles that tell more of the story.

If it's good enough for world-class pilots to develop their TQ, why not you? Find the folks in your company who are power users of the modern sales stack and ask them for hacks and techniques. Shadow them on setups. The sequencers (SEPs) are the next Salesforce, Hubspot, and Marketo for sales pipeline creation. Keep in mind that both Salesforce and Hubspot have released sales engagement offerings. The space is getting crowded just like CRM and Marketing Automation, but that's a good sign. Very few sales leaders are truly pushing them to the limit as outlined in this book. Most use automation poorly, because they botch their message and then fail with clumsy, inappropriate personalization. Yet SEP is crossing the chasm as a category, advancing into the early and late majority of adopters.

The majority of SEP or sequencing players offer onboarding and training programs, and third-party consultancies such as RevShoppe are cropping up to help train your people, run ops, coach you on how to build the sequences, and even build them for you. XANT has an excellent online university experience with self-guided courses, videos, and resources in addition to their help site, which includes a wealth of information. Larger customers who pay for their Prime service get white glove sales and process consulting, training sessions, and so on. They offer training and onboarding and dedicated account management to each customer. Take advantage of all that is available to you.

Learning tech stacks is just like the software demo process—it's about the repetitions needed to become good, and then, with practice, masterful. Don't worry, be crappy (for a little while), as Guy Kawasaki recommends. Launch a bunch of sequences, A/B test, and iterate. Get some verbiage out into the wild, see how it performs. Release early and release often, which is the "agile" way. During weekly team meetings, actually open up your SEP (Outreach, etc.) to review the metrics on how your outbound campaigns are performing. Understand the impact of pixel tracking and blended touches. Make sure your reps are trying new things, are A/B testing, and feel they have the autonomy to be creative. Meet with your AEs and coupled SDRs on Zoom and make sure there is alignment between the messaging, account lists, and tests that week. This is the new reality of sales engagement management.

When it comes to coaching and enablement when using the phone or even Zoom, use Gong, Chorus, Refract.ai, or ExecVision to record all your calls so you can coach yourself and others. If you want to take this a step further, use Wingman, not just to do postmortems on your calls but also suggest interventions in real time as if you were on each call with every sales rep. If your reps struggle from frequent long monologues or use some filler phrases you'd much rather they didn't, then these technologies remind them in real time to make a change!

Marc Bernstein says: "To date, post-call solutions like Gong and Chorus have been the clear winners, and that's because they have a handful of undeniably powerful advantages. For one, post-call solutions enhance *existing* workflows, like managers' processes for listening to call recordings. Because post-calls technologies save sales managers time by speeding up and enhancing their coaching processes, they produce clear and consistent ROIs for their customers. The realtime space, though, has been heating up with established contenders like Balto and high-profile contenders like Cresta producing double-digit sales lifts for their customers. The realtime space has a ways to go if it's going to catch up to the post-call space, where Gong and Chorus have raised hundreds of millions of dollars and earned spots as Silicon Valley sweethearts. Still, the emergence of realtime solutions is an interesting and promising trend. 'Realtime everything' might just be the catchphrase of our new, post-COVID world."[9]

There are huge advances being made in this area. One example is real-time cuing technology from Salesken.ai that transcribes what reps say in real time using natural language processing (NLP) and then provides cues for what to say next based on machine learning around context. Another innovation is Outreach Kaia. According to Sunny Bjerk: "To use Outreach Kaia, reps simply start a virtual meeting via Zoom and the product begins real-time transcription, and based on contextual conversation, Outreach Kaia dynamically surfaces information as soon as the reps need it, including product info, battlecards, and more. Now, reps are able to focus on having a conversation, while Outreach Kaia seamlessly collects action-items and displays key product info exactly when the rep needs it so they can focus on having a conversation with their customers."[10]

Imagine a flight simulator mode for sales training. Chad Nuss at InsideOut has an XDR Test Lab where he split-tests sequences and then releases them into the wild for top companies. The only person we know of who has built something like this for the individual rep is Mike Scher at Frontline Selling to help train phone reps. What if instead of ramping with live prospects, you could train *Top Gun* style in flight school against an AI assistant that spoke to you using natural language processing (NLP) plus deep learning / neural nets and even select the voice? It could sound like Jack Nicholson or Kim Basinger. This AI assistant could train you completely on product knowledge, critique your demo, role-play with you, and then follow you into the remote field. By this time, Zooms will happen holographically, and smartphones will be gone. Travel won't be necessary: there will be a virtual area, like a holodeck, where you can communicate with any prospect on this planet. The point being, it's very feasible that in the near future, AI assistants will be playing a key role with prediction, guidance, and live critical feedback to help sellers improve toward benchmarks.

Greg Meyer believes there is a great product waiting to be built using the Google Slides API so that templated presentations that use data from the account or from the sales motion are built automatically. This could then be shared with anyone who uses Google Slides instead of having to use a proprietary system.

TQ TAKEAWAY

Sales training and enablement is more about the do than the teach. Focus on enabling methodologies and processes within the features and functions. Clarity, context, coaching, and accountability is the key. Make sure knowledge is applied and practiced to become competent, then instinctive, and eventually masterful.

TQ for Recruiting

Are recruiters thinking about TQ as the new lens of sales aptitude? Tests around Challenger style selling and Dave Kurlan's OMG are popular yet fluency with tech platforms is now mandatory for rapid onboarding and sustained success. How can it be effectively assessed and measured? PerceptionPredict created a questionnaire for a seller that predicts how much revenue they will close once onboarded. The recruitment industry is using technology to sell to hiring managers, assess candidates, and streamline recruitment processes. Every person in every profession needs TQ to thrive.

Jeremy Siegel, experienced tech recruiter, says: "For SDR/AE hiring, it's necessary to ask what tools a candidate is using and how they are using them to get results. The candidates who will ramp quickest for our clients are going to be the ones that use multiple tools (Zoom/411, Sales Nav, Outreach, etc.) and forms of outreach (phone, email, social) to achieve their goals. We can often match candidates to clients based on the TQ."[11]

We've been spreading the word about TQ and it's becoming part of the vernacular. Jeremy continues: "This is why we love hiring SDRs and AEs from technology backgrounds. They have a huge advantage if they have utilized tech and social for outbound vs. recruiters who are late adopters of tech platforms. These 'next-gen super recruiters' can accelerate pipeline and produce more revenue earlier. They are the future recruitment leaders."

Filip Karwala posed the sixty-four-million TQ question for Founders: "Who should I hire as a VP of Sales to master organizational TQ?"[12] We believe the answer is a MacGyver for those at the angel/seed stage as this person can pick a lock with a sewing needle and create a grappling hook with an umbrella. They are able to single-handedly make all your home-spun, scrappy solutions (or non-solutions) somehow function so you can scale hyper-lean. Also consider outsourcing the SDRs by automating top of funnel.

If your revenue is between $3 and $10 million, then adopt a more process-driven approach. Build revenue operations (RevOps) capability with a leader who truly knows the tools and how to test sequencers, source the best data providers, implement the right BI systems, and drive insightful marketing attribution. Once any business grows above $20 to $30 million, fully commit to investing in all the power tools and even third-party consultants to drive growth with a killer machine of sales and marketing automation, augmented with the best specialist humans for insightful engagement.

The best sellers will be attracted to companies that have a platform that feeds the sales opportunity funnel. Jake Dunlap says: "If you're in sales today, I would only work for companies that heavily invest in sales operations and sales technology. You are going to have to become really proficient at executing various software as the manual skill of gathering and executing will be automated. There are three skills you are going to need—interpersonal, project management, and technical. Work at companies that invest in tech and operations as those are going to be the pillars of the modern sales org."[13]

Skaled is a VP of Sales resource on demand and can help optimize operations and sales stacks. Jake says: "Stop trying to hire full-time people and hire an agency that is an expert in this. Just like marketing and finance and every other part of an organization. That's the long-term play."

TQ BOOSTER

Some of the best AEs came out of project management (PM) roles as well as sales engineers. Take the time to learn these skills on LinkedIn Learning or Udemy. Become proficient in building Gantt charts in LucidChart. Non-technical folks can become phenomenal PMs to create mutual action plans and move in lockstep from scoping to redlines to contract sign and onboarding. That's what a close plan is—a mutual project alignment plan before the commit to buy.

New Models for a Post-Pandemic World

During the initial heights of the pandemic in early 2020, we gave a webinar for XANT where we highlighted three hidden keys for managers and reps to drive sales pipeline in a crisis. These are empathy, humanization, and personalization. Let these three principles be your guide and clarion call, whether during a crisis, recession, or even boom times. Ten days earlier, we had delivered a live webinar with thousands registered, *Selling During Tough Times*, and we had similar thoughts but went deeper to talk about the lens through which boardroom leaders view any request to invest in change during a crisis and difficult economic period. Here is a summary.

First, always engage with empathy. Most of your potential or current customers are worried about their own jobs, their teams, and the viability of their businesses. Where you have existing relationships, ask if they are okay and if there is anything you can do to help. Show the right intent. Beyond initial conversations, don't endlessly check in, reach out, or virtue-signal—there is no value in that for your clients. You need an actionable point of view on how you can help them improve results and reduce risk.

The best businesses in the COVID-19 crisis innovated with practical ways to help staff and clients, and they often did it for free. Zoom, Salesforce, and Qualtrics are excellent examples in offering free access to platforms for clients that made a real difference in collaboration and engagement for remote workers and customers. Go beyond empathy and proactively provide additional value so your customers lift their gaze up from the valley to new horizons.

Every board and senior leadership team is firmly focused on cutting costs, protecting cash flow, and creating lean business models. The new normal emerged in the back end of 2020 with harsh economic realities. Sellers who are unable to cocreate a vision for a better future with their clients, and then nail the business case for the customer investing, are in trouble. Commercial acumen is the new table stakes for business-to-business sales professionals. Ask yourself whether you address their drivers of reducing costs, improving cash flow, and operating lean business models for greatest efficiency and competitive advantage. Be brutally honest with yourself because this is what funds any transformation you seek to position.

For those selling to governments, be ready for austerity measures as they grapple with record levels of debt. All sellers must sharpen their conversations by honing their narrative around the commercial value of investing in what they sell, and do it in a way that aligns with their vision for a brighter future. Study the concepts of OKRs and learn to speak the language of leaders.

Software-driven automation will accelerate as white-collar job redundancies bite harder. Sales is not immune! Far from that, it is ripe for the picking by automation bots. Everyone needs to create the necessary level of value to fund their role, and they need to create that value for both their customers and employer. For any seller in the field as an AE, know that relationships alone will not save you if you operate as a "professional visitor" or "transactor of commodities." You must self-generate consistent opportunity pipeline that converts to serious revenue. To do this, and create the necessary value that funds your role, you need to be the very best of what has enabled you to succeed so far, plus TQ (technology quotient).

The fourth Industrial Revolution is already here, and all of us must up our game. Open your eyes and set a vision for you and your customers to emerge stronger. Those who fail to embrace technology are destined to be replaced by it. We are in the age of the machines, where the bots may reign supreme. Here are essential skills needed to survive and thrive in these new times:

- Go beyond IQ and EQ to now have TQ with superhuman levels of effectiveness. Can you build a Boolean search? Do you know how to use your own CRM, Sales Navigator, and sales intelligence tools properly? Can you build sequences in outbound automation tools? Invest in your own education and enablement as never before.

- Have empathy and insight in providing real value in conversations that *lead to*, not *lead with* the product, service, or solution you sell. Create a worthwhile point of view in your conversation narrative to earn engagement with decisionmakers. Make it all about them, not you.

- Become a masterful digital seller. Look them in the camera rather than the screen when on video calls. Encourage everyone to have their camera on and create engagement through participation. Don't deliver monologues or tortuous slides or demos. Regularly switch back to gallery view with everyone's face on the screen. Make sure your lighting and audio is good, mute when not speaking, frame yourself on the screen, and lift your energy.

Work harder and smarter to adapt and thrive. Invest in your TQ by learning and doing. Everyone is depending on you—family, colleagues, company, partners, and customers. Combine the timeless truths from past luminaries such as Zig Ziglar, Brian Tracy, Tom Hopkins, and Neil Rackham with modern technologies and contemporary techniques to break through and operate at new levels.

How are you feeling right now with all that you've read—bewildered and overwhelmed or maybe motivated and inspired to actually run with some of this? You cannot change the past, you can only control the present—yet the future is where we will all live. The incredible thing is that it is already here. We just need to open our eyes and minds to the possibilities.

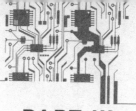

PART III

THE FUTURE OF SELLING

"The future is already here—it's just not very evenly distributed."

—William Gibson, the *Economist,* December 4, 2003.

William Gibson is arguably the greatest science fiction writer of all time. He wrote about all the concepts that led to the cyberpunk dystopia that has enthralled audiences for decades. Are we destined for a *Star Trek*–style utopia—all clean, bright, and shiny with humans enjoying lifestyle existences on the universal wage? Or will it be dystopia with an ever-widening social divide leading to a tipping point of inequality and dysfunction? Consider the future of professional selling and decide what you will embrace to prosper.

The day will come, sooner than you think, when you open your sales app and it starts popping up C-suite buyers within your ICP based on trigger events and referral opportunities. You'll be looking at baseball card–style summaries with relevant stats, paths of introduction, sales probability scores, and best conversation starters—Tinder for sales as you swipe left and right. The ones you swipe right go to your AI virtual assistant, and in a couple of days the meetings are booked with everything automated in the back end for the buyer and the seller!

Rather than the deepfakers with avatars, you just focus on turning up in person to nail the human elements of insightful empathic conversations while managing the complexities and politics of the engagement, engineering value, and outfoxing the competition. With the most intelligent and capable virtual assistant a human could ever wish for, you masterfully orchestrate your platform, and the bots do your research and admin, including CRM hygiene, follow-ups, and forecasting.

CHAPTER ELEVEN

A Day in the Life of Tomorrow

"Hi, Mary! Thanks for taking the meeting that Steve set up for us. Do you mind if he joins to take notes for follow-up?" Sally conducts her first discovery and qualification call with Mary while Steve monitors the conversation and transcribes notes for later. It goes swimmingly—warmed up before the call with context, and executed during the call to create real progression.

During the meeting, Steve was messaging Sally in a side-window beside the video call with a meter showing conversation engagement based on Mary's body language, facial expressions, tone of voice, and the actual language being used. Steve prompted Sally with the best questions to ask and reminded her to talk less whenever she was approaching more than one-third of the talking ratio. Steve popped best words and phrases on the side-screen and suggested the most relevant examples and case studies to support claims of improved results that Mary could achieve in working with them.

Although Steve is subordinate to Sally, she completely trusts him and his judgment. After the call, Steve asked Sally about what she thought went well, what could have been done differently, and the score she gave herself for the interaction. Steve then provided some coaching by discussing Sally's tone and pace, language, and words that resonated most with Mary, and those that . . . not so much. Even body language, energy, and eye contact was covered. Steve's advice included reminding her to look people in the camera more, despite all the information on the screens, and the need for Sally to invest more time with the briefing information he provided before the call. Both of their scores and comments were added into the CRM along with Steve updating the opportunity with all the discovery information, moving it to stage two, and assigning a conservative deal value and close date.

Before the meeting, Steve had created a "Mary profile" so that Sally was fully briefed. It was a hyper-personalized buyer persona and included a summary of Mary's personality style and values, including personal interests and affiliations. Steve also highlighted Mary's career successes and the relationships in common with Sally that were most relevant. Steve even took the time to analyze Mary's articles, posts, and comments in LinkedIn and found several videos in which Mary stated opinions that Sally could quote back to show alignment and spark the conversation to new levels. Most importantly, the profile included Mary's most likely performance metrics for how she was measured in her role, her company's performance stats, recent announcements, and industry trends with commentary from the experts most relevant to Mary. No wonder Sally nailed the meeting with an assistant like Steve and all that valuable information on-screen.

Three days earlier, Steve had called Mary out of the blue to set the meeting: "Hi, Mary. I work for Sally Philips and you both know Bill Thomas who thought you and Sally should talk. She has some ideas on how you could get runs of the board with your new Jabadoo product into the Canadian market where you just opened an office. I'm looking at Sally's calendar now—how's next week for a thirty-minute Zoom?"

Steve's Aussie ascent wasn't too difficult to understand and he dealt with Mary's questions without any fuss. Steve sent an email thanking Mary, created the Zoom meeting, and sent the calendar invitations. Steve then jumped in to ghost Sally's LinkedIn account and sent a connection request, plus updated the CRM with activity notes against the newly created stage one opportunity.

The day before the meeting, Steve ghosted Sally's IT accounts again, sent a text message and email saying she was looking forward to the call, and posed a few questions to set the agenda around what others in Mary's industry were doing to drive record growth. Like all good EAs, Steve did everything possible to ensure Sally's time was productive with people actually attending scheduled meetings.

So, who is this dream-come-true character, Steve? You guessed it—Sales Team Enablement Virtual Entity—STEVE, a DVSA (digital virtual sales assistant). STEVE doesn't arrive late, never has a hangover, doesn't get depressed or have addictions, nor does he complain about workload or targets or competition or territory or comp plan or the *hopeless boss* or *idiot customers* . . . STEVE can actually write, follows-up, and just works 24/7 doing everything in the Sally and Mary scenario and much more. Currently, one human SDR can effectively support a maximum of three

AEs, while STEVE could support every seller and customer-facing employee in an entire company. Current SDRs are ideally poised to become AEs because they are best equipped to feed themselves with great leads by managing STEVE for the most difficult phase of selling—opportunity pipeline creation.

STEVE not only books meetings and supports new sales and current account engagements, but also consistently creates quality opportunity pipeline by monitoring for thousands of trigger events and referral opportunities. STEVE makes the outbound phone calls and has relevant conversations, sends emails, texts, writes letters and social posts, schedules calendar appointments, updates the CRM, adjusts the forecast, highlights risk in accounts and deals, suggests best next steps, finds the ideal reference sites and tees them up for the prospect to validate. STEVE interacts with lots of DAVES (Digital Adaptive Virtual Entity For Sales) such as Einstein who lives within Salesforce or Cortana within Dynamics, plus the countless other AIs driving sales engagement and other platforms.

Think this is some ridiculous fantasy? Apart from one element, every single thing you just read is already here today. Just search YouTube for "Google Duplex makes appointments"...it's years old. In a post-pandemic world, we don't need geeky Google Glasses to feed the AI with images, audio, and data. This is because most of the meetings are now happening in front of a computer camera that could be seamlessly connected to an AI stack that can scrape everything automatically and provide the analysis, coaching, and data entry for sellers. The tricky bit for the human seller is to convince the customer to turn their camera on and give permission to have your DVA in attendance.

Right now, computers that watch and listen through a camera are already better than people at detecting and understanding human emotion, and whether someone is telling lies. Affectiva is one of the companies making huge inroads with AI that takes Ekman's Facial Action Coding System to anticipate human behavior based on observations. Geoff Colvin wrote the book *Humans Are Underrated*, and says: "So this mysterious human ability to read another person's emotions turns out not to be all that mysterious. Computers can do it too and it isn't even very hard."[1]

So, what is the one thing that's missing? It's the orchestration-bot. DARPA, the US military innovation arm, already has military-bots at sea, on the ground, and in the air that are terrifyingly effective. Imagine a mechanical hybrid dog-horse with Gatling guns as saddlebags that can run, crawl, and jump—it's real. Other drone-bots provide surveillance in the air and logistic-bots provide new batteries and ammunition from the rear echelon. In August 2020, DARPA's AI fighter pilot beat a human F-16 pilot 5–0 in a simulator, even when staying well within human performance limits. AI fighter pilots will be in the air before 2030 and will be using the full limits of aircraft design, unlike humans who pass out pulling too hard on the stick. DARPA knows that the specialist bots execute tasks better than humans but they need individual direction and group orchestration at lightning speed, a boss-bot of the worker-bots if you will, with real human commanders up the chain and at the top of this pecking order.

Yet DARPA sees a vital role for humans in war, even though there will be far fewer people needed. You may find this hard to believe, but amidst all the technology, DARPA is focusing on training human warriors for greater empathy and insight in their interactions with people. They are using actors and then digitizing them with deepfake AI to gamify survival and success in complex human interactions. The soldier of the future will operate more effectively in urban theaters where there are high levels of ambiguity with combatants disguised amidst innocent civilians. Soldiers will be equipped to influence (sell to) a crowd and individuals who are distressed, offended, or angry, and also negotiate difficult situations to de-escalate and save lives while achieving their objectives. The programs also teach soldiers how to identify the "friendly street vendor" who is going to unleash a hidden bomb when familiarity sets in. The model is human empathy and insight for urban domains with "mixed populations" packed with ambiguity; and AI automation for lightning-fast techno-mechanical dominance in open combat.

The DARPA model for war is not dissimilar to where B2B sales is going—brand marketing is the air cover and product marketing is the artillery, with sales being the ground force. Commercial soldiers will be trained on DARPA-like sales simulation platforms (SSP) to assess and hone the skills of sellers at all levels as they interact with virtual C-suite players who throw up objections, ask for proof, and terminate interactions that fail to meet expectations concerning empathy, insight, and value in conversations.

Changing metaphors, it will be a three-dimensional web of interactions for sales, rather than a production line, to bring Einstein, Watson, Siri, Duplex, and myriad specialist AI and automation elements together. Right now, effective orchestration of technology is the frontier for humans driving automation, in addition to actually getting it right in sales with relevant targeting and messaging to stop spamming the galaxy with dross.

The Winds of Change

There's more than pandemics blowing in the air—can you smell the coming change? Throughout human history, periods of great adversity or conflict have driven quantum leaps in innovation. The global pandemic and ensuing recession made 2020 a catalyst year in accelerating the fourth Industrial Revolution. Meetings moved online, behind computer screens, with ways of working and collaborating forever changed. Leaders took the opportunity to double down on channel shift initiatives, moving more engagement to digital online and mobile self-service platforms to reduce costs while improving customer experience.

With high failure rates of field sales roles in achieving revenue targets, their ranks began to be culled as resources shifted to inside sales operations powered by ever-improving tech stacks. One CEO said to us, "Why would I persist with an expensive field rep who can't feed themselves when I can have two inside salespeople with a killer tech stack for the same cost . . . and the inside sellers deliver triple the revenue opportunities that my managers in the field can then close?"

The year 2020 also revealed secondary consequences, some quite unexpected. Plastic surgery skyrocketed as people narcissistically gazed at themselves in Zoom meetings and didn't like what they saw. Physical money was seen as a dirty potential COVID spreader and momentum for a cashless world accelerated. Convenience started to trump concerns about data security and privacy. Avoiding the office and working from home (WFH) became a *perceived entitlement* and the "side hustle" grew as workers operated away from the gaze of the boss. Meetings became shorter online and with less real emotional connection. WFH became the norm and corporate offices became event and collaboration spaces instead of the daily place of battery hen–style work. Fringe real estate prices climbed as people moved farther away from the office knowing there would be far less hellish commuting because the majority of work would be from home. House and apartment design pivoted to include better work and study spaces. We also saw the rise of remote metrics management (and gaming them by employees) and the daily stand-up or check-in for all.

Sadly, screen fatigue set in and sellers became desperate, struggling to break through to remote and resistant buyers who were deadened by the sheer volume and amateurishness of most sales automation. Buyers discovered they could gain greater control of sellers, disempowering them, with shorter virtual meetings containing less emotion or "pitch," and instead demanding more evidence-based insights about others achieving real results. Buyers adopted a harder stance: "Don't sell to us and create unnecessary relationship overhead. Instead, prove your relevance and value before we decide whether to invest in any real face-to-face meetings."

Procurement processes became increasingly pre-vetted, selective, and prescriptive—social proof and strong brand became essential table stakes for sellers to even get to the starting line. Creating real engagement with a new person, when you're remote, is no easy thing to achieve. You now have to be great at digital selling to earn the right to real face-to-face with new people. It's an art to get them to turn on the camera and engage rather than half-listen while they scan email and other distractions.

Amid all the change, where is B2B sales going and what does it mean for traditional sellers? We believe one-third of current field sales roles will disappear in the 2020s. Yes, you read that right—33 percent gone. Expensive people who add little value and fail to create the sales pipeline needed to fund themselves are doomed. It's sad but real. Leaders will become the closers rather than expensive sir-lunch-a-lot relationship sellers. Empathy combined with business acumen and an insight-laden consultative approach is now a mandatory requirement in the field. Field sellers must therefore be cocreators of a vision for a brighter future with the client along with the business case and change management strategy required to close.

Make no mistake, field sales resources are shifting to inside roles with lower-cost people powered by ever-evolving tech stacks. Marketing and sales will finally fuse for content-driven demand generation with humans being injected at the right moments of a buyer's journey of enticement and discovery. The rise of sales/revenue operations (RevOps) with XDR roles specializing in all things top of funnel for inbound and outbound is here. To set the scene for what the not-too-distant future looks like for B2B sales, let's see what the Chief Strategy Officer at XANT, Dave Boyce, believes are the major trends:

1. The customer of the future controls when and how she interacts with salespeople. Having done most of her research online, she's careful who to engage, when, and how. The successful

salesperson is quick to respond, knowledgeable, and helpful. Marketing may have created content that helped the customer complete 70 percent of her purchasing decision, but for the last 30 percent she needs consultative expertise. The modern sales rep will spend less time selling and more time helping customers buy—a buying concierge, as it were.

2. The days of the road warrior are gone. The modern sales rep can do everything from her desk. She makes herself omnipresent through multi-channel networking. She makes herself relevant by staying on top of the trends in her industry—both for her customers and for solutions related to her own. She utilizes technology to stay on top of her funnel: top, middle, and bottom. AI helps surface the things she should be working on—the opportunities most likely to result in a purchase. Meetings are held remotely, approvals are secured remotely, signatures are delivered remotely. The modern sales rep spends in-person time with her customers only at their request, and sometimes not until after the purchase.

3. When it comes to AI for sales, it matters which type of AI. If you want to optimize words, use conversational AI. If you want to optimize process, use process AI. If you want to work on the right things—the things that will convert to sales—you must use behavioral AI.

   Behavioral AI is the only domain that contains signal about buyer behavior—the signal needed to prioritize the right buyers. Of all the potential companies, which ones? Of all the people at those companies, which ones? Of all the communication possibilities, which ones? Is this person an influencer? A decisionmaker? An approver? A tire kicker? When this person buys, how big are the purchases? Who else is typically involved? Behavioral AI processes signals like this and optimizes who, when, and how, based on likelihood of sales success. These signals are hard to get though—one must have a clean source of buyer behavior across the market. This is what XANT does—a kind of "Waze for Sales." XANT streams buying signal in real time across the industry so each individual sales rep benefits from those who've gone before.

4. When it comes to email prospecting, one must be careful what you put in the hands of reps. If reps had the opportunity to SPAM

their territory, would they? Some might. And that could seriously damage your reputation and maybe even get your email domain blacklisted. The key is prioritization—which accounts, which people, when, and how? This is a job for behavioral AI—the type delivered by XANT, 6Sense, Bombora . . . anyone who tracks customer behavior and prioritizes sales motions accordingly. With prioritization, you can target the right customers at the right time with the right message. Without it, you can scorch acres of earth with email and create reputational damage that will long outlast the reps and the technology that caused it.

5. Digital selling will evolve just like every other business application space. First, automation. Help one person do the work of ten. In marketing automation, this was powerful software that allowed you to blast your market indiscriminately. In sales technology, these are the generation 1.0 sales engagement platforms—those designed to SPAM. Next, intelligence. Intelligence governs what gets done, matching activity with outcomes. In marketing automation, this was web analytics, observing a customer and customizing an approach appropriate to them. In sales technology, this is behavioral AI—also observing the customer and customizing an approach appropriate to them. Finally, eCommerce. The buyer is in control. Research, comparative shopping, and transactions all happen online. Content is king, but the self-guided journey only takes a buyer 70 percent of the way. Sellers are then required to help the buyer fill in the last 30 percent. This is a consultative interaction, fully aware of the buyer's journey to that point. This is the future of B2B sales.[2]

Dave's comments show us the future of all sales even though, in our view, strategic enterprise selling will be a laggard.

Let's now extrapolate all road maps, beginning with sequencers. Toward 2025, sequencers and SEPs will automatically move cohorts into experiments (against hold-out control groups) for relevant A/B tests. They will then autonomously port those learnings back while actioning on the data. Better-performing sequences will get more leads while lower performers are paused. Full-blown automation!

By 2030, sequencers and SEPs can A/B test all the personalization variables, automatically picking winners based on not just vanity metrics like reply rates but instead digging into reply sentiment analysis to gauge the quality of replies. What to write, when to send and how often, what to personalize; these are all just levers for the AI to pull as it trains itself building upon years of human guided learning for improved neural net decisionmaking. Just as IBM Watson wins at *Jeopardy*, SEP sequencers will win at outbound. The SEP players will be acquired by the major CRM clouds and augmented with big data to feed the virtual brain trusts to become even more powerful.

That's where we move into the emerging science of sales engagement analytics (SEA), where every micro change in outbound can be tied back to revenue. We will then predict how slight changes made in emails impact close rates, velocity, and deal size. Can you imagine? If you mention actual relevant and trusted connection in common, propensity to close rises 12 percent and contract value is projected to increase by $35,600. It's based on your own historical CRM data and all the marketing cloud provider's anonymized data to benchmark.

Futurist Travis Wallis, CSO and cofounder of OutboundWorks and now CEO of Time Advisors, contributes: "I think about the use of corollary relationships using nodal architecture, particularly for leveraging existing relationships a lot. Social graphs are by far the most powerful tools for sales because relationships are simply a function of trust. LinkedIn, Facebook, and now platforms in sales like Bravado, People.ai, Affinity, and more are all leveraging data around relationships to speed up the sales (or in my case, the investment process). Where are social graphs going? Why did Microsoft spend $26.2 billion on LinkedIn? Why did all of the social networks shut off access to their data streams? It's because that's their greatest value outside of advertising. With regard to sequencing, the path forward is with chat like Drift where we will be able to know more about people from any platform by saying, 'Hey, Siri, start a chat with X.' The minute we can say 'Hey, Siri, who does X use for Y in my network?' that recommendation will be our decision. By 2035 email may be redundant like the fax, and the race will be around expertise, comparison, and mind-share in a different way than we ever imagined."[3]

Jeremey Donovan, SVP at SalesLoft, adds:

I would think in terms of two phases. The first phase is augmented intelligence. We are in that phase now but only at the beginning. Here, AI tells you which accounts and contacts to go after. When going after the contact, it tells you key information to personalize. In phase two, we cross the uncanny valley where prospects cannot tell if the person emailing them is AI or human. That is a 2035+ thing. Also, consider a scenario forecasting approach. If you want to project fifteen years, think back circa 2005. What is new, what is not?

One other major thing, circa 2025, is that we will have conquered (a) implementation (b) adoption. We will have also nailed augmented performance management (for example, by combining technologies like Atrium with a SEP).[4]

Mansour Salame, CEO of FrontSpin, believes AI will keep playing a more prevalent role. He has built a number of products that use math to optimize (similar technology to ML and AI), and they can quickly get in trouble without a human guiding them. He likes our cyborg analogy, believing the most successful sales engagement systems will allow humans to use their intuition and judgment to guide the AI to optimize the sequences and their content.

Sales Runner 2049

Back in 2012, Gartner predicted that by 2020, 85 percent of transacting between businesses would be without any human interactions. Futurist Kai-Fu Lee said in 2020: "Artificial intelligence will probably replace 50 percent of human jobs within ten years."[5] Here is the core issue for those seeking to evade the sales apocalypse—everyone needs to fund themselves from the value they create. Lynne Zaledonis captures the heart of the problem: "A rep can only be as productive as the time spent selling."[6] The big problem is that people are living in denial and it's causing them to fade away.

According to Kevin Dorsey: "Asking salespeople if they believe they will be replaced is like asking the factory worker if a robot could build a car. We will always put our perceived skill on a pedestal, assuming no machine or computer could match it, until it's already occurred. AI has already replaced reps, AI is already enhancing reps, AI is already anticipating need, and it's going to continue down this path. It's already happening."[7]

We believe 70 percent of the current sales development function is automatable right now, so how should we seek to evolve? According to Thomas Baumgartner: "Beyond their relationship skills, reps will succeed based on their ability to understand and interpret data, work effectively with AI, and move quickly on opportunities. That's a very different sales profile from the one many companies recruit for today."[8]

Just imagine in the not-too-distant future when the SDR-AE industrial complex crumbles like that scene in *The Matrix* to reveal the awe-inspiring possibilities far beyond. Is this plausible or from the lunatic fringe? Prospecting morphs into humans training algorithms, but one of the biggest challenges in training machine learning (ML) algorithms effectively is the massive amount of data plus human ingenuity needed for fine tuning. Training the bots could be as simple as human sellers *swiping right* a la Tinder. The sales development function as we know it today could fall away. Optimally, one sales AI could simply ping-pong with another buyer's AI to open the sales/buying cycle and warm up a qualified introduction for the humans.

In transactional sales, this includes (but is not limited to) negotiating and closing the deal at the speed of high-frequency trading on Wall Street. Cold calling becomes programming your AI's voicemail sequences (indistinguishable from the sound of the human voice) for 1:1-to-many personalization via voicemail drops at scale. The code can actually do that now.

Today's SDR or full-cycle AE are bogged down in nearly limitless research and list-building. The cognitive load of administrative tasks and switching UIs is so spellbinding it literally consumes the bulk of their time. The result is the confounding silence of the sales floor with SDRs creating email cadences with semi-automated sequencing as the primary channel. The actual emails that go out are usually well below par, but when they see any "proof of life" they then call to just hit voicemails and the machinery designed to block sellers all day long.

But what if an AI could go out and synthesize every possible data source on the internet, prioritize it all, and act on it with the relevant message, at the relevant time, with the optimal prospect in your ICP within a nanosecond, weaponizing relevant insight—and then only bother involving you when the potential buyer is ready, much deeper down the funnel? Attitudes toward AI are changing with people increasingly seeing technology as the enabler for improved results and greater productivity.

Could AI, fueled by smart ML and big data, deliver a return to innocence? A return to just, well, *selling*? Acronyms fall away—SD-this, AE-that. No need. Simplicity is the ultimate sophistication, per da Vinci. The right human receives the lead and engages after it's all been warmed and prepared for engagement. The majority of enterprises are already using AI technology in corporate apps and, according to Narrative Science, a storytelling data analytics company, marketing departments alone spent more than $2 billion on AI tools in 2020.[9]

According to Ben Daters at People.ai: "We will increasingly see the top human salespeople being asked to work with deep learning engineers to more-or-less teach AI algorithms how to understand human emotions, build relationships with customers, and fulfill the simplest parts of the sales process."[10] A human data scientist can help to fine-tune these analyses at scale, plus others at such a macro level that it's mind-numbing.

Anders Fredriksson, startup entrepreneur, puts it best: "Imagine a more senior Sales Development 'Operator' that will (eventually) have the efficiency of a hundred-person team of SDRs." Koka Sexton agrees: "I've seen how AI can more than triple the appointments being made by SDRs. It's a new field but it's going to transform how sales teams are structured."[11]

The SDR of the future will be an orchestrator of tools and a manager of messaging to drive sales bots that deliver leads at scale. They won't have to worry about whom to target anymore because the CRM AI will no longer be static—it will automagically deploy crawlers to harvest and analyze not only your sales team's own data but also to reach out and do look-alike pulls across the broader internet, capturing trigger events, buying sentiment, and finding other relevant information. It will then go out and drive opening conversations and set meetings with the precision of an atomic clock. The technology itself will handle that back-and-forth, even pinging reminders the day of or hours before to ensure the prospect shows up.

Is a data scientist the rep of the future? Will a face-to-face seller be a remnant of nostalgia of a bygone age, something akin to classic jazz music played whimsically on vinyl? "Would you like to pay extra for a live human to sell to you, miss?" Yet synthesized face-to-face interaction could be easily achieved through virtual reality.

According to Swati Sinha:

> We are seeing a paradigm shift in sales from being reactive to proactive, and from instinct-driven to insight and data-driven. AI can guide the sales journey from identification to customer retention. Sales applications can pick up each and every signal, in the form of any action, by any customer, community, or partner; while machine learning can continuously improve

actions, offers, and processes for your sales organization. AI can't replace the value of human interaction when it comes to building relationships with customers, but it can make them smarter and more productive through guided selling and automating the operational tasks, allowing sales reps to focus on their primary job—delivering value to customers and building loyalty that leads to organic revenue growth.[12]

Jill Rowley says: "AI is destined to be the perfect tool to fuel organizations' sales efforts and power sales teams with genuinely intelligent tools to more effectively organize their work and sell more."[13] Others think that AI will initially augment, then automate, then eradicate the need for most humans in the selling process.

There are really just two types of future environments portrayed: dystopia and utopia. When we think of the limitless possibility of quantum computing, the Singularity, and humanity melding with machines, we are left in awe of human potential. Peter Schwartz has a more pragmatic view: "I'd be more worried about being replaced by another salesperson who is empowered by intelligence than by a machine [alone]."[14]

We think there will be a marriage of AI and seasoned strategic selling experience into an entirely new fusion of the modern sales professional. The near-term augmentation of human capabilities with automation of low-value and time-consuming tasks is good news because it means less mundane work and higher value activity leveraging empathy and insights for emotional connection as the winning point of difference. Technology will free us to do the vibrant piece we love most about professional selling. Having qualified conversations with the right people at the right time in the right companies to solve really thorny problems—that's the stimulating and rewarding part of professional selling.

We've focused on sales, but marketing is making huge strides ahead. According to Falon Fatemi: "Historically, there's been a longstanding tension between marketing and sales . . . AI has the potential to rectify this longstanding tension."[15] Dharmesh Shah says: "In the next few years, we are going to have autonomous, self-driving, marketing automation. Machine learning will improve sales and marketing software by giving it the ability to do things without us explicitly telling it what to do. As a result, tasks such as predictive lead scoring, content recommendations, and email acquisition will get a lot better."[16] Another interesting example is Match.com for automatically routing leads to the right salesperson based on analysis of the data about the lead and about the salespeople.

Keith Rabois is dead right when he says: "If you want to know where to make money over the next two decades, look for companies that are finding ways to automate jobs that are currently being done by humans . . . that you wouldn't have thought previously could be done by a machine. Truck drivers are one thing and Google, as well as Tesla, have a great head start in disrupting that market, but lawyers, doctors, teachers, customer service and sales reps—there are companies that are turning these professions into lines of code, and they're going to make a lot of money."[17]

Back in 2013, Tomasz Tunguz said this: "The startup that disrupts Salesforce will be worth much more because instead of simply recording leads and sales, the next CRM will create business for its customers leveraging social proof. It won't be enough for a CRM to inform a salesperson which potential customer to call the way Salesforce's task list operates today. This new CRM will scour the web to find potential customers, discover points of social proof with potential customers, increasing close rates, and finally record the transactions in the system."[18]

Salesforce evolved, embraced AI with Einstein and other incarnations, built their own SEP called High Velocity Sales (HVS), and made many strategic acquisitions, including Slack. They are disrupting themselves and defining the future of customer experience for the entire life cycle of marketing, sales, service, and support. One of the best ways to de-risk your sales future is to hitch your wagon to Salesforce, as they are innovating for you at levels you could never achieve on your own. You then focus on the edge cases for innovation that highly differentiates you in your industry or market, while always bringing data, reporting, and process automation into the Salesforce core.

Amara's Law states: "We tend to overestimate the effect of a technology in the short run and underestimate the effect in the long run." Marc Benioff, CEO of Salesforce, puts it another way: "We overestimate the change that will occur in the next two years and underestimate the change that will occur in the next ten." With all that said, here are our **twenty predictions for B2B selling in the roaring 2020s**:

1. Remote working and virtual selling become the norm as the war for sales talent changes. Companies hire people from almost anywhere in the world with the right communication skills and with the necessary technical and commercial capabilities or acumen.

2. Revenue operations (RevOps), incorporating sales operations,

reports directly to the CEO and rules the fiefdoms as the lines between sales and marketing blur beyond recognition.

3. The rise of mega inside sales tech stacks with RevOps driving customer and sales experience, messaging, campaign design, orchestration of technology, and wrangling data will occur.

4. The investment and op-ex mix for sales and marketing swings from salaries toward technology and from field sellers to inside sales.

5. Channel-shift strategies mature to move prospect and customer engagement to automation with select human interaction at high-impact inflection points. Technology becomes the front end of interactions and then real human conversations "pop up to delight" with seamless machine handoffs across engagement channels.

6. The decade finishes with 33 percent fewer field salespeople as resources shift to inside sales with next-generation tech stacks. Field selling transitions to "domain expertise with commercial acumen." Managers and leaders become the closers of enterprise deals in the field.

7. Five billion dollars in VC capital goes into sales tech tools creating a Cambrian explosion of sales technology—five hundred vendors in 2020 explodes to five-thousand-plus by 2025, spurred by advances in AI, ML, NLP, neural net, and even neurolink core tech. Fewer IPOs after the WeWork and Uber issues, and secondary markets thrive fueled by 40 to 50 percent megarounds of unicorn, decacorn, and hectocorn valuations.

8. By 2025, a startup proves it is successfully running "SDR ex Machina" with fully autonomous top funnel and closing—no humans with SDR-as-a-service needed with software instead running the entire sales revenue supply chain.

9. By 2027, digital virtual sales assistants (DVSAs) are a real thing, a la the STEVE or DAVES mentioned earlier. Sellers focus more strongly on the human meta-skills of empathy, insights, storytelling, influence, and leadership.

10. Having already passed the Turing test on the phone and text-based chat, Sales AI passes the Turing test on a Zoom call . . . the

customer was ninety-six, partially deaf, and visually impaired but bought the encyclopedia set on a payment plan . . . "Eve seemed like such a lovely, thoughtful girl, and promised to come visit in Zoom anytime I feel a bit lonely or confused."

11. AI automated email and sales outreach becomes regulated by the Federal Trade Commission (FTC) and others. Warning labels are required on all AI-generated content.

12. Government regulators around the world ban deceptive fake human outreach on video or phone, and legislate warnings to consumers that they are interacting with a bot.

13. CRM morphs into full-blown customer experience (CX) and the segment stratifies with two gorillas dominating the market, Salesforce and Microsoft, followed by Hubspot plus myriad niche players for industry vertical solutions.

14. CRM cloud wars heat up with an avalanche of acquisitions. Potential examples could be Salesforce going beyond Slack to also sweep up players such as Outreach, ZoomInfo, Gong, and Bombora to roll them all up in a new cloud SEP offering.

15. Sales management returns to the age of innocence as player/coaches and focus only on large deals that need to be closed in the field.

16. Sales enablement focuses on eLearning and virtual engagement, blending methodology, tools, and tech to provide real-time coaching and feedback, along with flight simulator–style role-plays with AI avatars on Zoom calls to enable and certify sellers.

17. AI bots buy and sell to each other at the speed of high-frequency trading. Humans rarely get involved in selling anything deemed to be a commodity.

18. Mega corporations dominate as governments struggle to regulate the sea of ambiguity in a borderless world with democratized data and self-enabled individuals and movements.

19. The socioeconomic divide magnifies with salaries for skilled workers going backward while unemployment hits record levels. Resentment of technology builds and societies polarize.

20. The Singularity horizon comes into sight along with a resurgence

in debates about values, purpose, and meaning to define what is truly human and right amid breathtaking advances and possibilities of the future.

Choices and Actions

We opened the book with Morpheus asking about which pill—red or blue? You, too, must make a decision. Automation is real and many jobs are gone. All knowledge workers, including salespeople, must save themselves by identifying the tasks within their roles that can be enhanced, automated, or outsourced to technology. Time is running out to create and execute your plan. The earlier you develop your TQ and double down on the human skills of empathy, insight, and storytelling, the less risk you have and the brighter your future.

Professor Rita McGrath believes business management has moved from eras of industrial-style execution and then knowledge worker–style expertise, to a new era of empathy. She argues that organizations are now seeking to create meaningful experiences for customers and that business has entered this era of empathy despite all the automation.[19] Empathy, rather than mimicry, is a uniquely human capability.

Right now, machines already execute "games of intellect" better than humans, with chess conquered by the machines when IBM's Deep Blue computer won a quarter of a century ago.[20] In more recent times, computers have also defeated the very best people on the planet at *Jeopardy* and Go![21] In war, AI can outfly a *Top Gun* fighter pilot in simulated air-to-air combat. In business, computers are already better at fraud detection, financial operations, and share trading (faster and more consistently picking winning stocks). Machines can execute data entry in the back office with accuracy and speed no person can match.

In medicine, a computer can diagnose an image thirty times faster than a human radiographer and with 99 percent accuracy—no person, no matter how talented and qualified, can compete with that. Technology is literally saving lives when you consider that, in the USA alone, 5 to 10 percent of trips to an ER are the result of misdiagnosis and fourteen million diagnostic mistakes contribute to almost five hundred thousand deaths each year. Self-driving cars are already safer than humans: 94 percent of car accidents with a person behind the wheel are caused by human error—if you can call deliberate distraction with texting, watching videos, eating breakfast, road rage, being drunk, falling asleep, and doing dumb stuff "an accident."

Every single day, we all interact with technology and algorithms that make our lives easier. Artificial intelligence with machine learning is pervasive in LinkedIn, Facebook, Amazon, eBay, Google, Netflix, navigation apps, smartphones, and cameras. Anywhere you touch technology, AI is there and growing in capability. Every platform company on the planet is investing their future in algorithms and machine learning fed with big data to be surfaced with easy-to-use apps or interfaces. Add to this the forty billion devices constantly connected to the internet of things (IoT) that automatically send data, and you get the picture.

Humans are hopeless at wading through huge amounts of data to find insights . . . and even worse at creating accurate data in a CRM or expense report! The fourth Industrial Revolution is accelerating and it is like nothing before. In the first Industrial Revolution, one power loom replaced forty textile workers, and one steam engine replaced fifty horses. The decimation of jobs was visibly obvious and that's why the Luddites sought to smash the machines. It's why, in the third Industrial Revolution, the auto workers went on strike and lobbied governments to save their jobs. But now the change is almost invisible as jobs are quietly automated away. For the first time in human history, we have a tool—self-generating software—that can create and then improve itself. Think about the implications of this, given that physical machines are increasingly controlled by software executing with fly-by-wire orchestration rather than cumbersome mechanical linkages that go back to a clumsy primate.

So, can a salesbot really replace a human? Yes, if the buyer is seeking a commodity. It's already happening. Think about how you buy books, music, and anything on Amazon or eBay . . . no human sales assistant needed. We've even seen a digital person (AI avatar) sell a credit card on a video call, and although creepy, the technology will only become more realistic. You can see an example from back in 2017 by searching YouTube for "IBM Watson presents Soul Machines." Think about how the *Avatar* movies trick your brain into ignoring the fact that the characters are computer-generated instead of real, live humans . . . it all just blends into your immersive experience. Look at Synthesia and Soul Machines with their amazing capabilities in creating digital employees that communicate and sell.

Technology is moving fast and computers have the advantage of being able to deal with huge amounts of data, automate processes, and make well-informed recommendations. But what about where there is a need for empathy, discovery, problem identification, solution design, consensus-gathering, business case creation, navigation of political agendas, and then instilling confidence to close the deal? Right now, these things are the domain of humans, and that is where you must focus—the truly human elements of business. The meta-skills that save humans in a sales career are empathy, insight, and storytelling—they are how you create emotional connection to transfer belief and build trust.

Many predict approximately 50 percent of white-collar jobs will disappear in the coming decade, but Malcolm Frank, Paul Roehrig, and Ben Pring believe that is a bit extreme. In 2017, they coauthored the book *What to Do When Machines Do Everything*, and they wrote: "AI will eat existing jobs in a 'slowly, slowly, suddenly' manner. Certain tasks will quietly and increasingly become automated and will then hit a potential tipping point that will fundamentally impact the very nature of certain jobs."[22] They go on to say that changes in Western labor forces will occur in three distinct ways: 1) job automation, with approximately 12 percent of jobs being disrupted/taken out of existence, 2) job enhancement, with approximately 75 percent of jobs being enhanced/altered and delivering greater output or improved quality, and 3) job creation, with approximately 13 percent new jobs created.

Whatever the degree of impact, know for sure that someone is seriously working on technology that ultimately replaces you. We think change will be more extreme for B2B sales with 33 percent disruption of field sales roles. Most of the carnage will be with expensive field sellers, but also with some inside roles being impacted. Regardless of job categorization, if all you do is provide information to people and give them pricing, you're in trouble.

Technology will steadily take over the role of transacting for buyers. All B2B selling will be impacted with AI, machine learning, big data, algorithms, and automation all having the potential to increase the efficiency and effectiveness of high-value professional salespeople. Or sweep away many people's jobs if they don't evolve with TQ. The most successful sellers of the future will be masterful with people and politics, empathy specialists with genuine insights and awe-inspiring stories, and uber-orchestrators of the platforms and technologies that enable them.

Importantly, as you think about your future in sales, don't confuse *job* with *task*. Your job is safe if you automate as many tasks as possible . . . the ones where technology can do it for you better, acting as your virtual assistant. Right now, we are in the era of "narrow AI," where machines focus on narrow tasks such as flying, driving, sorting, processing, recommending a similar book or complementary product, or serving a relevant new item or advertisement. Think also about how Salesforce automation with Einstein can automatically log phone calls, emails, do your forecast, remind you of tasks, and even prompt you when a deal is at risk because it's been stuck in a stage for too long or there has been no contact for a while, or because an email mentions a dangerous competitor.

Narrow AI will give way to general AI (also known as strong AI) around 2035, with powerful contextualization across multiple domains—and ultimately super AI, which is also known as the Singularity and could occur as soon as 2050. Stay alert because nasty change sneaks up on us: technology will initially complement or assist you, then augment the way you operate, then potentially replace you altogether. If a sinister super AI were here today, its business plan could be simple when it comes to the humans who add no value and merely deplete the planet's finite resources: engage–enhance–eradicate. Enlightened super AI, on the other hand, would seek to augment, empower, and protect humans and the biosphere.

Let's revisit the military analogy because sales success is really a commercial war, battling the competition. This book initially hit the stands at the same time *Top Gun: Maverick* was released in theaters in mid-2021. Most know about *Top Gun*, but few understand the full story. In Vietnam during the 1960s, the USA paused bombing, and therefore fighter operations, for a year. The "exchange ratio" before the pause was 2.3 enemy aircraft downed for each US aircraft lost. The performance of the US Navy compared with the US Air Force was almost the same. During the one-year cessation period however, the US Navy decided to build stronger capability into the human pilots with high-pressure, hyper-real simulations in the air—Top Gun was born. The US Air Force was bemused and instead maintained the status quo. When fighter operations recommenced in Vietnam, something interesting happened. The US Air Force exchange ratio got worse, dropping from 2.3 to 2.0—I guess their pilots were a bit rusty. The US Navy exchange ratio rose from 2.4 to 12.5—more than a 500 percent improvement!

The lesson here is that having the best technology or equipment gives you an advantage that can be massively amplified with masterful execution by humans. But that is not the end of the story. Technology initially enabled pilots (e.g., radar and navigation), then augmented their abilities (e.g., targeting and firing systems), and will now replace them (DARPA AI) because humans cannot cope with the capabilities of the tools they need to control. The g-forces are just too great in pulling the maneuvers. No job is safe, no profession immune from AI. Selling is not as complicated as you imagine—it's just insanely difficult getting out of your own way and breaking through the apathy of the person you seek to help.

It's a bizarre paradox that scripts are needed to scale, but they also kill creativity and empathy in engagement. Never phone someone and read a script unless you've also taken acting classes—they can almost always tell it's not real even though you're human. Also, don't fall into the trap of becoming like everyone else who reads this book, using the same techniques and messaging. You are the unique point of difference, so make your voice count.

Change always creates opportunity, and you can choose your future. An example is the newspaper business and how it was hammered. There were huge opportunities for established publishers and disruptive entrepreneurs alike to provide personalized news and tailored advertising rather than the old model with "one set of content and ads for all." Many new jobs and businesses have been created as a result. Change is an opportunity for those with the right mindset. How do we humans continue to provide meaningful contributions that fund our existence, and avoid a tipping [out-of-the-boat] point driven by "the machines"? In our opinion, the answer is to:

1. **Focus** on the truly human attributes of empathy, insight, and storytelling to create emotional connection and trust, powered by your vision, curiosity, imagination, creativity, innovation, belief, and passion.

2. **Target** customers and environments where there is significant complexity, ambiguity, risk, and politics that must be navigated, and where trusted relationships are needed to build a business case and secure consensus for change.

3. **Avoid** the drift toward commoditization and elevate all you do by becoming a consultative domain expert in how a business or organization can transform results with lowest risk. Master your message and relentlessly build your brand and network.

4. **Embrace** change with every fiber of your being and build your TQ and become hyper-effective by automating tasks and all non-creative work. Design your own tech stack and become masterfully adept in all aspects of design and orchestration.

The year 2020 was one in which change dramatically accelerated. Your time is now for embracing the daring concepts in this book. Be the best you can be in your career by becoming a salesborg fusion of human and machine. So dust off your technology stack and dive deep to thrive where others fail. Be unique and bold in how you message and execute while upgrading yourself to superhuman status.

Finally, how does it feel? Is your skin starting to peel back to reveal the metal parts and circuits that are now part of you? Or, maybe they've always been there? Either way, you're now on your way, but the real transformation takes place when you start to apply what you've learned. When you earn the attention, trust, and respect of more people than you were capable of before. When you start to be able to contribute more to our world. When more people and organizations are able to achieve a better future-state because of your superhuman vision and effort.

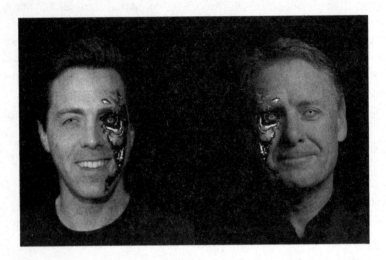

Justin Michael (left) and Tony Hughes (right)

We hope you won't forget that to sell is to be human and it can be a noble endeavor. The bots will never truly replicate empathy or love or even a real desire to serve. We also hope you've learned that in this day and age we all increasingly need TQ. Despite dystopian fears, the world is actually a better place because of technology—one simply needs to think a bit more like Tony Stark than Henry Ford to adopt the right mindset.

As Spock says: "Live long and prosper." Sell on, salesborg; many people depend on your success for their livelihoods. Join the Salesborgs.ai community, led by Justin, to continue your journey and achieve superhuman results.

Final Thoughts

You're still here—wow, thanks for hanging in there. It can all seem bewildering, but once you dive in fearlessly and immerse yourself in the waters of intelligent doing, rather than pontificating at the edge, you'll see whole new layers and nuances to what's in this book and how it can help you thrive in the age of the machines.

Honestly, collaborating on this work took us down many rabbit holes over many years with hundreds of people. Between us, we've lived everything in this book and been on the bleeding edge of accountability for sales results and how to crack the bizarre code of B2B sales success in crazy, competitive markets.

But maybe you are wondering what to make of all this—it's all real. Amid the fake tech of algorithms dressed up as AI, and Mechanical Turks beavering away to create the illusion of technomagical sophistication, behind the facade of hype, there is actually the very real ability to become superhuman with technology today. Ignore it and your economic existence is under serious threat—you'll wake up one day and be redundant. Run with this and you'll grow and prosper; just make sure you do it with soul and integrity.

Here in this book, we strived to deliver killer ideation with practical application, all for the purpose of saving an industry that is in deep trouble. Failure rates in B2B selling are staggering. Sadly, many salespeople will fade away. But not you, because you are here and you are now more enlightened with how to evolve. Our goal is to awaken you with the *why* while showing you the *how*. We would love to hear about your success, so connect with us, Justin Michael and Tony Hughes, on LinkedIn.

Acknowledgments

To the more than a hundred leaders and experts who read, commented, and contributed to this work, thank you! Your real-world experience and insights into cutting-edge technology and road maps provided powerful examples and informed our thinking as we took this book to new levels. We especially thank these individuals.

Lars Nilsson for providing generous insights and wisdom. He is a friend, mentor, and advisor for True Ventures, and one of the world's leading consultants on account-based sales development (ABSD).

Wesley "Meep" Pennock is the future of sales and he has been a technical advisor so this book can *pass the sniff test* with software engineers, computer science majors, CTOs, coders, hackers, growth hackers, and SaaS software architects.

Remington Rawlings for being a fellow journeyman in the insane world of tech-driven sales and contributing so much of his cutting-edge real-world wisdom within these pages.

Daniel Gray, masterful Chief Customer Officer, for sharing his tech stack and insights.

Greg Meyer from Data Czar for generously sharing inside knowledge and years of experience in delivering amazing results.

David Boyce, Chief Strategy Officer at XANT, for sharing the trends he believes matter most.

Mary Shea, PhD, the intrepid analyst at Forrester helping to analyze and shape the space so buyers can make the best decisions for their business.

Matthew Kloss for helping edit early drafts of this work. He has achieved salesborg status as an army of one to embody all the principles herein.

Sydney Sloan, CMO of SalesLoft, for believing in the universal application of sales engagement to all modern business.

Mateo Elvira for content marketing assistance.

Patrick Joyce for helping prove out many of the concepts.

Kyle Rasmussen, rock star in applying these principles.

Most importantly, we thank our families for tolerating the time commitment and insanity of writing a book while continuing to deliver in the real world for clients.

Honorable mentions: cutting-edge consultants and leaders

Aaron Ross—Consultant and author of *Predictable Revenue*

Anthony Iannarino—Sales community leader and author

Amir Reiter—CEO at CloudTask

Ben Collins—Advanced Google Sheets strategies

Ben Salzman—DogPatch Advisors

Ben Sardella—Cofounded Datanyze and OutboundWorks

Brendan Short—Ops and enablement at Zoom Video Communications

Catarina Hoch—VP at Operatix.net

Chris Ortolano—Community leader at SalesStack.io and OutboundEdge.com

Cian McGloughlan—CEO at Trinity Perspectives

Cory Bray—ClozeLoop

David Dulany—Founder and CEO at Tenbound

David Skok—For Entrepreneurs VC with phenomenal sales and marketing insights

Eric Quanstrom—CMO at CIENCE

Gabe Villamizar—LinkedIn Sales Navigator YouTube tutorials

Guillaume Moubeche—Cofounder & CEO, lemlist (Automation Community on FB)

Hilmon Sorey—Managing Director at ClozeLoop

Jake Dunlap—CEO at SKALED Consulting

Jason Bay—Blissful Prospecting

Jason Vargas—Cofounder at RevShoppe

Jeb Blount—CEO at Sales Gravy and author of *Fanatical Prospecting* and other books

Jeremey Donovan—SVP Strategy at SalesLoft and author of *Leading Sales Development*

John Barrows—CEO of JB Sales

Josh Braun—SalesDNA

Josh O'Brien—Cofounder RevShoppe

Julia Nimchinski—Founder, RevGarage

Kyle Coleman—VP Revenue Growth & Enablement at Clari

Kyle Williams—DogPatch Advisors

Lars Nilsson—VP, Global Sales Development at Snowflake

Lee Gladish—CEO at AirborneApp

Luigi Presinenzi—Cofounder at Sales IQ Global

Luis Batalha—Founder at AmpleMarket with goodsalesemails.com content for sellers

Marc Benioff—Founder, Chairman, and CEO at Salesforce

Mary Shea—VP, Global Innovation Evangelist at Outreach.io

Marylou Tyler—CEO at Strategic Pipeline, author of *Predictable Prospecting*

Miles Veth—CEO, Veth Group

Patricia McLaren—Cofounder and CEO at RevShoppe

Remington Rawlings—Cofounder, Advanced Revenue Consulting

Ryan Reisert—CEO of Reisert Consulting

Sam Feldotto—Head of Sales & Growth, SalesHive.com

Scott Britton—Cofounder, Troops.ai

Scott Mark—Sales Director at XANT.ai

Shawn Sease—Head of Sales at ScaledOn

Steve Richard—Chief Evangelist and Cofounder, ExecVision and Vorsight

Sujan Patel—Cofounder of Mailshake (The Cold Email Masterclass)

Tito Bohrt—CEO, AltiSales

Tomasz Tunguz—Managing Director at Redpoint Ventures

Vlad Voskresensky—CEO and Cofounder at Revenue Grid

Yelena Reese—Chief Creative Officer at Persuasion Studio

Check out these collectives and communities: Salesborgs.ai, Wizard of Ops by Brad Smith, RevGenius by Jared Robin and Galem Girmay, SDRevolution by Greyson Fulbright, Sales Enablement Society, Revenue Collective, Modern Sales Pros, Bravado, many sales leader Patreons, Gain Grow Retain by Jay Nathan and Jeff Breunsbach.

Thank You

Our families: Eloise and Julia plus Gail, Annie, and Josh. Lars Nilsson, Aaron Ross, Max Altschuler, Manny Medina, Kyle Porter, Jeremey Donovan, Chris Harrington, Howard Brown, David Boyce, Mary Shea PhD, Sean Parker, Mark Whalberg, John Barrows, Tiffani Bova, Morgan Ingram, Bryan Franklin, Ryan Buma, Lucas and Lee Brown, Jason Bay, Doug McMillen, Steve Richard, Cory Bray, Hilmon Sorey, Jackson Lieu,

Derek Jankowski, David Dulany, Elay Cohen, Anders Fredriksson, David Boyce, Aaron Janmohamed, Richard Harris, Scott Leese, Marylou Tyler, Amy Volas, Luigi Prestinenzi, David Brock, Matthew Kloss (editing), Jake Housdon, Chris Ortolano, Wesley Pennock, Jake Dunlap, Josh Braun, Becc Holland, Neil Rackham, Charles H. Green, Dale Dupree, James Buckley, Emanuel Carpenter. Ryan Reisert, Shawn Sease, Scott Barker, Justin Welsh, Keenan, Cian Mcloughlin, John Smibert, Mike Weinberg, Anthony Iannarino, Jeff Thull, Jim Holden, Mike Bosworth, Ben Zoldan, Jacco vanderKooij, Craig Rosenberg, Bryan Kreuzberger, Scott Britton, Jim Mongillo, Garrett MacDonald, Jim Thoeni, Christian Hunter, Tom Adams, Stephanie Leffler, Peter Hamilton, Charles Manning, Bryan Franklin, Ben Sardella, Marcus Sandberg, Wesley Pennock (technical advisor), Dyer Whitt, Eric Quanstrom, John Girard, Dyer Whitt, Remington Rawlings, Ewing Gillaspy, Micah Zayner, Scott Lichtenstein, Julia Nimchinski, Amy Quick, Francois Bourdeau, Jared Robin, Brendan Short, Luke Anderson, Leo Giel, Nancy Roberts, Alec Baker, Patrick Joyce, Mateo Elvira, and Kyle Rasmussen.

Appendix

TQ Application Case Studies

Case Study: Rep on a Performance Review Becomes Top Rep

Ironically, a rep at one of the big four SEP companies was struggling and called. We helped him add in phone strategically to his cadences and refine his value messaging so it was more fear based (loss) versus ROI (gain). He embraced the *COMBO Prospecting* ethos and methodology, and in four months he went from a performance review to the top rep in the company and got flown to Vegas to get the award. True story!

Here are some of the changes that we made. The sequences were way too salesy and read like a marketing brochure. We shortened them to make them more conversational. Next we nailed the message and conversation narrative by making it about sharing ideas on growing the business, reducing risk, saving FTE costs, reducing ramp time costs, and so on. He then started to triple his prospects (phone, voicemail, email with ninety seconds). Anyone who viewed his profile or viewed a sequence four times was tripled, starting with the phone. He was rewarded for this persistence by getting nicknamed "Triple Timmy!" He described the reason for success as an application of COMBO to the sequencer modality of preprogramming mass email.

Case Study: Six Years of Pipeline in Six Months

A company in NYC had feedback that their prospects hated receiving cold calls so they did away with it as a practice. A new seller joined and subscribed to a semi-automated email sending technology via Groove and an effective data source in ZoomInfo. He parked himself in a cubicle and made thirty calls first thing every day and sent out sequences every forty-eight hours to a targeted list of buyers. The response to this activity from peers and management: "This guy is not a cultural fit. He just bangs the same script out all day in a cubicle." But he soon set meetings with Coca-Cola, McDonald's, Home Depot, you name it. Within six months, he set the record for the most pipeline ever generated in the company and was promoted and relocated to Seattle to create a worldwide sales development operation covering six countries.

What techniques actually worked? Combination effect: call, vmail, email, InMail, liked a tweet, added personalization across the board. He also created shared Google sheets to work ABM/ABSD style on a finite list of contacts into the top two hundred accounts matching ICP. He went deep into the accounts and booked on-site meetings using the neighborhood technique doing COMBO triples and launching sequences at Atlanta, Chicago, Toronto, or NYC for upcoming travel. He was monitoring the pixel firing (tracking) every day on all outbound email and then reacting to views of his profile and high opens on email. He was also leveraging TeamLinks to triangulate his way into technical mobile orgs through the engineering arms via common connections in his own organization.

When he built the team in Seattle, he included a tech stack to enable them, including Sales Navigator, ZoomInfo for direct dials and emails (Lusha for the EMEA region), and Groove was handling the sequencing. Results were okay but a light-bulb moment happened reading an article by Tony Hughes titled "The Rise of the Silent Sales Floor Is Killing Business." The job of SDR had become one of listening to Spotify while cruising around Navigator (building lists and endlessly researching), using LeadIQ or ZoomInfo to batch load into sequencers, and then utilizing some crowdsourced templates. People were treating the phone like it was covered with spiders, fearing rejection or suffering from performance anxiety in wielding their voice.

To change things, he hired forward-thinking reps who embraced the old-school phone as the primary connector, on the back of better keyword targeting in advanced Sales Navigator settings. Some were even using exotic B2C media like Skype and Facebook Messenger to land meetings all over the world with harder-to-reach stakeholders in the affiliate marketing space—Isle of Malta or Cyprus. The operation was a raving success after ensuring a proactive culture in sales development that did not cower behind email sequencers and grooming social media.

Case Study:
Liquid Syntax in Personalization for Warm Outreach

The best way you can impinge into any market when you join a company is to find all the past buyers and map them to LinkedIn. We call this a trigger diaspora. Within platforms like Apollo and lemlist, you are able to use "liquid syntax." This is a set of encoding where you can preprogram when certain prospects reach a condition and the personalization changes.

Ben Harbert shares how this transformed results. "We'd been Apollo users for three months when I caught a webinar with Krishan Patel and he shared liquid syntax. He starts the webinar talking about how Apollo was able to book more outbound meetings with liquid syntax and zero SDRs than when they were with six SDRs working independently. Of course, I was like, 'Holy crap! How can I use this now?'"[1]

Krishan's advice was to build rules based on known personalization points (e.g., persona, hiring, funding, tech stack, location, and vertical) and then use liquid syntax to have multiple variations of an email housed in one step in Apollo. Figure A.1 presents his example of a rule that automatically updates custom fields in Apollo or a CRM. These are updated continuously, so when companies fall out of the recent funding window of two months, the custom field will be reset accordingly and will be gated to prevent triggering the wrong message.

---

1. Rule Details ⓘ

Rule name:	Hiring: Sales Operations
Folder:	Hiring
Activity from:	Contact
Rule type:	Triggered

2. Triggers ⓘ

• Contact Added To Sequence

3. Filters ⓘ

• Currently Hiring For: **sales operations** **sales ops**
• Job Posted At: **From: 2 Months Ago**

4. Actions ⓘ

Actions: • Set Contact Field | Field: Custom Field Hiring: Sales Operations | New value: True
       • Wait 1 months
       • Set Contact Field | Field: Custom Field Hiring: Sales Operations | New value: False

5. Schedule ⓘ

Run: • Every time

Figure A.1

Figure A.2 is an example of the messaging framework that would be built using the above rule and any others that we may want to configure.

```
{{#if Persona == CMO}}
{{#if Hiring Marketing == TRUE}}
{{#if Using Marketo == TRUE}}
        Message for CMOs growing their marketing team and using Marketo.
{{#else}}
        Message for CMOs growing their marketing team and not using Marketo.
{{#endif}}
{{#else}}
{{#if Using Marketo == TRUE}}
        Message for CMOs not growing their marketing team and using Marketo.
{{#else}}
        Message for CMOs not growing their marketing team and not using Marketo.
{{#endif}}
{{#endif}}
{{#endif}}
```

Figure A.2

Even though this is a very basic setup for making liquid syntax work, you can begin to imagine how much more flexible this makes the messaging to prospects, because each message can be limited to only prospects meeting a certain set of variables. Ben learned not to insert too many custom fields into the message, and instead create more segmented value propositions that are controlled by rules triggered on custom fields. "I learned my lesson—'less is more'! We created outreach for very specific segments of companies that matched our clients who were growing fast."

Ben made personalization and the narrative more targeted and succinct, and also used that framework to revamp outreach to companies who were probably not in the buying zone and started conversations that won new customers. "We learned to use liquid syntax messaging, controlled by rules, to make sure the right messaging went to the right people and not just custom field vomiting at them."

Ben became adept at using the tool and techniques and says: "When I started creating rules and complex liquid syntax templates, I moved into an area where the support team had a hard time knowing how to help me. But finding external experts to help makes all the difference!"

Krishan Patel, Director of Growth at Apollo, is one of those experts and he found that in order to replicate the results of his previous SDR team, it took hyper-personalization at scale.

There's more than one side to the personalization. Personalization that SDRs do based on information they already have. For this type of personalization, we can use Apollo's Rules Engine to enrich and check each lead as soon as it's added to a sequence to fill out certain custom fields based on data. This can include whether the company is hiring in certain positions, has raised funding, is using certain technologies, is in specific locations, is new to its role, etc.

Much personalization that SDRs do is based on researching and finding new data not currently in the system. For this type of personalization, we hand over a huge list of accounts to a low-cost offshore team to do deep account-research and fill out custom fields for us. For example, if you were a web design agency, maybe you would have the researchers take a screenshot of each company's website and place the URL in the custom field which can then be used to personalize an email to anyone within that account.

If you can afford to invest more in acquiring customers (CAC) or already have a relatively high ACV, then this entire process shouldn't have the goal to replace your SDR, but instead it should save significant time for SDRs so they can focus more on calling and doing the things that only they can do. The overall SDR team doesn't need to be as large because each SDR can cover more accounts since they don't have to spend as much time researching, personalizing emails, and wrangling data.

In Apollo, driving account-based sequences then allows accounts to be managed in a playbook. Manual researchers input personalization data and people are then added to the account with them being in correct sequences based on their persona. We can run the campaign as top-down, bottom-up, or scattershot.[2]

Apollo is excellent and we've seen WYSIWYG (what you see is what you get, pronounced wis-ee-wig) in email marketing automation canvas builders and visual editors to coordinate emails, social touches, push notifications, and so on. There are simple templates now for non-technical marketers to customize. Salesforce Journey Builder is an excellent example. This type of thinking will come to personalization at scale with drag-and-drop ease for parameters to personalize. UIs will be so smart and facile that a child could build hyper-touch sequences in minutes toward 2025.

TQ TAKEAWAY

Use platforms such as Apollo with Zoom (Scoops) and Triggr to automatically receive lists of people to target, with their contact details, based on automatically analyzing a combination of attributes and trigger events. This gives you ongoing funnel for driving outreach where there is relevance, context, and higher propensity to buy. You can even automate cohorts into various sequences based on how the personalization should take place—and in real time.

Case Study:
The Power of Baseline Content for Buyer Personas

We strongly advocate that you absolutely nail your ICP and buyer personas to then create strong baseline value narratives (messaging) to which you can add relevant personalization. Remington Rawlings shared his views on this topic: "When you are creating personalization at scale, you don't have to personalize a huge portion of the email if the parts of the email that aren't personalized are highly impactful to the person in their role. This obviously requires tight alignment between marketing and whoever is writing the sequences with custom personalization fields."[3]

Remington provides the following anonymized real example of what he helped a company build and deploy with great results.

- [1] INTRO/PERSONALIZATION: You personalize the beginning of the email using account/persona/contact specific attributes or triggers. These can either come from a manual email where you find details and add them as the first step in any sequence, or from an account field you map over that contains specific wording that is good for anyone in the whole account.

- [a], [b], [c], [d]—BENEFITS/VALUE (meat of the message): You make a strong value pitch for the persona, articulate the product benefits, not the features. Personalization is icing on the cake to get them to feel you know them *and* you brought value.

  [a] PAIN: For instance, you have to know their role, share what their problems usually are.

[b] FUNCTIONAL BENEFIT: Talk about the literal operational/ organizational/technological changes they will see because of whatever you're positioning—i.e., what they stand to see change at work because of the thing you offer.

[c] EMOTIONAL BENEFIT: What they personally would see if they had this functional benefit—i.e., more time for strategic work, less stress managing employees, less frustration because of constant change you didn't see coming, etc.

[d] PERSONAL VALUE: Share what they will end up walking away with from working with you and gaining those functional and emotional benefits—i.e., you end up being a strategic leader, promotion, lead change initiatives in your org with ease, etc.

- [e] CALL TO ACTION:

  [e] should include a specific ask, as well as a *when* question between two options, not an *if* question or a soft/flimsy ending that has no backbone. Unless you are doing a thought leadership campaign that you want to provide value and lead only to awareness, your CTA has to be on point if you want them to take a next step seriously.

Remington goes on. Put it all together and what do you get? Everything from [a] to [e] can be the same for every email within a single persona (supply chain executive/champion for example, or IT executive/champion). Here's an example of an email:

"Hey {{first name}},

[1] INTRO/PERSONALIZATION {{company}} seems to be going through some change as the market shifts and new laws are going to make your situation harder. [a] I know with your background of leading teams at multiple global enterprise companies like Salesforce, LinkedIn, and a couple others that this won't be a first for you. But with your CRO leaving recently, I am sure that makes it interesting.

[b] FUNCTIONAL BENEFIT: At [name of our company], we are spending lots of time putting effort toward understanding the way people work and why their jobs are harder following COVID. With the shift in the economy, you and your managers have had to cut costs and maximize profits. Our goal is to give you complete visibility into the ROI of your production line.

[c] EMOTIONAL BENEFIT: We know if you can see that better, and manage work cross-functionally, you won't feel the frustration of wondering where the friction points are in the business.

[d] PERSONAL VALUE: Through our technology, we have empowered executives at other companies like X, Y, and Z, companies to be the strategic leaders that take 50 percent less time to understand their ROI/problems.

[e] CALL TO ACTION: It would be important that I have fifteen minutes with you to understand what specific initiatives you are working on that [name of our company] can help with. Would Tuesday afternoon or Wednesday morning be better? I can send an invite.

Remington says: "This approach appeals to some of the various aspects of an executive's desires. You may find another framework is more beneficial for you. And you have to remember that frameworks can be combatants to brevity: don't make it too long! The point is that you have a framework that you can use to apply your personalization at scale." So, courtesy of Remington Rawlings, the skeleton is:

[1] INTRO/PERSONALIZATION

[a] FUNCTIONAL BENEFIT, [b] EMOTIONAL BENEFIT, [d] PERSONAL VALUE; (include case studies where applicable in any of these portions of the framework)

[e] CALL TO ACTION

Case Study: Spears™ and Signature Sequence

Justin (coauthor here) originally wrote this for Sales IQ Global, the sales enablement and eLearning platform we partner with to help people learn at scale without expensive consulting. *Spears* is a term coined by Justin, just as *COMBO* is coined by Tony. The quirky grammar is deliberate.

DAY 1—THREAD ONE:
A Subject Line 1: Growth for {{Company Name}}
B Subject Line 2: 3-5X pipeline for {{Company Name}}?
C Subject Line 3: Top Funnel Growth Training for your reps, {{first name}}?

Hey {{first_name}}, Are you struggling to generate top funnel growth and can't enable your people in ways that stick?

SalesIQ has trained leaders including {{reference_cust_1}}, {{reference_cust_2}}, and {{reference_cust_3}} with a virtual learning environment with reinforcement training to lead to double digit increases in sales team performance leveraging the principles of *COMBO Prospecting*. This can allow your reps to go full bottle on outbound with phone and multi-channel and build a 3-5X pipeline.

Are you the best person at {{company name}} to talk about this? Thanks, JM

DAY 4—REPLY BUMP

{{Customer_name}} Thoughts on this?

DAY 7—LINKEDIN SOCIAL TOUCH: FIRST DEGREE OR SECOND DEGREE (EXAMPLE IS SECOND DEGREE)

Dear {{first name}}—I see you are responsible for sales enablement at {{company name}}, and at SalesIQ, we help companies like {{reference_cust_1}} and {{reference_cust_2}} train their reps in top funnel growth. Makes sense to connect here?

DAY 11—LINKEDIN FOLLOW-UP 1

Hi {{first_name}}, I'm still shaken with what's happened (and happening) but I'm beginning to find my feet in this "new" normal. How are you doing?

If you've checked out my profile you can see that at SalesIQ, we have trained reps at {{competitors}} on top funnel growth techniques. The current scenario has ensured that SDRs are either:
- Complaining that no one's taking sales meetings
- Wasting AE's time on meetings that don't go anywhere, or
- Simply pretending to work from home :)

Essentially, companies may be spending >6k a month per rep that's currently producing zilch. I want to propose that we set up a call to:
- Identify areas you need the most help
- Understand your prospects' world and product market fit
- Propose a training program for your SDRs (if applicable)

Do you have some availability early next week? JM

DAY 14—LINKEDIN FOLLOW-UP 2

Hey {{first name}}. Can we hop on that call anytime soon? (totally understand if you are preoccupied w/ other priorities and would love a response when you catch a moment)

Now starting a whole new email and sequence with email thread two.

DAY 1

Subject Line 1: 50% missing quota, {{first name}}?
Subject Line 2: Can't generate pipeline fast enough, {{first name}}?
Subject Line 3: {{First Name}}, Training won't stick?

Hey hey {{first.name}}—We read wild stats on this every day with up to 70% of hunting reps missing quota. It's a scourge in high growth orgs—the churn rates and low morale.

We've developed a SalesIQ platform that teaches reps the fundamentals of outbound prospecting with an interactive online learning environment that cements results. The most cutting edge startups in the world use this. It's from the crack team of Tony Hughes and Luigi Prestinenzi, and is an affordable scalable way to upskill your global sales org virtually at a fraction of the cost of traditional sales training.

If it makes sense to talk, how does your calendar look? Thanks, JM

DAY 4—BUMP

{{first.name}}, Imagine the implications of improving your middle performers by 20%?

DAY 7—BUMP

{{first.name}}, It's about opportunity cost. Imagine not doing anything while the low performers are managed out and the middle is mediocre.

Shall we talk about helping your top performers double or triple pipeline with the right training in place?

DAY 10—THREAD THREE

Subject 1: {{full name}}: Not your Dad's sales enablement platform
Subject 2: {{full name}}: Cutting edge training on demand
Subject 3: {{First Name}}: Public Review on SalesIQ?

{{Prospect.name}}, We have helped many companies like {{customer.name}} drive distributed sales enablement with SalesIQ. Why is it different?

Here's a 2 minute video from James Bond, VP, Sales Enablement at Megacorp: https://video.com

If you prefer reading, here's a transcript: https://transcript.com

In essence: It's simply a better training experience—the production quality, the quizzes, the content itself, all produce the result of long term learning where reps actually upskill remotely.

Their reps produced real revenue outcomes.

Thousands of reps are using this platform to upskill their game at the most prestigious tech companies in the world.

The response is glowing, "Best training ever received, best quality I've ever seen." Why does quality matter?

Because with SalesIQ lasting results, adoption and participation in on-line sales training sets up your organization for top line success. I won't waste your time, can we connect on this?

Thanks, JM

DAY 13—BUMP

Hey {{first name}} Have been reaching out to you for about a month now. Is Sales training for {{company name}}'s SDRs relevant to you?

Wanted to check one last time to see if you may be interested in an exploratory call.

Let me know if we can set up a time to talk sometime soon.

All the best, Justin

Real sequences just like these yielded millions of dollars in revenues for those using them, and they were purely digital. These sequences often set at a mind-blowing 80 percent open rate, 10 to 15 percent reply rate, and 25 percent conversion rate. We have seen ten qualified opportunities on a thousand contacts per month, all hyper-personalized digital sequencing. (The industry hovers around ten opportunities per three thousand contacts.)

TQ TAKEAWAY

Seth Godin came up with the concept of "The Purple Cow." It's all about pattern interrupts. Can you think differently? Open your own inbox and look at the last dozen emails from vendors that were sent automatedly. "Hope you're doing well. Reaching out." Sea of sameness. Now think of anything you can do to make your email opening line look different—the syntax, linguistics, structure. Less formal, more conversational. Be yourself; everyone else is taken.

Case Study: First Ninety Days— Checklist for New SDRs and SDR Leaders

The following list is what we've seen work well and what to be aware of in kicking off in the new role. It's open-sourced content from hundreds of those who've been down your path before. The premise of this section is that you will get the support and funding you ask for in the first ninety days, then it all goes downhill with the boss. Although numbered for reference purposes, it is not in priority order.

1. Get your tech stack in place including Sales Navigator, a sales engagement platform (SEP), a data source (direct numbers and emails), and a means to listen to remote calls (conversational intelligence). Sort out your CRM to enable sales process and marketing collaboration, and also moving data bi-directionally with your SEP.

2. Make your sequences painfully short with one-to-three-word subject lines, and two or three sentences maximum content so they are optimized for mobile responsive design. Consider avoiding bullets or dashes in early emails: massive tests by SalesLoft conclusively prove they decrease deliverability. Instead of a three-paragraph marketing email, go for something that looks like this. "Hey, Bill, noticed your sales team grew from 3 to 15 reps, which means you may need to de-risk scaling so the majority hit their numbers, similar to how we did this for Acme, Beta, and Zeta Corp—unlocking a 245 percent increase in revenue. When's a good time to talk? Thanks, Justin."

3. Deploy Reisert Buckets, a priority classifier that structures your process and how you work each day. Bucket 1—your evergreen TAM. Bucket 2—in ICP, in sequence. Bucket 3—priority, you've connected. Bucket 4—booked meeting. The system is designed to be worked from Bucket 4 to Bucket 1 as you prioritize the most engaged first.

4. A/B split test everything methodically, especially focusing on subject lines, opening sentences, and calls to action (CTAs).

5. Avoid using links, images, or a cluttered signature. Use text only in first and early sends to appease the SPAM gods!

6. Make your cadences assertively high frequency (every forty-eight to seventy-two hours) so you get routed—referrals in the replies are huge! The goal is "proof of life" in any form, even a hard *no*.

7. Make sure you are doing triples on high opens. So if you see three or more opens of a sequence, you need to manually call that prospect, leave a voicemail, and send an email within ninety seconds (*COMBO Prospecting* technique). Engagement of any kind with your triple deserves follow-up. You can automatically set tasks to remind you whenever a prospect opens a sequence more than three times; optimally five or more is a leading indicator. In Outreach, this is in Settings / Ruleset 3)

8. Consider ORUM, ConnectAndSell, and ConnectLeader to get "speak live" contacts per day from five to more than twenty, leveraging parallel assisted dialing (PAD) from offshore and hot-switches unbeknownst to the prospect.

9. Think from the viewpoint of the prospect. Send test email sequences to friends and family, then be open to super-candid feedback. Send it to your VP of Sales, CRO, and CMO. Make sure your outreach sounds authentic and conversational, not like a marketing brochure. Drop your own personal email into all initial sequences.

10. Make a judgment call on how much to personalize. It is best done at the technographic, psychographic, and firmographic levels. A/B test hyper-short compacted messaging against these methods. You need to be savvy with adding custom fields and importing these fields into an Excel column, normalizing the data, and assigning them to a custom field you map on a bulk create import where you line up a column such as "friend in common" to that field. Other examples include first-degree connection (but vet these for actually having a real relationship), alumni, head count growth, job change {{Former Company}} to company.

11. Study Becc Holland (Chorus.ai YouTube: Flip The Script Calls and Emails), Josh Braun (Bad Ass B2B Growth Guide), and Sam Nelson (Agoge Sequence). An example of what good could look like is: "Hey, Jessica, looks like we both know Jon Selig. I noticed you just moved from {{former.company}} to {{company}} and {{former.company}} was a satisfied customer of {{my.company}}.

Shall we find some time to talk about conversational intelligence at {{company}}? Best, JM." One of the super cool things we saw with Hexa.ai technology at OutboundWorks was that it could map entire AI-written sentences into custom outreach fields.

12. Basic messaging that always works is "social proof." "Mr. Prospect, here are three famous names that we drive these valuable outcomes for." The demand types you should focus your message on are: make money, save money, reduce risk, satisfy a regulation.

13. Remember the 80/20 rule: An effective SDR outbound motion is asymmetrical by definition. Therefore, 80 percent of each day is wasted. It's your job to hone in on the levers that work and 10X them. Be maniacally focused on identifying and cutting waste from the system, then prioritizing what's converting to results.

14. Sales development and revenue operations (RevOps) requires rigorous commitment to the scientific method so don't fall into the trap of a spray-and-pray approach. Change one thing at a time to hone in on the streaks using the process of elimination. If you test six subject lines and clone the email, see which has the highest reply rate, then analyze sentiment. SDRs need to see themselves as data scientists, always yearning to break new ground, discover uncharted territory, but keen on self-control, wisdom—and patience, persistence, and perspicacity (the three Ps).

15. Understand your budget for tech stacks and hiring. You need to bring in Drift front-of-site chatbots so they can float on your website, chatting and bringing in business with highest value prospects *as they presearch in real time* at the ZMOT (zero moment of truth). Subscribe to Vidyard, Loom, or BombBomb for video emails. Buy Chili Piper for high show rate calendaring. One of the top reps ever that we worked with came from DocuSign, which had over two hundred SDRs. He had been passed up for a promotion and therefore moved to a new company. He was the heaviest cold caller on the block and became a legend for it. Once we trained him on responding to social signals, COMBO, and key elements of TQ—game over, he was hands down the top performer every single month. As Kevin O'Connor, founder of DoubleClick, says: "Hire smart athletes." Work ethic is even more important as self-motivation and discipline is the prerequisite for everything in this book.

16. Study *The Bridge Group SDR Metrics Report* for SDR SaaS Metrics. Based on these benchmarks, establish your baseline KPIs—calls per day, emails per day, social touches per day, outbound emails per day. Follow what VC David Skok, the oracle of SDRs, says.

17. Know the math of sales! Ryan Reisert's mantra is to define your TAM, ICP, and IPP/buyer personas and build out touch patterns for these. Then actually follow-up in a disciplined programmatic manner . . . every quarter for every contact.

18. Get your social strategy in place so it's measurable. There are many systems like Skylead.io, DuxSoup, and Kennected.org that automate LinkedIn—but major warning, be careful about this as there are stringent guidelines around automating LinkedIn interaction. You can do this safely manually. Have a template for the first custom LinkedIn invite and subsequent manual touches. Understand throttles, caps, and how to rescind LinkedIn invites to stay compliant.

19. Be smart about targeting and trigger events. In Navigator, this means mastering Boolean searches. This also means considering Bombora intent data. Understand job changes, the most powerful trigger event. Take the approach of top-down, middle-out, and bottom-up. Understand flanking if you are selling at senior levels. Make sure you are hitting up the marketing leaders, as they have cyclical budgets, which the sales leaders often pull from for tool budgets.

Glossary

Buzzwords and acronyms galore! This book is an insider's guide for sellers and sales leaders seeking to take a quantum leap in revenue generation. There is a high level of assumed knowledge, but here is your survival guide. Note that the inside sales function is highly fragmented, with many companies thrashing around with different models and acronyms—which is why we provide the following list. Be ready to use the most basic TQ tool, Google, to hunt down anything else you need to know as you read.

Sales Industry Nomenclature

Inside sales roles: ISR (Inside Sales Rep) is mainly known as an SDR (sales development rep) for inbound and BDR (business development rep) for outbound. Inside sales roles are also called MDR (market development rep) or MRR (marketing response rep) or LDR (lead development rep) or ADR (account development rep). These roles are sometimes supported by SDAs (sales data analysts) in large companies. The main distinction between ISR roles is whether they are focused on qualifying inbound enquiries or marketing leads, versus driving outbound activity to create qualified leads that are given to more senior salespeople in the field. Inbound reps sometimes report in to marketing because they are qualifying the marketing department's leads to move them from MQLs to SQLs. Outbound reps usually report to sales because they feed the field reps (AEs) with qualified leads. Got it? . . . good luck . . . it's an acronym soup swimming in a morass of metaphors and insider jargon. XDR can refer to any of the above!

Sales lead types: MQL (marketing qualified lead) and SQL (sales qualified lead). Someone downloading a white paper, registering for a webinar, or signing up to attend an event are all examples of marketing leads that need to be qualified and turned into sales leads. Someone requesting a demo or quote would be a sales lead that needs to be qualified. The goal is to move MQLs to be SQLs.

Field sales roles: AE (account executive) and also known as a field rep, BDM (business development manager) or sales executive. It is common for these sellers to have fancy titles that make them appear senior in the eyes of prospective buyers.

Sales support roles: SE (sales engineer, solutions engineer, or systems engineer) also known as an SA (solution architect) or sometimes called pre-sales consultant or solution sales specialist.

Acronyms and Defined Terms

ABM: Account-based marketing.

ABS: Account-based selling (not automatic braking system).

ABSD: Account-based sales development.

ACV: Annual (or Average) contract value.

ADR: Account development rep.

AE: Account executive. Sometimes called a BDM or field rep.

AI: Artificial intelligence—machines that learn and self-improve. Don't say "AI" to a farmer or breeder; they'll think you mean artificial insemination.

AM: Account manager. Sometimes known as CSM.

API: Application program interface (often incorporates web services and other forms of software systems integration).

ASD: Automated sales development.

B2B: Business-to-business.

B2C: Business-to-customer/consumer/client.

BDM: Business development manager. Sometimes called an account executive (but not an AE) or field rep.

BDR: Business development rep. Inside sales role with outbound focus.

BPM: Business process management.

Buyer Persona: Archetype of buyer roles (technical buyer, financial buyer, etc.) See IPP.

CAC: Client/customer acquisition cost.

Cadence: The rhythm or frequency in which you drive outreach. Some SEP companies use the term interchangeably with *sequence*.

CCO: Chief customer officer or chief commercial officer.

CDO: Chief digital officer.

CMO: Chief marketing officer.

Conversational or **Revenue Intelligence:** These are systems that record and transcribe all the rep calls to analyze the listen-to-talk ratio, question frequency (open or closed Qs), objections, sentiment, and so on. Players include Gong, Chorus, Refract.ai, and Execvision.

CPL: Cost per lead.

CPO: Chief procurement officer.

CRM: Customer relationship management. System of record for all customer information and interactions. Salesforce, Microsoft Dynamics, and Hubspot are leaders.

CRO: Chief revenue officer.

CSM: Customer success manager. Sometimes known as account manager.

CSO: Chief sales officer.

CTA: Call to action.

CTO: Chief technology officer.

CX: Customer experience.

CXO: Chief *anything you pick* officer.

DAVE/S: Digital Adaptive Virtual Entity for Sales.

DB: Database.

DM: Direct message (not direct marketing).

DNC: Do not call (*take me off your mailing list and database*).

DSP: Demand side platform.

DVA: Digital Virtual Assistant.

DVSA: Digital Virtual Sales Assistant.

EBS: Equal business stature.

EIEIO: As in the "Old Macdonald" song. Used when highlighting acronym overload.

EX: Employee experience.

Firmographics: Information about an organization's industry vertical, geographic locations, number of employees, clients, and so on. Everstring and ZoomInfo (Datanyze acquisition) are good sources.

GIGO: Garbage in, garbage out.

ICP: Ideal customer profile.

IFTT: If this, then that (machine logic to trigger actions).

Intent/Surge Data Platforms: Assess anonymized surge data to identify which types of accounts are searching for your category on Google. Quantcast and Bombora are examples.

IP: Internet protocol or intellectual property.

IPP: Ideal prospect profile. See buyer persona.

ISR: Inside sales rep. Often with an inbound response focus and also known as SDR.

LDR: Lead development rep. Mainly dealing with inbound inquiries.

MDM: Market development rep.

ML: Machine learning—often with human assistance and guidance.

MQL: Marketing qualified lead. Also known as "fake leads from marketing so they can claim to hit their metrics."

MRR: Marketing response rep.

Navigator or **Nav:** LinkedIn Sales Navigator platform for B2B business intelligence.

NLP: Natural language processing (not neural linguistic programming as used in the field of phycology).

NPS: Net promoter score (a way of quantifying customer satisfaction from an interaction).

PAD: Parallel assisted dialing—sometimes called the Bazooka™. Companies including Orum, ConnectLeader, and ConnectAndSell have developed proprietary technology where an offshore team can dial thousands of times and seamlessly hot-switch when the actual prospect answers without the prospect realizing. Some use hardware and software dialers, or a combination. How? It's proprietary; ask them.

Psychographics: Information about consumer or corporate emotions and values.

RPA: Robotic process automation.

SA: Solution architect. Pre-sales person designing and documenting "solutions."

SAM: Serviceable addressable market.

SDK: Software development kit.

SDR: Inside sales rep. Often with an inbound response focus.

SE: Sales engineer, solutions engineer, or systems engineer, usually not used for sales executive.

SEO: Search Engine Optimization.

SEP: Sales engagement platform. These platforms focus on automating aspects of outbound business development—sending emails, monitoring opens and replies, and building personalized messaging segments.

Sequence: The order in which you send outreach or use content. Also known as a *cadence* or *play*. Sales engagement platforms (SEPs) use different terms. Outreach calls a series of touches a *sequence*. SalesLoft uses *cadence*. Groove uses *flow*. XANT uses *play*. FrontSpin uses *playbooks*.

Sequencer: Part of what is incorporated with an SEP.

Smarketing: Utopian coining claimed by Peter Strohkorb. The heart of RevOps, where sales and marketing fuse into a synergistic whole.

SMM: Social media monitoring or social media management.

SNAFU: Situation normal all fudged up (a military term, only they don't use *fudged* in the military).

SQL: Sales qualified leads.

SSP: Sales Simulation Platform.

STEVE: Sales Team Enablement Virtual Entity.

System of Engagement: SalesLoft, Outreach, Groove, XANT.

TAM: Target or total addressable/available/attainable/actionable market.

TAM: Target account marketing.

TAM: Technical account manager.

TCV: Total contract value.

Technographics: Information about the technologies they are using in their stack.

TOFU: Top of funnel.

UI: User interface.

VM: Voicemail or videomail (not virtual machine).

WFH: Work from home.

WYSIWYG: Pronounced *wizeewig*. What you see is what you get. Simple editor in a UI.

XDR: *Anything* development rep.

ZMOT: Zero moment of truth.

Further Reading

Take courses, engage a mentor, read and apply everything you can to absorb all facets of sales-development strategy. The following are highly recommended: Sales IQ Global online courses, Trish Bertuzzi's *Sales Development Playbook*, Mark Roberge's *Sales Acceleration Formula*, Bryan Kreuzberger's *Breakthrough Email*, Scott Britton's *Crack Cold Emailing*, Aaron Ross's *Predictable Revenue*, Marylou Tyler's *Predictable Prospecting*, Jeremey Donovan's *Leading Sales Development*, Max Altschuler and Mark Kosoglow's *Sales Engagement*, Josh Braun's *Badass B2B Growth Guide*, Becc Holland's *Flip the Script* YouTube series. Do all the Salesforce Trailheads you can gain access to. Become savvy with Outreach, XANT, and SalesLoft Universities. Let your curiosity drive you wild!

Personalization is everything. Google and purchase "Josh Braun's Badass B2B Growth Guide." Also follow Becc Holland from Chorus.ai, Dan Swift from Empire Selling, and Jaker Dunlap from Skaled. Do this on LinkedIn and with their blogs, podcasts, and videos.

Here are some great references, organized by topic:

Prospecting

Predictable Prospecting by Marylou Tyler
Fanatical Prospecting by Jeb Blount
COMBO Prospecting by Tony J. Hughes
How to Get a Meeting with Anyone by Stu Heinecke
New Sales. Simplified. by Mike Weinberg

Cold Calling

Smart Calling by Art Sobczak

Qualification

Addicted to the Process by Scott Leese

Negotiation

Never Split the Difference by Chris Voss

Neuroscience

Persuasion by Dr. Robert Cialdini
The Science of Selling by David Hoffeld

Sales Engagement

Sales Engagement by Max Altschuler, Mark Kosoglow & Manny Medina
Leading Sales Development by Alea Homison and Jeremey Donovan

SDR Organizational Design

Predictable Revenue by Aaron Ross
Sales Development Playbook by Trish Bertuzzi
Sales Acceleration Formula by Mark Roberge

C-Level Strategy:

New Power Base Selling by Jim Holden
The Joshua Principle by Tony J. Hughes
What Great Salespeople Do by Ben Zoldan and Mike Bosworth
Mastering the Complex Sale by Jeff Thull
Eat Their Lunch by Anthony Iannarino

SDR Management

Cracking the Sales Management Code by Jason Jordan & Michelle Vazzana

Sales Execution

Four Disciplines of Execution by Chris McChesney, Jim Huling, and Sean Covey
SPIN Selling by Neil Rackham
The Science of Selling by David Hoffeld
The Perfect Close by James Muir

Trigger Events:

Shift! by Craig Elias and Tibor Shanto

Consultative

Consultative Selling by Mach Hanon
Same Side Selling by Ian Altman and Jack Quarles
Let's Get Real or Let's Not Play by Mahan Khalsa and Randy Illig
Founders at Work by Jessica Livingston
The Challenger Sale by Brent Adamson and Matt Dixon
The Challenger Customer by Brent Adamson, Matt Dixon, Pat Spenner, and Nick Toman
VCs at Work by Shital Shah and Tarang Shah
The Trusted Advisor by Charles H. Green, David Maister, and Robert M. Galford

Scaling SaaS

The Discipline of Market Leaders by Michael Treacy and Fred Wiersema
From Impossible to Inevitable by Aaron Ross

Time Management

The 80/20 Principle by Richard Koch

Mindset

Mindset by Carol Dweck

AI Movies to Expand Your Thinking

Ex Machina
Automata
iRobot
A.I.
Alien Covenant
Blade Runner 2049
Her
Transcendence

Notes

Introduction

1. Matt Bertuzzi, "The 2018 SDR Metric Report Is Here," The Bridge Group, May 9, 2018. Accessed at https://blog.bridgegroupinc.com/2018-sdr-metrics-report.
2. "COVID-19 Economic Benchmarking Survey Summary Results," Revenue Collective, April 9, 2020. Accessed at https://drive.google.com/file/d/1aaP_x4492IviAU4_91UorRHLCGhoyKqj/view.
3. "Gartner Customer 360 Summit 2011," Gartner Summits. Accessed at https://www.gartner.com/imagesrv/summits/docs/na/customer-360/C360_2011_brochure_FINAL.pdf.
4. Michael Schrage, "Why Your 'TQ' May Matter More Than Your 'IQ,'" *Harvard Business Review*, November 3, 2011. Accessed at https://hbr.org/2011/11/why-your-tq-may-matter-more-th.html. The quote seems to originate with "Technology Quotient (TQ) and the Digital Skills Gap," NPI working paper, n.d. Accessed at https://www.hbhriq.com/sites/default/files/John%20Burton%20Technology%20Quotient%20Session%20Summary-final.pdf (JohnBurton, NPI? Maybe an HBR publication).
5. Ken Krogue, "Why Sales Reps Spend Less Than 36% of Time Selling (And Less Than 18% in CRM)," *Forbes*, January 10, 2018. Accessed at https://www.forbes.com/sites/kenkrogue/2018/01/10/why-sales-reps-spend-less-than-36-of-time-selling-and-less-than-18-in-crm/?sh=812be45b998f.
6. Jill Rowley, "A Fool with a Tool IS Still a Fool," LinkedIn, November 12, 2014. Accessed at https://www.linkedin.com/pulse/20141112151556-320966-a-fool-with-a-tool-is-still-a-fool/.

Part I

1. "Clarke's Three Laws," New Scientist, n.d. Accessed at https://www.newscientist.com/term/clarkes-three-laws/.
2. Matt Bertuzzi, "The 2018 SDR Metric Report Is Here."
3. Brian Anderson, "SiriusDecisions' Dana Therrien Discusses New Revenue Operations Charter, Highlights the 'Sirius Seven' to Alignment," Industry Insights, DemandGen Report, May 15, 2019. Accessed at https://www.demandgenreport.com/features/industry-insights/siriusdecisions-dana-therrien-discusses-new-revenue-operations-charter-highlights-the-sirius-seven-to-alignment.

Chapter One

1. See, for instance, Chelsea Mize, "Jill Rowley and Getting to Know Your Buyer: STAGEnext 2016 Keynote Recap," PGI, August 24, 2016. Accessed at https://www.pgi.com/blog/2016/08/jill-rowley-getting-to-know-your-buyer-stagenext-2016-keynote-recap/. There are various sources where Jill talks about this topic, but the quote seems to be from Andrew Walker, CEO of Shift7. See Andrew Wheeler, "Manufacturing, the Empowered Buyer, and Shifting into the Future," Shift7 Digital, July 31, 2019. Accessed at https://www.shift7digital.com/manufacturing-the-empowered-buyer-and-shifting-into-the-future/. For the platinum rule, see Tony Alessandra, "The Platinum Rule," Alessandra.com, n.d. Accessed at http://www.alessandra.com/platinum_members/platinum_short_article.asp

2. Garrett MacDonald, personal commentary.

3. Jason Hubbard, personal commentary.

4. Remington Rawlings, personal commentary.

5. Remington Rawlings, personal commentary.

6. Alexander Low , personal commentary.

7. Justin Michael , personal commentary.

8. Lars Nilsson and Travis Henry, "The Ultimate ABSD Tech Stack," SalesSource infographic, n.d. Accessed at https://salessource.com/resources/the-ultimate-absd-tech-stack-infographic/; Lars Nilsson LinkedIn page. Accessed at https://www.linkedin.com/in/lanilsson/; Dave Dulany LinkedIn page. Accessed at https://www.linkedin.com/in/davidkdulany/.

9. Wesley Pennock, personal commentary.

10. Lumascapes homepage, Luma Partners. Accessed at https://lumapartners.com/luma-content/.

11. Mike Brooks, "Why Most Inside Sales Reps Fail," National Association of Sales Professionals, n.d. Accessed at https://www.nasp.com/blog/why-most-inside-sales-reps-fail/.

12. Jason Hubbard, personal commentary.

13. Ken Krogue, "Why Sales Reps Spend So Little Time Selling," *Forbes*, February 15, 2018. Accessed at https://www.forbes.com/sites/kenkrogue/2018/02/15/why-sales-reps-spend-so-little-time-selling/?sh=3c9a99371051.

14. Aaron Janmohamed, personal commentary; Aaron Janmohamed LinkedIn page. Accessed at https://www.linkedin.com/in/aaronjanmohamed/.

15. Anastasia Voitehina, "The Bridge Group 2018 SDR Report's Must-Know Takeaways for CEOs," CIENCE, May 18, 2018. Accessed at https://cience.com/bridge-group-2018-main-takeaways-ceos/.

16. "Understanding Buyer Behavior with Marc McNamara," Marylou Tyler podcast, episode 41, 2018. Accessed at http://maryloutyler.com/portfolio/episode-41-marc-mcnamara/.

17. Kenny Madden, personal commentary.

18. Eric Quanstrom, personal commentary.

19. Rahul Rajvanshi , personal commentary.

20. Stephen Chase, personal commentary.

21. Justin Roff-Marsh, *The Machine*, Greenleaf Book Group Press.

22. Read *Machine, Platform, Crowd* by Erik Brynjolfsson and Andrew McAfee for a distillation of these themes.

23. Pete Caputa, "BANT Isn't Enough Anymore: A New Framework for Qualifying Prospects," HubSpot, June 12, 2018. Accessed at https://blog.hubspot.com /sales/gpct-sales-qualification.

24. Tomasz Tunguz, personal commentary.

25. Jason Hubbard, personal commentary.

Chapter Two

1. Anders Frederiksson, personal commentary; Anders Frederiksson LinkedIn page. Accessed at https://www.linkedin.com/in/andersfredriksson/.

2. Greg Meyer, personal commentary.

3. Greg Meyer, personal commentary.

4. Ryan Chisholm, personal commentary.

5. John Barrows, "The #1 Thing I Would Tell My 22-Year-Old Self," jbarrows .com, n.d. Accessed at https://jbarrows.com/blog/split-test-everything-you -do/.

6. Lars Nilsson, personal commentary.

7. Craig Rosenberg, "The Age of Multi-Channel Prospecting: Despite the Hype, Nothing is 'Dead,'" TOPO, n.d. Accessed at https://blog.topohq.com/age -multi-channel-prospecting-despite-hype-nothing-dead/.

8. "Aragon Research Says Sales Engagement Platform Market Value to Reach $5.59 Billion by 2023," CISION PR Web, press release, October 4, 2018. Accessed at http://www.prweb.com/releases/aragon_research_says_sales_engagement _platform_market_value_to_reach_5_59_billion_by_2023/prweb15814073 .htm.

9. Micah Zayner, personal commentary.

10. Jason Hubbard, personal commentary.

11. Daniel Gray, personal commentary.

12. Daniel Gray, personal commentary.

13. Daniel Gray, personal commentary.

14. Remington Rawlings, personal commentary.

15. Remington Rawlings, personal commentary.

16. Lars Nilsson and Travis Henry, "The Ultimate ABSD Tech Stack."

17. Lars Nilsson and Dave Dulany, personal commentary.

18. Remington Rawlings, personal commentary.

Chapter Three

1. Klaus Schwab, "The Fourth Industrial Revolution: What It Means, How to Respond," World Economic Forum, January 14, 2016. Accessed at https:// www.weforum.org/agenda/2016/01/the-fourth-industrial-revolution-what -it-means-and-how-to-respond/.

2. Lars Nilsson, personal commentary.

3. Brock Anthony, "5 Minutes or Less: Risk and Reward in Lead Response Time," Vendasta blog, n.d. Accessed at https://www.vendasta.com/blog/lead-response -time/#78.

4. "Engage Every Customer at Any Time with Drift Automation," Drift homepage, n.d. Accessed at https://www.drift.com/platform/automation/.

5. Aaron Janmohamed, personal commentary.
6. Conversica homepage. Accessed at https://www.conversica.com/; Zoe Enterprise Conversation AI homepage. Accessed at https://zoebot.ai/.
7. Lars Nilsson, personal commentary; Affinity / Nudge homepage. Accessed at https://nudge.ai/; People AI homepage. Accessed at https://people.ai/.
8. Everstring LinkedIn page, https://www.linkedin.com/company/everstring -technology/about/; Everstring home page, https://www.everstring.com/; Everstring Topio Networks page, https://www.topionetworks.com/companies /everstring-52a554e81dedae53f9000acf.
9. Aaron Janmohamed, personal commentary.
10. Greg Meyer, personal commentary.
11. Sam Feldotto, personal commentary.
12. Jason Hubbard, personal commentary.
13. Lately homepage. Accessed at https://www.trylately.com/.
14. Jason Vargas, personal commentary.
15. Micah Zayner, personal commentary.
16. Guillaume Moubeche, personal commentary.
17. Timothy Ferriss, *The 4-Hour Workweek* (Harmony, 2009).
18. Remington Rawlings, personal commentary.
19. Remington Rawlings, personal commentary.
20. Remington Rawlings, personal commentary.
21. Stephen Chase, personal commentary.
22. Ryan Chisholm, personal commentary.

Chapter Four

1. Paraphrase from a personal conversation with Marylou Tyler.
2. Jason Hubbard, personal commentary.
3. Ewing Gillaspy, personal commentary.
4. Ewing Gillaspy, personal commentary.
5. Greg Meyer, personal commentary.
6. Billy Sturgis, personal commentary.
7. Bryan Gonzalez, "Sales Development Technology: The Stack Emerges," TOPO, n.d. Accessed at https://blog.topohq.com/sales-development-technology -the-stack-emerges/.
8. Vlad Voskresensky, personal commentary.
9. Steve Richard, personal commentary.
10. Greg Meyer, personal commentary.

Chapter Five

1. Craig Elias "Finding the Hottest Prospects Is as Simple as ABC," LinkedIn, July 25, 2017. Accessed at https://www.linkedin.com/pulse/finding-hottest -prospects-simple-abc-craig-elias/; "2019 Purchasing Power Survey," DiscoverOrg, n.d. Accessed at https://page.discoverorg.com/purchasing-power-survey-kn -1.html.
2. Nelson Gilliat, personal commentary.
3. Tom Rielly, personal commentary.

4. Cory Bray and Hilmon Sorey, "Why No One Rereads Your 17-Page PDF (And What They Need Instead)," Sales Enablement Playbook, KIITE, n.d. Accessed at https://kiite.ai/why-no-one-reads-your-17-page-pdf-and-what-they-need -instead/.

5. Steve Richard, personal commentary; Steve Richard, "The Four 'Sales' Demand Types," Vorsight, June 15, 2020. Accessed at https://www.vorsight .com/single-post/2020/06/15/The-Four-Sales-Demand-Types.

6. Robert Cialdini, *Influence: The Psychology of Persuasion* (revised edition, HarperCollins, 2009); "Principles of Persuasion," Influence at Work, n.d. Accessed at https://www.influenceatwork.com/principles-of-persuasion/.

7. Sam Feldotto, personal commentary.

Chapter Six

1. Jeremy Donovan, personal commentary.
2. Aaron Janmohamed, personal commentary.
3. John Girard, personal commentary.
4. Grace Gagnon, "Jeremey Donovan on Data Driven Prospecting," Profitwell.com, January 28, 2020. Accessed at https://www.profitwell.com/recur/all/data-driven -prospecting; Jeremey Donovan LinkedIn page, https://www.linkedin.com/in /jeremeydonovan/detail/recent-activity/shares/.
5. For more on Bryan Kreuzberger, see Breakthrough Email homepage, https:// breakthroughemail.com/; for more on Art Sobczak, see Business by Phone homepage, https://businessbyphone.com/.
6. Sam Nelson, LinkedIn article excerpt edited—The Agoge Sequence: A Blueprint for 2X Response Rates. www.linkedin.com/pulse/writing-copy -closers-blueprint-2x-response-rates-sam-nelson/
7. Remington Rawlings, personal commentary.
8. Jason Bay, personal commentary.
9. Guillame Cabane, "The 4 Rules for Sending Cold Email That Converts in 2018," Clearbit, January 30, 2018. Accessed at https://clearbit.com/blog/the -4-rules-for-sending-cold-email-that-converts-in-2018/.
10. Chris Orlob, "Cold Calling Is Dead, Unless You Follow These Rules," *Gong* blogs, March 29, 2018. Accessed at https://www.gong.io/blog/is-cold-calling -dead/.
11. Jason Bay, personal commentary.
12. Jason Bay, personal commentary.
13. Lars Nilsson and Travis Henry, personal commentary.
14. Ernie Santeralli, personal commentary.
15. Wesley Pennock, personal commentary.
16. Matthew Kloss, personal commentary.
17. "A Little Personalization Goes a Long Way. A Really Long Way," SalesLoft, June 13, 2018. Accessed at https://salesloft.com/resources/blog/sales-email -personalization-research/#:~:text=By%20personalizing%2020%20percent %20of,reply%20rates%20increased%20112%20percent.
18. Max Altschuler, Mark Kosoglow, and Manny Medina, *Sales Engagement* (Wiley, 2019).
19. Jake Dunlap LinkedIn page, https://www.linkedin.com/in/jakedunlap/ https://skaled.com/.

20. Nadir Mansor, personal commentary.
21. Guillaume Moubeche, personal commentary.
22. Greg Meyer, personal commentary.
23. Guillaume Moubeche, personal commentary.

Chapter Seven

1. Nick Bonfiglio, personal commentary.
2. Greg Meyer, personal commentary.
3. Sam Feldetto, personal commentary.
4. "Outreach Announces 'Outreach Kaia,' Real-Time Knowledge AI Assistant Which Helps Customer-Facing Reps Sell Smarter and Close Deals Faster," CISION PR Newswire, press release, May 4, 2020. Accessed at https://www .prnewswire.com/news-releases/outreach-announces-outreach-kaia-real -time-knowledge-ai-assistant-which-helps-customer-facing-reps-sell -smarter-and-close-deals-faster-301052017.html.
5. Aaron at XANT, personal commentary.
6. Chris Beall, personal commentary.
7. Ryan Reisert, personal commentary.
8. Amir Reiter, personal commentary.
9. Aaron at XANT, personal commentary.
10. Lars Nilsson, personal commentary.
11. Greg Meyer, personal commentary.
12. Max Altschuler, personal commentary.
13. Greg Meyer, personal commentary.
14. Ryan Reisert, personal commentary.
15. Greg Meyer, personal commentary.
16. Greg Meyer, personal commentary.
17. Mark Chaffey, personal commentary.
18. Timothy B. Lee, "LinkedIn: It's Illegal to Scrape Our Website Without Permission," Ars Technica, July 31, 2017. Accessed at https://arstechnica .com/tech-policy/2017/07/linkedin-its-illegal-to-scrape-our-website -without-permission/#:~:text=%22You%20can't%20publish%20to,more%20 than%2030%20years%20ago.
19. Ingrid Lunden, "LinkedIn Steps into Business Intelligence with the Launch of Talent Insights," Tech Crunch, September 25, 2018. Accessed at https:// techcrunch.com/2018/09/25/linkedin-talent-insights/?sr_share=facebook &utm_source=tcfbpage.
20. Victor Antonio and James Glenn-Anderson, *Sales Ex Machina* (Sellinger Group Publishing, 2018).

Chapter Eight

1. Ryan Reisert, personal commentary.
2. Jack Kosakowski, "Real Sales Talk" podcast. Accessed at https://www.youtube .com/watch?v=ARTVNi8dpcc&ab_channel=RealSalesTalkPodcast.
3. Reid Hoffman, "The 3 Puzzle Pieces That Shape Your Career Path," LinkedIn, October 9, 2012. Accessed at https://www.linkedin.com/pulse/20121010022430

-1213-the-3-puzzle-pieces-that-shape-your-career-path/; Reid Hoffman, *The Start-Up of You* (Currency, 2012). Accessed at http://www.thestartupofyou.com/.

4. Tony Hughes, "An Open Letter to Social Sellers Everywhere," RSVP Selling, February 22, 2018. Accessed at https://rsvpselling.squarespace.com/tony -hughes-blog?offset=1519296552288.

5. Ryan Reisert, personal commentary.

6. Laurence Minsky and Keith A. Quesenberry, "How B2B Sales Can Benefit from Social Selling," *Harvard Business Review*, November 10, 2016. Accessed at https://hbr.org/2016/11/84-of-b2b-sales-start-with-a-referral-not-a-sales person.

7. Eric Quanstrom, personal commentary.

8. Marylou Tyler, personal commentary.

Chapter Nine

1. Chris Marin, personal commentary.

2. Sam Feldetto, personal commentary.

3. Sam Feldetto, personal commentary.

4. Brent Adamson, Matthew Dixon, Pat Spenner, and Nick Toman, *The Challenger Customer* (Portfolio, 2015).

5. VITO Selling homepage, https://www.vitosalestraining.com/.

6. Patricia McLaren, personal commentary.

7. Brigid Archibald, personal commentary.

8. Jason Oakley, personal commentary.

9. Ryan Reisert, personal commentary.

10. Todd Caponi talks about these breakthroughs in his book, *The Transparency Sale* (Ideapress Publishing, 2013).

11. Ryan Reisert, personal commentary.

12. Joe Benjamin, personal commentary.

13. Josh Braun homepage, https://joshbraun.com/ https://academy.joshbraun.com/.

14. Luigi Prestinenzi, personal commentary.

15. Guillaume Moubeche, personal commentary.

16. Guillaume Moubeche, personal commentary.

17. Brendan Short, personal commentary.

Chapter Ten

1. Greg Meyer, personal commentary.

2. Ryan Reisert, personal commentary.

3. Brendan Short, "The Most Important Outbound Metric That No One Is Talking About," The Revenue Playbook, May 8, 2020. Accessed at https:// www.therevenueplaybook.com/blog/the-most-important-outbound -metric-that-no-one-is-talking-about.

4. Sam Feldetto, personal commentary.

5. Kristin Hersant, personal commentary.

6. Chris Bealle, personal commentary.

7. Zack Gasaway, personal commentary.

8. Manish Goel, personal commentary.
9. Marc Bernstein, personal commentary.
10. Sunny Bjerk, personal commentary.
11. Jeremy Siegel, personal commentary.
12. Filip Karwala, personal commentary.
13. Jake Dunlap, personal commentary.

Chapter Eleven

1. Geoff Colvin, personal commentary.
2. Dave Boyce, personal commentary.
3. Travis Wallis, personal commentary.
4. Jeremey Donovan, personal commentary.
5. Kai-Fu Lee, personal commentary.
6. Lynne Zaledonis, personal commentary.
7. Kevin Dorsey, personal commentary; Kevin "KD" Dorsey LinkedIn page, https://www.linkedin.com/in/kddorsey3/.
8. Thomas Baumgartner, personal commentary.
9. Narrative Science, personal commentary.
10. Ben Daters, personal commentary.
11. Anders Fredriksson, personal commentary.
12. Swati Sinha, personal commentary.
13. Jill Rowley, personal commentary.
14. Peter Schwartz, personal commentary.
15. Falon Fatemi, personal commentary.
16. Dharmesh Shah, personal commentary.
17. Keith Rabois, personal commentary.
18. Tomasz Tunguz, personal commentary.
19. Professor Rita McGrath, personal commentary.
20. "Deep Blue vs Kasparov: How a Computer Beat Best Chess Player in the World," BBC News, May 14, 2017. Accessed at https://www.youtube.com/watch?v=KF6sLCeBj0s&feature=youtu.be.
21. "IBM's Watson Supercomputer Destroys Humans in Jeopardy," Engadget, January 13, 2011. Accessed at https://www.youtube.com/watch?v=WFR3lOm_xhE&feature=youtu.be.
22. Malcolm Frank, Paul Roehrig, and Ben Pring, *What to Do When Machines Do Everything: How to Get Ahead in a World of AI, Algorithms, Bots, and Big Data* (Wiley, 2017), p. 42.

Appendix

1. Ben Herbert, personal commentary.
2. Krishan Patel, personal commentary.
3. Remington Rawlings, personal commentary.

About the Authors

Justin Michael has set records over the past decade for full-cycle revenue creation in cutting-edge AdTech/MarTech and SaaS startups, both as an individual contributor and global team leader (leading teams of field-based and inside sellers). He also received a prestigious 10X Award from a top-20, Tier 1 VC-backed Seattle startup. Justin was the inspiration behind *COMBO Prospecting*, an acclaimed sales pipeline methodology used by some of the most successful brands globally. He lives in California, where he consults leading corporations on top-of-funnel revenue operations.

Tony Hughes has thirty-five years of corporate and sales leadership experience, having generated record-breaking results as a salesperson, head of sales, and CEO leading the Asia-Pacific region for multinational corporations. He is a bestselling author, consultant, trainer, and keynote speaker. Tony is cofounder and sales innovation director at Sales IQ Global and also serves on advisory boards. He has taught sales at Sydney University, the University of New South Wales, and within the MBA program at the University of Technology, Sydney.

Uplift your strategic selling knowledge and learn how to elevate engagement in how you open by reading *COMBO Prospecting* and following Tony Hughes and Justin Michael on LinkedIn.

Go to Sales IQ Global (www.salesIQglobal.com) and complete the Create Pipeline Program. (Special offer for book readers at www.salesIQglobal.com/TPS.)

Sales IQ Global is the best eLearning and sales enablement platform on the planet for B2B selling. Our affiliation with them enables us to offer you free access to their *Selling in Tough Times* course, which includes free access to a module, Sales Success Plan. Simply go to https://info.salesiqglobal.com/webinar-selling-during-tough-times. What you create will blow your boss away.

All these together will enable you to apply the concepts and lead your company, even your industry.